WHY BUSINESSES
FAIL

. . . AND THE
JOURNEY THROUGH OUR
IRRATIONAL MINDS

- BOB WEIR -

A catalogue record for this book is available from the National Library of New Zealand.

Published by R.J. Weir Ltd, trading as Pinpoint Business.
Design by Nick Turzynski, redinc. Book Design, www.redinc.co.nz

www.whybusinessesfail.co.nz

DEDICATION

To all those people battling mental health issues.
Don't be silent. Talk about it. Turn to loved ones.
Ask for help. Hang on to hope.
It is out there — believe me, I know.

Bob Weir

Contents

PROLOGUE: THE AUTHOR'S THOUGHTS AND EXPERIENCES. **9**

My interest in business 9
Who am I to comment?. 10
Depression — the greatest irrationality 11
The world of senior management 13
The mythical business leader 14
What is business success? 14
How irrational are we? Let's test. 15
How this book is presented 16

SECTION 1: INTRODUCTION. **17**

Chapter 1: What is business failure — and what is success? **18**
Some definitions. 18
Defining success and failure can be very personal 19
What is business failure as defined in this book? 20
It's very easy starting a business in New Zealand 21
Some statistics. 22
The only common factor in failures. 25
They say to succeed we must first fail — or maybe not? 27
The high cost of business failures 28
A history of business failures 30

SECTION 2: THE BUSINESSES THAT GOT IT WRONG — AND FAILED . . . **34**
Why these examples? 35
Business failure is about people 35
Other common contributing factors. 36

Chapter 2: The failure of New Zealand's coal miner — Solid Energy. **37**
Some history 37
Solid Energy's leadership 39
Challenges of coal mining in New Zealand 41
New developments 43
National Resources Company — Solid Energy's "audacious" goal. 48
Shareholder's influence and its impact on Solid Energy. 49
When others were finally able to take a closer look 52
World coal prices and what the business was worth 53
How did other coal businesses fare?. 58
What can we learn from the Solid Energy failure?. 59
Saying sorry is not always enough. 62

Chapter 3: Death of a Kiwi icon — Pumpkin Patch and the risk of growing 63
A star is born 63
Aggressive growth, debt and decline 64
Staying relevant 66
The end was nigh 66
What might Pumpkin Patch have done differently? 67

Chapter 4: When businesses fail, who decides the truth? — Salthouse Marine . . . 69
The Salthouse Marine story 70
Entry of a new investor 73
The courts and the wine tycoon 75
What can we learn — what might the truth be? 76

Chapter 5: Dishonesty, fraud, and Ross Asset Management 78
Breaking the law and business 79
Fraudulent behaviour and the Serious Fraud Office 80
Inland Revenue fraud 81
New Zealand's biggest individual fraud — David Ross 82
Why do people commit fraud? 89
Dishonesty in different cultures 91
How honest are we — really? 93

Chapter 6: Allan Hubbard and the failure of South Canterbury Finance 98
Allan Hubbard — the man and the business owner 99
The Global Financial Crisis and New Zealand finance companies 102
The rise and fall of an icon and finance giant 103
Mr and Mrs Hubbard's businesses — the final straw for SCF 111
Accusations of fraud and failed legal action 114
Why did SCF fail and what can businesses learn from this? 116
There were no winners from SCF's failure 123

**SECTION 3: HOW WE MAKE BUSINESS DECISIONS —
AND WHY WE GET THEM WRONG 124**

Chapter 7: The brain of the business owner 127
Some basics about our brains 127
Three s within one 129
The brain basics — a summary 132
Facts and myths about our brains 133
Our inner mental conflicts and mental fatigue 136
Our senses 137
Practice makes permanent 137
Evolution of our brain (and of the modern business) 139
Nature versus nurture? 141
Our automatic brain versus our reflective brain 142
Attention — what's important and what is not 144
The shortcomings of our memory 146
You are human — be humble, be kind to yourself 150

Chapter 8: The simple mental shortcuts we use to survive each day **151**
   Heuristics and biases. 151
   Examples of the many biases we suffer 153
   Reducing the impact of our biases 167

Chapter 9: How we decide **168**
   Rational decisions — what are they? 170
   When deciding, we compare — it's all relative 173
   Emotions and business decisions 175
   The science behind, and risk of, going with your gut 177
   Making instinctive decisions under pressure 179
   Fatigue, stress and the impact of wellbeing on decisions. 180
   So how can we make better decisions? 181

Chapter 10: Employees — they are irrational people too **183**
   Remember the human in human resources 184
   What motivates staff? 185
   Rewards and compensation 190
   Managing and supporting your staff's performance. 193
   Our management and leadership skills 194

Chapter 11: Self-awareness, personality, and what we stand for **197**
   Know thyself. 198
   Our values and what we stand for 200
   Our personality 203
   Intelligence. 205
   Arrogance, stubbornness and the Dark Triad 207

SECTION 4: WHAT WE NEED TO DO DIFFERENTLY **214**
   It's more than our irrationality we need to address 215

Chapter 12: Know why the business exists, where it is heading — its strategy . . . **216**
   Strategy and too many choices 217
   What is business strategy? 219
   Why does your business exist? 220
   Your business goals 222

Chapter 13: Health, wellbeing, and their impact on business **224**
   A few sad examples 226
   So, what to do? 227
   Sleep. 227
   Stress 228
   Happiness. 232
   Building resilience 234
   My brutal lesson — and advice 236

Chapter 14: Controlling the controllable, risk, uncertainty and luck **237**
    What part does luck play in business? 240
    Regression to the mean 244
    Scenario planning — a technique to contemplate the future 245
    Control the controllable … and ask, "What if?" 246
    If you were lucky, enjoy it — don't rely on it 247

Chapter 15: Cash and the mouse that sank the boat **249**
    Profit and cash — you need both 251
    Taking too much money out of the business 255
    Managing the money you owe, and money owed to you 257
    And when you can't pay the bills 258

Chapter 16: Paying taxes — the cash of last resort **261**
    What is the IRD all about? 262
    It's simple — really 265

Chapter 17: Debt and how to kill a 1400-year-old business **266**
    The debt burden 268
    A common source of funding for a small business — the family home 270
    What you must pledge to secure debt 271
    When the debt starts mounting 272

Chapter 18: Doing the little things really well **274**
    Time — it is everything 275
    Procrastination — eat the big frog first 275
    Multitasking — doing a lot of things badly 276
    Prioritise 278
    Identifying and removing waste 278
    Habits and rules to assist in overcoming our irrationality 279

SECTION 5: WHAT HAVE WE LEARNED? **281**
    To conclude and summarise 282

Acknowledgements 284

APPENDIX: South Canterbury Finance — structure of entities 285

References 286

PROLOGUE: THE AUTHOR'S THOUGHTS AND EXPERIENCES

My interest in business

I've been privileged to have almost 30 years in and around businesses, of all shapes and sizes, in different countries. I have worked with, and worked for, some amazing and inspiring people. I have also worked for some very flawed and unpleasant souls. I'm sure there are many who enjoyed working for me and some who I am sure are glad to be rid of me as their boss.

I have been fascinated with the business world throughout these years. My fascination has been less about the business process but more about the human being within that process.

I've always found life within business to reflect life more broadly. We cannot separate the two. In my MBA, which I completed many years ago, a good cost benefit analysis was the solution to most things and good industrial relations and human resource policies were all you needed to get the most from people. I have developed a very different view now.

Of particular interest, and what inspired the many years I have spent researching this book, was a macabre fascination we have with the failure of businesses and the downfall of those within such businesses.

I believe running or leading a business is intensely personal, as our lives, self-esteem, even our families could depend on it. Even the leaders of large organisations find it difficult to separate the business from themselves, as these roles involve a significant level of personal investment.

Throughout my career, I have worked very hard (too hard, as I will soon explain) to ensure every business I owned, I worked for, or with, was a success.

So, in combining my desire to see people and the businesses they operate within succeed, and combining the interest we have in failure, I decided to see what I could learn about the many business failures out there. I wanted to see if we could understand why they failed, prevent future failures and, in turn, be more successful in business.

Who am I to comment?

Many may ask, as I asked myself, what right I have to write about the failures of other business owners and leaders and to speak of the irrationality of others, which I do throughout this book.

Well, I probably have no right except that I felt it was a story that needed exploring. I felt some comfort in doing this when I considered that I have been an employee, an engineer, a university student (a few times over), a business manager, a senior executive, a small business owner, a small business advisor and an author.

After some further reflection, rather than challenging what right I had to tell this story, I felt that if I didn't tell it, then who should?

My initial research started looking at the inner workings of small, medium and large business entities and the mechanics of business failure. However, it very quickly became clear that this was more of a journey into the mind of the business owner, the business leader, employee and all our minds, than a journey through the mechanics of business.

It became clearer the more research I did that success or failure in business was indelibly linked to the mind of the people involved — and a very imperfect mind it is.

Hence, I commenced my journey through the not so pleasant world of liquidations, receiverships, fraud insolvency practice, and business failures — an enriching journey it has been and one I want to share.

During the years of research into this book I had the privilege of talking to a huge array of amazing and intriguing people. The owners and leaders of failed businesses, people who have committed fraud and been jailed, journalists, insolvency experts, lawyers, psychologists, accountants, and many more. I hope I have done their input justice.

I also researched as much information as I could to do this topic justice. I read the reports of over 1000 liquidations, and hundreds of news articles and press releases. I read or listened to over 700 books and hundreds of academic papers. I read through many court proceedings and hundreds of documents released by various government agencies under the Official Information Act — and more.

I also drew on my experience as a person who paid a heavy price for pursuing what I thought was success in business and in my career. In my case, the failure I was confronted with was not of the businesses I worked in but the failure of my health and mental wellbeing trying to make them a success.

Depression — the greatest irrationality

In August 2012, I fell into a very dangerous and severe depression. I recall collapsing in a heap one Saturday afternoon that August after a work phone call, which I can't fully remember, but it was the trigger. I had my very worried wife drag me to a doctor on the following morning at which time we both learned what depression was, and we also realised that I had a very long road ahead of me.

Depression sufferers become entirely focused with what's happening within their minds, being trapped in their dark thoughts, lacking hope and becoming oblivious to the world around them. After all these years, I now realise how selfish an illness depression is. The sufferer is completely self-absorbed, battling thoughts and uninterested in the world around them. They may also be oblivious to the pain this is inflicting on loved ones struggling to make sense of what is going on.

All this describes me.

I, like many depression sufferers, became overwhelmed with suicidal thoughts.

Suicide became an option that seemed like a perfectly rational way to end the suffering I believed I was going through. The experts explained to me that I was simply working through solutions to my issues. Sleep was a great escape, until I woke each morning dreading the day ahead. The natural next question I asked was "Hey, what if I didn't wake up — isn't that problem solved?".

People often believe suicide is a coward's way out. For me I look back on the planning I was working through in my mind simply as a process, a decision, to escape the pain I felt and to remove the burden I had become to my family and friends — at least that was what I thought.

There is no greater example of irrationality than such thinking.

Everyone around me could not understand or rationalise why I could think in this way. The more they tried to reason with me, the further I slipped into my irrational thoughts.

"Bob, you have a loving family, including your wife and two amazing kids and your extended family in Australia", "You have great people you call friends who care about you", "You have achieved so much in your career", "You have a great job that pays really well and you have many more opportunities ahead of you", "You own your homes and have no money worries", and so on.

Unfortunately, all I did was take these comments and rationalise them in my mind as "that's all bullshit, because I know I'm really just a useless piece of crap". Yep, pretty bizarre stuff but that's the power and irrationality of our minds.

> **A QUICK NOTE.**
> **PLEASE, if you or anyone close to you shows signs of depression, mentions self-harm or suicide, treat it seriously. Talk to these people. Ask them what they are thinking and, most of all, seek help.**

Only after this event did I look back and realise it had been coming for a long time. The many years that I had been fighting my way out of this situation since that August 2012 date (with the unconditional love of my family) reinforced how very fragile and irrational we can be.

The fallibility of humans and our irrationality is a central theme in this book.

I will discuss in some detail the contribution the irrationality that exists in all of us contributes to the success or failure of the businesses we are associated with.

Hopefully, this in not through the extreme irrationality of a mental health event like I experienced but just the day-to-day irrationalities that we all share.

The world of senior management

My arrival into executive management, after many years in other senior management roles, was at a time when things were good and money was readily available — it was a bit like arriving in Camelot.

The focus people placed on the role I held and the money and privilege it provided was very satisfying. The photos in annual reports, the functions, the influence of my decisions, and the ability to make a significant impact were very rewarding. There is no question that I enjoyed people asking me what I did at social events — people were impressed with the role I held.

Many felt the business world was at my feet and greater heights in corporate life were just around the corner. I shared this view.

I did love what I did, to an extent. I learned so much and with an exceptional team around me, we did achieve a great deal. Unfortunately, it came at a significant cost for me personally.

What it also showed me was how people in these roles can get things very wrong.

In the role of an executive manager, we can blur the lines between meeting the needs of those we report to, preservation of our positions, and what really needs to be done. Sometimes it becomes harder to establish what is fair and even what is right. Determining what is the right thing to do and deciding what choices we should or shouldn't make may not be so clear.

During my research for this book I met with many executives and board members close to the failure of the businesses they led. For those who had some distance between the failure events and the time to reflect back on them, almost all accepted they could have done better. Almost all accepted the impact these positions of power had on elevating their self-image and self-importance. It takes very strong and self-aware individuals to take on these roles and not allow what they offer to impact their view of themselves.

I often remember getting feedback that I was too nice, that I needed to be tougher to achieve the greater career progression that I felt I was due. At that time I believed to succeed as an executive I had to act on people who were not performing, often to satisfy the view of others — to be colder and less caring. I feel I hurt people along the way in meeting these expectations. I guess I learned how to play this role as I truly believed it was for the greater good of the business — and my career.

Eventually I think this created huge inner turmoil that I was not aware of at the time.

The mythical business leader

While researching this book I saw the damage failures had on so many people but I also couldn't help but empathise with the leaders in big business and the hundreds of thousands of small Kiwi business owners. The pressure that these roles can subject us to, in the face of our irrationality, fallibility, pride and ego, can result in poor decisions being made.

There is a huge amount of literature on leadership and entrepreneurship, describing a persona that leaders should strive to become. I have lost track of how many books, blogs and academic papers I have read on what attributes make a great business leader.

Such expectations are almost describing mythical individuals and put extraordinary pressure on people.

Having seen what rock bottom looks like, I now have a very different view of what true leadership and business ability requires — an acceptance of our humanity. The humility to accept we don't know it all and need to call on others to help us. The reality that, as humans, we are imperfect, fallible and wired to make mistakes.

In a funny way my struggle to overcome depression has been what I now describe as an *"ironic gift"*. The depth of love for those who stood by me is deeper than ever; the lack of tolerance I now have for those people who put their career and personal gain ahead of the welfare of others, including my own; and the brutal reality that I am human, as we all are. This has now replaced my previously held view, from my days as a senior executive, that failure was for others, not me.

I would love to believe this book will contribute to many fewer business failures but I am a realist. Business failures will keep occurring while people continue to be people — but I hope that, like in many other aspects of my business life, on this point I am mistaken.

What is business success?

There are many books, articles and pieces of work that try to simplify how to make your business successful and how to prevent it failing. Some often try to pin it down to one or two things that contribute to business success or failure. Unfortunately, running a business of any size is not that simple. The reasons businesses succeed or fail is not that black and white.

What became very clear from the research into this book is that there is no basic formula that, if applied by each of us, will guarantee success or prevent failure in business.

I will present some very critical aspects of running a business that will reduce the likelihood they will fail and, more importantly, hopefully, help people achieve the success sought from business.

One overwhelming theme that became clearer with every new person I spoke to, or every piece of information I read, was the role the business owners or leaders played in a business failing. While this may seem self-evident, it was not so obvious when many of the failures were made with very clever, experienced business people at the helm.

In digging deeper into why businesses fail, I realised I needed to understand more about how we interpret the information presented to us, how we process that information, recall it, form judgements based on it, and then make decisions.

In the end, what will determine if a business succeeds or fails will be the decisions the owners or leaders of that business make.

How irrational are we? Let's test

The decisions and the actions (or inactions) of the leaders and owners of businesses are a major contributor to the failure of businesses. I will be going through, in some detail, many examples of businesses that got it wrong and the people who contributed to this.

All of us will, and should, sit in judgement of these people, as I did when carrying out this research. We should ask "Why did they do what they did?", "How did they not realise what would happen?", "How could they have done that to all those people?", and more.

However, in asking these questions we should pause and consider what might we have done if we were put in the same situation as these people.

How rational are our own decisions in our daily lives and in our businesses?

In the latter chapters of the book I will provide a few samples of the many tests that researchers like Daniel Kahneman, Amos Tversky and Dan Ariely carried out over many decades to assess how our minds work when we filter information and make decisions. That is, how irrational are we?

Take a few minutes to answer these. Don't dwell on them too much. They are a bit of fun and hopefully will trigger a little more self-awareness about how we are wired.

How this book is presented

This book is broken into five sections.

Section 1 provides some introductory background on business in New Zealand, some statistics, and what defines success and failure.

In **Section 2**, I discuss a selection of high-profile business failures that have occurred within New Zealand.

In **Section 3**, I spend several chapters exploring the mind of people in business and how we make decisions. This is to help us understand the limitations we all face and why such limitations regularly fail us all.

In **Section 4**, I discuss the business practices that ultimately triggered the failures. While the central cause of all failures is people, there are aspects of business we should devote our attention to that will reduce the chance of failures occurring.

Finally, in **Section 5**, I wrap it all up with a summary of the key things business owners and leaders should consider to avoid failure, and deliver success.

There is an associated website you can spend some time on. I'd love to hear your thoughts and share your business stories, so we might all learn. Check it out at:

www.whybusinessesfail.co.nz

I hope you enjoy the book and learn a little more about yourself and your business activities.

BOB WEIR

SECTION 1:
INTRODUCTION

1 WHAT IS BUSINESS FAILURE — AND WHAT IS SUCCESS?

When discussing business success or failure, there are often very different views on what each means. I first need to define what I mean by business failures, and in turn business success, for the purposes of our discussion.

Some definitions

The *Oxford English Dictionary* defines "failure" as:

> 66 *The neglect or omission of an expected or required action.* 99

> 66 *The action or state of not functioning.* 99

In turn, it defines "success" as:

> 66 *The attainment of fame, wealth, or social status.* 99

So, what is business success? When can a business be considered a success? Is it wealth, status and fame, as the above definition would state? We often look upon those who have achieved these things as successful. So, does that in turn mean the rest of us have failed, or at least not been successful if the business we are involved in doesn't achieve this? I think not.

I much prefer another *Oxford* definition of success:

❝ *The accomplishment of an aim or purpose.* **❞**

My definition of success in business is when a business has a clear view of the reason that business exists, has specific goals it wishes to achieve, and achieves those goals, no matter how humble or audacious those goals might be.

Defining success and failure can be very personal

The most critical part in this definition is that the success is defined *only* by the business and not by what people perceive success to be.

Far too often we define business success based on what social expectations define it to be — for small businesses this is typically significant growth in terms of sales and staff, which in turn sees the owners reaping significant financial rewards.

In the extreme, there is a breed of businesses that started from nothing and became billion-dollar businesses — these are called unicorns because they are so rare. There were only about 175 unicorns in existence when I wrote this (although the number was growing each year). Well known examples have included Airbnb, Uber, Google, Pinterest, Dropbox, Spotify and Evernote. (Businesses are no longer included as unicorns when they list on the stock exchange.)

Considering the millions of businesses that start every year around the world, this level of extreme growth is indeed a very rare thing, yet they take up a lot of the space on bookshop shelves and discussions on what business success is.

If the definition of business success relates only to businesses that experienced significant growth and brought wealth to its owners, then it would imply that all the other businesses have not experienced success or indeed would be considered failures. This would then represent the clear majority of businesses on the planet — which means we must all be a pretty sorry bunch if it were true.

On this basis, I believe that growth and wealth are far from the only definitions of business success.

Many businesses, especially small businesses, do not want their business to grow. They do not want to employ more staff. The profit motive may in no way reflect the purpose of the business. It may be driven by a social good. They may deliberately avoid debt and therefore limit growth. They may simply want to be profitable enough to sustain their lifestyle and keep the business going for as long as possible.

If the business owners have set out with these goals and vision for their businesses and they achieve them, then they are successful.

What is business failure as defined in this book?

For the purposes of this book, I define business failure as when a business has gone into liquidation or receivership.

It is difficult to see any positives in a situation where a third party, such as the bank, a creditor or the Inland Revenue Department (IRD), acts through the courts to liquidate the business. It could be the shareholders who decide to liquidate before others do. Even if the shareholders voluntarily liquidate the business, it is usually their only option and not exactly voluntary.

Liquidation

The more detailed **definition of a liquidation** is provided by the New Zealand Companies Office:

> *Company liquidation can occur voluntarily or by court order where it has been established a company is unable to pay its debts as they fall due.*
> *A liquidator is appointed to:*
> - *investigate the company's financial affairs*
> - *establish causes of failure*
> - *investigate possible offences, and*
> - *identify and sell assets for the benefit of creditors.*
>
> *Liquidation is immediate and serious. Trading companies are usually closed. From the date of liquidation, the liquidator takes custody and control of all the company's unsecured assets and assists secured creditors where necessary. The assets are collected and sold for the benefit of the company's creditors. When the liquidation is completed the company is removed from the Register of Companies.*

(Just to clarify, liquidation relates to a business, bankruptcy relates to an individual.)

What about just walking away?

If a business owner has a go at running a small business, decides after some time that it's not for them, and walks away without any debts or without owing anyone money, one could argue this is not failure but a great learning opportunity. Perhaps this was all the owner wanted to do and achieved all the goals they set out to achieve.

A business owner may have had clear goals for the business when they started but did not achieve these goals. If the owner decided to walk away from the business without achieving these goals, it could be argued that the business failed. There is merit in this view. However, as there are no details on such businesses, I excluded them from my definition of "business failure". They may also fall into the category of a positive entrepreneurial endeavour that we discuss shortly.

Receivership

One step short of a liquidation but also very undesirable is **receivership**.

The Companies Office defines receivership as when:

> *Companies may offer security against assets such as plant and equipment to obtain finance or assist with cash flow. The creditor then has an interest in that security. In the event of default the creditor can appoint a receiver to collect and sell the asset in which they have a security interest.*

We discuss various failures throughout this book. Some of the businesses that were liquidated occurred after receivership. However, there are cases where a business may be forced into receivership but does not go into liquidation. I consider both scenarios to be a sign that a business has failed.

It's very easy starting a business in New Zealand

It is very simple to start a business in New Zealand to pursue a goal, a dream, an idea, to work for oneself, or to escape a work situation that we are less than happy with.

We can decide at any time to start a business activity without permission of any kind from anyone. This is how sole traders spring into life. You just start.

Even if you then want to register as a company, it is very easy in this country.

The World Bank, in its "Doing Business 2017" report, outlines which of 190 economies it researched is the easiest place to do business.[1]

The World Bank report focuses on regulations that affect small and medium-size businesses operating in the largest city in these countries, considering a range of regulatory processes. These include the ease of starting a business, getting permits to build, accessing electricity, getting credit, paying taxes, enforcing contracts, labour market regulation, resolving insolvencies and more.

New Zealand, across all criteria, is listed as the easiest of all these 190 countries to do business. Singapore is number two. The UK is seventh, the USA eighth, and Australia 15th. In case you were curious, the five places in which you least want to do business are Sudan, Venezuela, Libya, Eritrea and Somalia.

To register a company in New Zealand, we require the smallest number of procedures (only one) and the shortest time to fulfil them (half a day). By comparison, the global average is seven procedural steps. Have some sympathy for countries like Argentina, which requires 14 procedural steps to set up a company.

We don't score as well when it comes to resolving the failure (insolvency) of businesses. This considers the time, cost, recovery rate of losses and insolvency regulations. We are ranked 34th, recovering about 83 cents in the dollar, while Norway is ranked first on this criterion, recovering 93 cents in the dollar.

This World Bank report does not consider the impact of corruption in doing business. We cover this in more detail in a later chapter. On most corruption indices, New Zealand scores as one of the least corrupt countries in the world to do business.

Therefore, to get into business in New Zealand is very easy, and it's also one of the easiest countries in the world to carry out business.

Some statistics

Throughout this book, we will discuss the mind of the business owner. We also share some stories about real business failures. Throughout the evolution of our species, people have passed on information from one generation to the next through stories, songs and pictures. We are more likely to remember things if it is through a story or conversation rather than data and facts.

However, to substantiate the stories we need to back them with data. My aim, where possible, is to back my discussion with data.

❝ *There are three kinds of lies: lies, damned lies, and statistics.* **❞**
— Benjamin Disraeli, former British Prime Minister

New Zealand is a place of small businesses. In February 2016, there were 515,000 enterprises in this country. Of these, 70% had no employees, and 97% had fewer than 20 employees. There are only a little over 2300 enterprises in New Zealand with more than 100 staff.[2]

The Companies Office develops trends of the health of business in New Zealand, as shown in Figure 1. The trend shows the increase in businesses that came into existence from 2001, peaking at 74,239 in 2007. This is when the Global Financial Crisis (GFC) hit and incorporations dropped considerably (to 48,078 in 2009).

In 2001, company liquidations amounted to nearly 5% of the companies that were incorporated that year. It improved until the GFC hit. During the height of the GFC, the percentage increased to 8.1%. Since the GFC, the proportion of companies going into liquidation, relative to the number of companies in existence, has been slowly improving.[3]

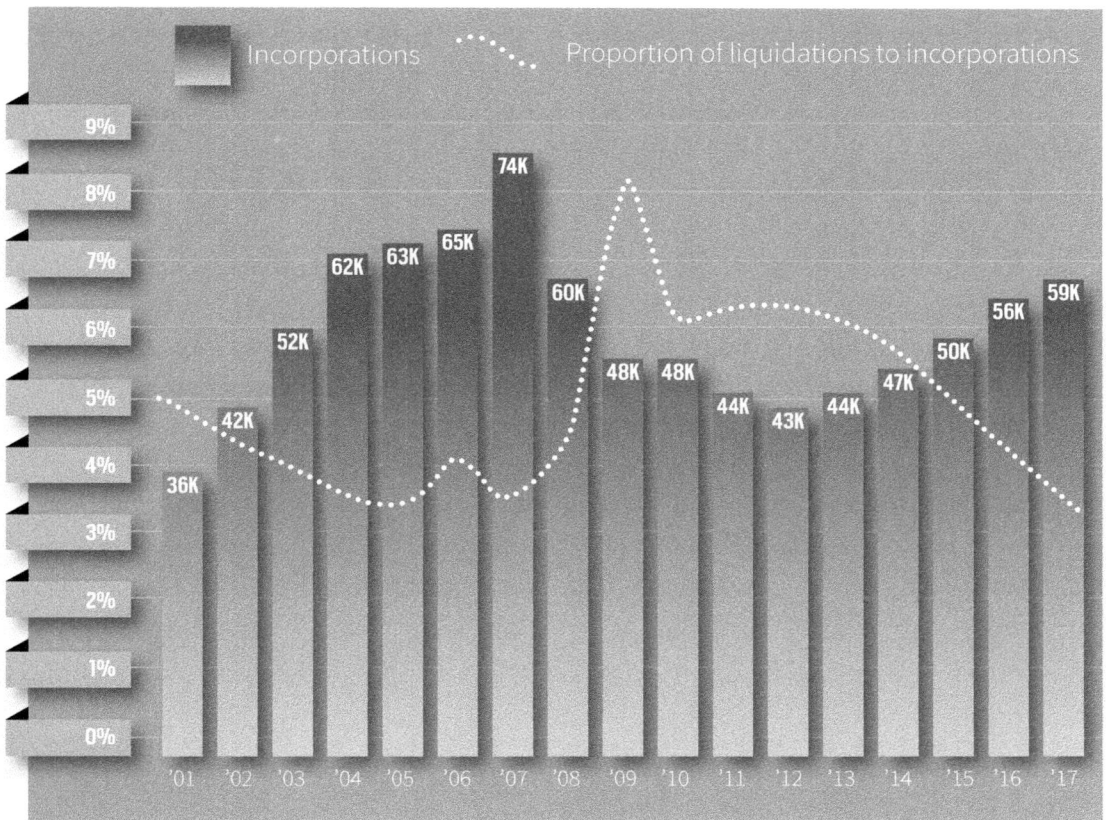

Figure 1. Companies that form, fail and last. Companies Office

Business births and deaths

There are also many businesses that simply disappear in New Zealand that Statistics New Zealand defines as business "deaths".

Statistics New Zealand defines a business **"death"** as an enterprise that ceases operation. This doesn't include businesses that have temporarily stopped activities, merged, been taken over, broken up, or been through some other restructuring of a group of businesses linked by ownership. It will include liquidations but these are a small percentage of total "deaths".

Likewise, Statistics New Zealand defines a new enterprise that starts operation as a business **"birth"**.

In 2016, about 58,500 enterprises came to life in New Zealand. In the same year, just over 53,700 died. Over the last 10 years, on average, business birth rates have been about 11% of the total businesses and death rates at about 10%.

So almost as many businesses start each year as disappear.

The statistics on business deaths, while not fitting into the definition of failure for the purposes of our discussion, are still a telling piece of information we can't ignore. It shows that a huge number of businesses start in this country and just as many disappear for reasons we are unlikely to ever collectively understand.

The smaller the business, the shorter its life

Most businesses that are born tend not to last that long. Statistics New Zealand indicates that about 20% of businesses disappear 12 months after starting. By 10 years, only about 25% of business remain.

Unfortunately, these statistics are dominated by small businesses. Businesses with more than 20 staff tend to hang around much longer than businesses with fewer staff. Over 50% of these businesses are still in place 10 years after starting. It's even higher for businesses with over 100 staff.

The *only* common factor in failures

The only thing all businesses have in common is that they all have people who make decisions about the business. The success or failure of the business will rest on the quality of the decisions the owner or business leader does or doesn't make.

Larger companies have a management structure, usually reporting to a position like a Managing Director or CEO, who in turn reports to a board of directors. There are usually a wide range of processes that must be followed in a large organisation before

critical decisions are made.

Unfortunately, while statistically more small businesses fail than large organisations, many large organisations also fail and this comes back to the decisions made by the leaders of those organisations.

So, the only common theme that relates to every failure is that it rests with human beings — the owners or managers of the business, and the decisions they did or didn't make.

Acts of God

Let's exclude those failures that can be linked directly to "acts of God".

These are defined as "an instance of uncontrollable natural forces in operation". These are those rare events where a business could rightly say the business failed due to events completely out of their control.

In saying that, there are business people who blame these "acts of God" as the reason for the failure of their business, yet it was the choices they made, rather than the event itself, that was the true cause of the failure. For example, a fire, a break-in or a flood where the business was uninsured.

There are significant economic or market-triggered events that will result in higher numbers of failures. Figure 1 illustrates that the GFC did result in more failures, although underlying failures occurred irrespective of the economic environment.

The agricultural sector in New Zealand is heavily impacted by world commodity prices such as beef, lamb or milk solid prices and by the introduction of diseases (such as the Psa bacteria that hit the kiwifruit industry in 2011) as well as the impact of extreme weather events.

I do have empathy with businesses impacted by these circumstances. However, while the size and timing of such events is unpredictable, the likelihood they will happen is high. As such, business people do have some ability to factor such events into their thinking.

We will discuss the role that luck, risk and uncertainty play in business failures a little later.

Where we attribute blame

Many business owners claim the factors leading to their demise were unforeseen and out of their control, when that is often not the case.

When things go wrong and a business fails, the business people, like any human being, will often look to external factors as the cause of the failure, rather than looking within. In some ways, this helps us cope with the difficulty of accepting failure.

This is sometimes called **_attribution error_**, where we attribute our failures to external forces. We will discuss this in more detail later when we go through the many biases that can impact our thinking.

They say to succeed we must first fail — or maybe not?

I am very conscious that our discussion is not misinterpreted as discouraging the entrepreneurial spirit that needs to exist to lead or run a business.

What I am aiming to do in this book is to assist business owners and leaders from making those mistakes that need not be made and, when made, could spell the end of their business — those events that the business cannot recover from.

Unfortunately, neither this book nor any other will prevent the failure of more businesses. The pace of change is unlikely to slow. Scarcity of resources and the basis of economic theory will live on. And people will be people, so failures will keep happening.

No legitimate business person ever sets out to fail in business. Each of us will have different appetites for risk, different creative capabilities, and different levels of comfort for making mistakes.

To build stronger and better businesses, people will continue to take risks — that is business. In taking risks businesses will get it wrong so mistakes are, unfortunately, inevitable. These mistakes result in learnings and these learnings should, in theory, lead to better businesses.

We will make mistakes — this is human, and the frailty of our humanity is a strong theme throughout this book. We must try things in business and take risks, as this is a fundamental part of achieving a business's goals.

So, is it legitimate to argue that business failure, as I define it, is a necessary process for being successful?

I strongly challenge this view.

We must take risks. We will make mistakes. However, the hope is the risks we take are well considered and their implications, both good and bad, are considered, and not fatal to the businesses we are involved in.

The high cost of business failures

Far too many businesses fail that should not have failed.

There is often admiration for business leaders who have failed, but have then recovered and gone on to greatness, claiming that success only came because of the failure. Henry Ford and Walt Disney are examples of this.

I do admire the resilience of those who recover from failures and then thrive. However, after researching this book, I found no reason to celebrate business failures or see them as a necessary contributor to success.

Unfortunately, those who were directly impacted by business failures, including the managers, owners, their staff and creditors, are unlikely to look upon the failure in any positive light — and this can be the case many years after the event.

I never spoke to anyone involved in a liquidation or receivership who looked upon it in any positive light.

> **❝** *If you've never experienced a failure like this, it is hard to describe the feeling. It's as if the world were falling out from under you* **❞**.
>
> — Eric Rees, *Lean Start-up*.[4]

The numbers

I have reviewed over 1000 liquidations from 2014 to 2016 from the Companies Office website. (Yes, if your business is liquidated, it is available for the world to see — forever.) I also researched the impact from the failure of many large New Zealand companies, a selection of which we will discuss shortly.

Here are a few reasons why we need to care about these failures and work to see them reduced:

- Of the 1000 liquidations I reviewed, 75% were single-director companies. This is likely to indicate the majority were small businesses.
- A further 12% had two directors with the same address, indicating they were in a personal relationship, typically married.
- Total losses to all creditors from these 1000-plus liquidations were over $500 million. There is some uncertainty around these figures as many liquidations were still in progress, not all creditors put in their claims, and reports were not always clear on money recovered. However, these numbers do give us a sense of the size of the losses (remembering there have been over 2000 liquidations every year for

the last 10 years — and I only looked at half of them).

- Over the four years from 2013 to 2016, the Inland Revenue Department (IRD) was out of pocket from liquidations by around $940 million.[5]
- Finance company failures in New Zealand during the period 2006–2010 resulted in government bailouts of more than $9 billion, the biggest being South Canterbury Finance (the biggest failure in New Zealand's history) at $1.5 billion. (Some of this money was later clawed back during the liquidations.) To put this in perspective, this is over four times the amount of money the government has paid out in settling claims under the Treaty of Waitangi with New Zealand Maori (at $2.2 billion).[6,7]

The flow-on effect of failures

The cost of large corporate failures can be huge, financially, on lost jobs, and often on the communities where their corporate profile was large.

Unfortunately, not only might those directly involved in the business suffer from a failure, often the impact, even from a small business failure, can be widespread.

Those affected will include the owner's families; employees; those who had personal guarantees over unpaid debts (at times this may not be the owners, but parents, friends or family); and creditors, many of whom are also struggling small businesses.

Often one failure may trigger other failures. The banks are impacted. While we may not shed too many tears for the banks, the more they lose, the more it impacts their behaviour toward the rest of business. The IRD is usually one of the biggest losers, which impacts all of us in loss of tax revenue.

The personal impact

The owners of small businesses invest at a very personal level in their business and it can lead to what is called ***identity fusion*** — the owners struggle to distinguish between their personal identity and the identity of their business.

Senior managers in large organisations can suffer the same identity fusion, as these positions expect significant commitment.

So, when the business fails, the owners or leaders are impacted heavily, because they feel part of their identity has been removed or irreversibly damaged.

Therefore, business failures may be a learning experience, but the learnings have come at too great a cost to accept.

> 66 *Remember that failure is an event, not a person.* 99
> — Zig Zigler

My hope is that we can reduce the number of failures.

When they do occur, I do hope those impacted have the resilience to come back from them and move on in life.

A history of business failures

> 66 *Those who cannot remember the past are condemned to repeat it.* 99
> — George Santayana

Considering the role people play in business failures, it is no surprise that it has been happening since the concept of business first existed.

Our first ancestors were making tools about 2.5 million years ago. We left Africa around 2 million years ago. Neanderthals evolved in Europe and the Middle East about 500,000 years ago and *Homo sapiens*, the modern human, can be tracked back to Africa about 200,000 years ago. Recent finds suggest it may even be much earlier than this.[8]

However, economics and business are very recent concepts, in evolutionary terms.

We only started making metal coins as currency about 2500 to 3000 years ago.

Business throughout the Middle Ages (fifth to 15th centuries) was characterised by great innovation and inventiveness as the world's cultures crossed through Europe, Asia and the Islamic nations.

However, at this time business was only carried out by the wealthy and social elite and was essentially out of the reach of most people. The elite supplied the force behind economic development. Their dietary preferences shaped the evolution of agriculture; their desires for luxury foods, apparel, and symbols of prestige laid the foundations for international business.[9]

Businessmen (and they were almost exclusively men back then) were also often part of the bureaucracies and government and had significant power. This political power, in turn, gave them control over commerce.

This era gave birth to many corporate giants. While they were well resourced, controlled and owned by governments or the elite, they were not immune to failure.

Famous historic failures — a small sample

Here is but a small sample of the many large corporate failures from the Middle Ages through to more recent centuries.

The Medici Bank was started in Florence, Italy, in 1397 by the Medici family and operated for around 100 years. It was the largest and most respected bank across Europe during its prime, having significant political influence, particularly with the Vatican. It was an institution whose practices still exist today in modern banking and accounting. As the expertise of its early founders disappeared, and new generations took over, issues started to emerge — not unlike in many modern businesses. Branches progressively failed across Europe until the empire collapsed in 1494.

The Company of Scotland, created by the Scottish parliament in 1695 to trade into Africa, the Indies and settle parts of South America, failed in 1707. The losses were so great it played a key role in encouraging Scotland to remain in the Union with Britain.

The South Sea Company, founded in 1711 as a private-public partnership, gave the company monopoly rights to trade into South America but was mainly set up to manage government debt (like a central bank). Shares in the company grew, and many benefited personally through insider trading, but it triggered a share market collapse in 1720 (the South Sea Bubble). This collapse triggered legislation, which gave Parliament significant power over company formations (e.g. The Bubble Act) and slowed freedom for new private companies to be formed for a century.

The Company of the West (previously the Mississippi Company) was founded by John Law in 1717 as a trading company and to settle the Mississippi Valley. John Law was a big believer in bank notes and paper money as a means of trade and had huge influence. He issued more and more of it. Unfortunately, it was not backed by physical wealth and he exaggerated the success of the business, which ultimately collapsed in 1720.

The Dutch East India Company was founded in 1602 when the Dutch government granted it a monopoly over the spice trade. It was the first company to issue shares and bonds to the public and was a truly transnational corporation — perhaps the first. Between 1602 and 1796, the company sent almost a million people to work in the Asian trade markets on nearly 5000 ships and generated huge wealth. It established what is now the city of Jakarta and lasted over 200 years. Changes in the trading markets, too much central control in the remote Jakarta, internal corruption and a dividend policy that sucked wealth out of the company led to its ultimate failure in 1799.

Thomas Russell and the Bank of New Zealand

New Zealand, while a much younger country, has not been immune to business failures.

Thomas Russell, the high-profile lawyer, businessman and politician in the late 1800s, and a strong supporter of the confiscation of Maori land, was the main force in starting the Bank of New Zealand in 1861. He was also the founder of various other businesses and speculative land deals in the Waikato and the South Island. He achieved great personal gain through his political influence. Russell overreached himself with his complex investments and faced insolvency and fraud charges. His activities contributed to the near collapse of the Bank of New Zealand in the late 1870s. If not for his involvement in the Waihi gold mine in the later years of his life, he may have been a poor man at his death in 1904.[10, 11]

The landscape for companies was changing — but only recently

The ease and freedom individuals have today to get involved in business and the structured legal and economic framework we now take for granted were not so common in past centuries. Corporations were traditionally owned or controlled by governments.

The right for individuals to own their own property was the basis of philosophical and religious debate around the 1700s by people like John Locke and Adam Smith. This was at a time when ownership and trade rested with the state. People, like Locke and Smith, debated that private people should also own that property.

Private ownership of companies, free from government control, was almost non-existent until the Joint-Stock Companies Act was passed in Britain in 1844. This is also seen as the birth of modern company law. Around this time, the Industrial Revolution was gaining momentum and with it came significant increases in disposable wealth, the birth of the modern cities, as well as economic, political and legal changes.

In 1855, the Limited Liability Act was enacted by the British parliament. Until then setting up a company required a special act of Parliament. This new act allowed people to start their own companies.[12]

As growth occurred with the Industrial Revolution, there was an associated desire to free up business to support that growth, with many laws being eased to allow ordinary people to start companies.

Not surprisingly, none of these reforms prevented company failures — humans are humans no matter the legal framework or the time in history — and businesses have continued to fail.

While people have been involved in trade and business enterprises for millennia, the concept of small business, companies as entities and the modern economy we take for granted has only been part of the landscape for a little over 150 years.

So, as we start our conversation on modern business failures, let's not forget that failure in business is not a new phenomenon. Let's also keep in mind that as humans, we may not yet have mentally evolved to a level that allows us to easily succeed at business in our modern world.

SECTION 2:
THE BUSINESSES THAT GOT IT WRONG — AND FAILED

Why these examples?

To discuss why businesses fail, we need to look at real examples.

Sadly, there is a wealth of examples of failed businesses I could have used for our discussion. The examples I chose were because of their profile, the accessibility of information in the public domain, the complexity, the relevance to our discussion, and access to people willing to talk about and share their experiences.

The more recent the failure, the more difficult it was to get to the issues — for many involved, the events were still too raw and the investigations were still in progress.

Business failure is about people

Humans were involved in every failure, so all the irrationalities and limitations that come with being human contributed, in some way, to these failures.

These failures hurt a lot of people, including those who were at the helm of the businesses that failed. While these people may have been directly to blame, they paid a heavy price, emotionally, professionally and financially, for their and their business's failure.

Most people involved in the failures I researched were happy to talk about what happened. For others, they simply couldn't bring themselves to discuss the events for many different reasons.

We are all different and we all respond to difficult events in our lives differently. I found exploring these failures to be no different.

The larger the failure, the more complex the factors contributing to the failure and the greater the diversity of views on the cause of the failure. These large failures also involved many more parties who played some part in the final demise. These larger failures also tend to have far more lasting impacts many years after the event, including ongoing legal battles.

Small business failures, and there are thousands each year, are usually simpler, especially as they involve only one or two key people. While the impact is far more contained than the larger failures, they are no less devastating to those involved. When discussing the failures with these owners, it involved their view, which may or may not reflect the true reasons for the failure.

**It became very clear to me that every person who had a view was correct —
from their perspective.**

I believe people were honest with me, even if the stories were different, depending on who I spoke to. It was simply that they recalled events differently and responded to them through their own biases, memories and filters.

So not only do our limitations as human beings contribute directly to failures, they also contribute to the differing recollections of why they failed.

Therefore, when we analyse and discuss the reasons behind these failures in Section 2, it requires a thorough look inside our minds, as it is there that decisions are formulated that ultimately decide a business's fate.

Other common contributing factors

As well as the contribution of people to the failures, and the decisions they made, there are other themes that continually repeat in almost every failure.

These include the impact of large debts, uncontrolled growth, external economic factors, high fixed costs, gaps in skills, weak governance and oversight, failure to assess and manage risks, and poorly managed tax obligations.

In **Section 3**, we will discuss these themes in greater detail and how we can better manage them in our own businesses.

2 THE FAILURE OF NEW ZEALAND'S COAL MINER — SOLID ENERGY

Some history

Solid Energy was formed in 1987 from the former State Coal Mines, a government department. It is a State-Owned Enterprise (SOE). (I say "is" rather than "was", as it was still limping along when I wrote this.)

An SOE is a business that is 100% owned by the government but is run by an independent board of directors and managers. The government has limited ability to influence the day-to-day operation of the business. The government was the company's only shareholder.

Solid Energy extracted, processed, marketed and distributed coal for steel production (coking coal) and coal for power generation (thermal coal) from underground and opencast mines around Huntly in the Waikato, Greymouth and Westport on the West Coast of the South Island, and New Vale in Southland.

Its sales within New Zealand were to New Zealand Steel, Fonterra's dairy factories and Genesis Energy for the Huntly Power Station. It also sold coal to a range of smaller coal users in the South Island, most notably dairy factories.

It exported coal from its South Island coal mines through Lyttelton Port near Christchurch into Japan, India, Chile, South Africa and China and had been doing so for decades.

A business saved from the ashes

In 1999, Solid Energy faced significant issues resulting from the Asian crisis. Poor-performing foreign currency deals resulted in the board being replaced, banking facilities being renegotiated, and the Crown offering support. The new chair initiated a strategic review and restructuring and soon after appointed Don Elder as the new CEO.

When Don Elder became CEO of Solid Energy, his role was to look seriously at breaking up the company and selling it. However, Elder saw the potential in the business and argued for a different strategy. His vision would ultimately see the business grow and deliver many successful years, before its demise in 2012.

Between 2003 and 2012, it averaged annual coal sales of between four and five million tonnes.

Historically, it generated very strong financial results. In the ten years prior to 2012, it had been profitable.

The cracks started showing

The shareholder, the New Zealand government, became aware of the serious underlying problems with the company when it organised a review of the business in preparation for its partial sale in late 2011.

In early 2012, Solid Energy started to report the potential for significant downturns in its profits and write-off of assets as world coal prices continued to fall.

In June 2012, the government put Solid Energy into what they called "intensive monitoring" where Treasury took a more active role in overseeing Solid Energy's activities, with the support of Deutsche Bank.[1]

Solid Energy started reducing costs but even as late as August 2012 remained committed to its growth strategy and was not prepared to bring third parties in to advise the board.[2,3]

The chair, John Palmer, who joined the board in 2006, resigned on 31 August 2012. Four other board members resigned in November 2012.

In late 2012, with the fall in world coal prices, Solid Energy was forced to mothball its Spring Creek Mine as it was bleeding cash without producing the coal volumes it had projected. It also announced changes to its operations with further widespread cost reductions including loss of staff.

By the end of this process, over 900 people would lose their jobs.

In its 2012 results it announced a loss of $40 million. By early 2013, the size of the company's debt and the overall state of the business played out in the headlines. In 2013, losses ballooned to $335 million, followed by a $182-million loss in 2014 and a loss of $177 million in 2015.

Elder backed the strategy to the very end. This is highlighted in a CEO announcement in August 2012 where Don Elder said:

"Our long-term business strategy remains fundamentally sound, based on global economics and our very significant coal resources. Demand for energy and coal will grow …"

Forensic accountants were engaged in October 2012.

Don Elder resigned in February 2013, having served as the CEO since May 2000.

In August 2013, the board announced it had placed the struggling company and all its associated companies in voluntary administration.

The company's debts had grown from zero in the early part of the decade to over $400 million in 2013.[4]

The creditors of Solid Energy and those of its non-coal subsidiary businesses engaged administrators in August 2015 to recover the money they were owed. The subsidiary businesses were liquidated while Solid Energy limped on.

So why did this happen?

Solid Energy's leadership

A high-profile CEO

The CEO, Don Elder, described the factors contributing to these problems at the time of the failure as *"the perfect storm"* of coal prices dropping, sales reducing, and the exchange rates reducing the value of the coal they sold. Elder stated that the coal industry around the world suffered a *"stunning blow"*, with coal prices falling faster and further than anyone expected.

Don Elder graduated as an engineer and received a Rhodes Scholarship to Oxford University in 1980. He worked internationally before taking over the helm of Solid Energy in 2000, which he held for 13 years.

Don Elder's original brief was to close the business or sell off what he could to gain as much as possible for the government. This included a possible sale of North Island mines to Genesis Energy.

However, Elder saw far greater potential in the business than others saw and proposed a different scenario for the business, one the government supported.

Don Elder was a highly intelligent man, a big personality, high profile, and a visionary leader. His vision extended well beyond what was best for Solid Energy but also what was best for the country. He had a very strong relationship with the most senior political people in both sides of politics, including Prime Minister John Key.

Don Elder was very unlikely to sit on his hands. Solid Energy would not have been lifted from its near death in 2000 to what it became had it not been for Don Elder.

An extract from a personal report he published in November 2009 and submitted to government on the challenge for New Zealand was subtitled *"Be bolder than a 'stand back and wait' approach"*. Don Elder was never going to be a CEO who was going to "stand back and wait" for things to happen.[5]

Working for a person like Elder could inspire, which it did, but his intellect and drive could also be intimidating for those less confident. This meant many were disinclined to challenge him, including members of his executive team and the board.

The board supported Don Elder's strategy throughout his time as CEO.

All correspondence between the board and government leading up to the failure was aligned with Don Elder's vision.[6]

If the strategy a CEO is progressing is not one the board supports, while acting in the best interests of the shareholder (in this case the government), then the board cannot simply let it continue. The board must instruct the CEO to change tack, or they must replace the CEO with someone who is more likely to adhere to the wishes of the board and shareholder.

The board, especially the chairman, John Palmer, supported Elder and backed him to the very end.

A talented board of directors

The chairman, John Palmer, was a highly successful, experienced and respected board member. He was also very well regarded by other board members, the CEO and the management team. In 2017, he was recognised with the Institute of Directors' highest accolade, the Distinguished Fellow Award, for his contribution to governance. Unfortunately, he was at the helm when Solid Energy failed, and he and five other board members left the board in the latter half of 2012.

The Solid Energy board members were very experienced people. Combined, they had held over 100 directorships, on some of the most prominent, long standing businesses in New Zealand. These included Fletchers, Air New Zealand and Heartland Bank. It was a diverse board including both genders, members from the oil and gas and resources sectors, construction, coal, finance, and legal businesses. Such diversity and experience would be deemed best practice for any board.

The board could be criticised for not challenging the CEO and the chair more, and may have had insufficient experience to understand the high-risk growth strategy Don Elder wanted to lead the company into.

For a large, complex business like Solid Energy there were several factors that contributed to its demise and a range of parties, who together, contributed.

Challenges of coal mining in New Zealand

While the quality of coal in New Zealand is high, it was not an easy place to mine coal. The beauty of the New Zealand countryside and its geological history make it a stunning place to live and visit. However, it makes it a tough place to mine coal, to both extract the coal and meet environmental standards. Solid Energy faced major challenges, particularly with its South Island facilities.

There were two distinct parts to Solid Energy's coal business. There were mines producing coal solely for domestic customers. These were backed by longer term contracts, provided the underpinning cash flow for the business, were profitable, and were cushioned from world coal prices.

Other West Coast mines, like Stockton and Spring Creek, sold coal into the international market and were exposed to the volatility of world commodity prices. They also involved very short-term contracts that could be renegotiated or changed at short notice.

Stockton — the more successful mine

Solid Energy spent around $128 million on the coal-processing plant at Stockton Mine, an opencast mine 35 kilometres north of Westport on the New Zealand West Coast. This project aimed to process and reclaim large volumes of stockpiled coal that historically could not be sold to customers. While the investment was significant, it was based on a short payback period, and, as it processed already mined coal, it did not require high mining costs.

The headache that was Spring Creek Mine

The Spring Creek underground mine in the hills north of Greymouth on the West Coast promised great returns from excellent coal resources when it opened in 1998. The geology was very difficult and initial production levels were below forecasts.

In April 2006, Solid Energy informed ministers that the existing operation at Spring Creek was no longer economically viable. They stated: *"In 1998 the mine was opened, but by 2000 it had become obvious that opening the mine had been the wrong decision"*.[7]

In 2006, Solid Energy planned to cease production at the mine. Elder and the management recommended to the board that the mine be closed but the board rejected this in a close vote. Instead, the board hoped to find an investor to buy or at least partially underwrite the development costs and risks of the mine.

In 2007, Solid Energy sold 49% of the Spring Creek Mine to Cargill International. (Cargill) sold its share in 2012 when prices dropped, claiming it lost $63.5million from the venture.[8]

In late 2012, Solid Energy closed the Spring Creek Mine, hoping it might be reopened at some future date.

Solid Energy had invested significant sums into the venture over its life. One review stated the mine had *"failed to deliver on a single plan submitted during its 12-year life"*.[9]

Finally, in February 2017, Solid Energy announced that, despite an exhaustive sales process, they were unsuccessful in securing a buyer for Spring Creek Mine and closed the mine.[10]

Living within their means

These mines demonstrated the high risk associated with mining in New Zealand, especially when the revenue to be gained from the sale of that coal faced the further uncertainty of world market prices.

Venturing into even riskier ventures would seem unwise.

Solid Energy had traditionally followed a very conservative approach to the core coal-mining business considering these challenges. They lived within their means, carrying no debt, and only committed to projects with very short payback periods, especially if the projects were exposed to world coal prices. There was a clear understanding of the risks in the decade prior to the failure. In this period, the company ran a very difficult coal portfolio but did it profitably.

They couldn't last forever

Solid Energy, especially Elder, realised that their mining activities were getting increasingly expensive as reserves reduced. The Rotowaro Mine at Huntly had less than 10 years of supply left; Spring Creek would only get more difficult to mine. There was an increasing reliance on Stockton Mine and Huntly East Mine to fund the business.

Solid Energy would eventually be unable to sustain itself solely as a coal-mining business. It needed to look to scale down the company or look to new strategies.

Not consistent with "100% Pure"

Solid Energy faced direct pressure from environmental groups. In 2008, Greenpeace blocked the departure of Solid Energy's coal shipments from Lyttelton Port. Environmental groups also clashed with Solid Energy over its impact on West Coast habitats, both on site and in the courts.

Solid Energy faced the challenge of surviving in an industry under huge pressure and scrutiny as the greenhouse gas debate and the environmental impact of opencast mining increased. The mining and exporting of coal was also at odds with a country branded as 100% environmentally pure. At the end of the 1990s and in the first decade of this century, significant political and public debate about New Zealand's role in climate change and switch away from thermal fuels played out heavily in mainstream media. Energy companies, especially Solid Energy, were thrust into the middle of this debate.

New developments

Solid Energy had access to large reserves of lignite coal in the South Island and gas locked in deep coal seams that they could not access. Finding ways to turn these reserves into cash was one underpinning goal for Solid Energy's future.

Other options were needed

With these issues and a more expensive and increasingly difficult coal business, it was not surprising that the board and management looked to other strategic options in the first decade of the new century.

The government (and shareholder) supported Solid Energy's ideas, as it indicated at its 2009 shareholders meeting:

> 66 *We encourage the Board to continue its investigations into new energy uses for coal — the potential benefits for the company are significant, as they are for contributing to economic growth …* 99 [11]

The rationale for the move was summarised in the CEO's statement in a 2007 media release:

> 66 *… we identified some time ago that we wanted to build a diversified portfolio of energy businesses alongside our existing coal mining operations. This strategy,*

and our increasing presence in the bioenergy sector, support national objectives to increase energy security and affordability in future through utilisation of diverse indigenous energy resources while also increasing renewable energy and reducing energy-related emissions. **99** [12]

Solid Energy pursued these options alone, with their own funding, and went well beyond their core strength, which was mining coal. Elder did spend significant time pursuing partners and possible funders, particularly in China.

The company expected to gain good returns from these projects, would fund them through their existing business but would also need to increase its lending, as was highlighted by the chairman:

> **66** *These projects will have good prospective returns. The capital demands will be largely supported by strong operating cash flows from our existing operations but our debt will also increase significantly.* **99** [13]

Rather than using the huge fall in coal prices in 2008 as a warning to be cautious (see Figure 2), they instead increased their lending from near zero to $220 million by 2011.

The importance of keeping the cash rolling in to the company is evident in the above statement from the chairman. These cash flows came from selling large volumes of coal at a good price. It would therefore seem self-evident that a fall in the amount of coal being sold or the price it attracted would have a direct impact on Solid Energy's ability to fund the new strategy.

A lack of transparency

Solid Energy's annual reports did not provide separate financial details on the performance of these new non-coal developments. The more stringent approval processes normally used in the traditional mining part of the business were not followed for the new developments. This created resentment within Solid Energy — the frugal coal business was less than impressed with the cavalier approach of the new project processes.

As they progressed, with performance below that expected, the outside world was none the wiser.

Board members who joined the board after these projects had started said there was little discussion about them at the board table. They had not reached the next stage of approvals so did not involve detailed debate about them — spending simply continued with limited board scrutiny.

By the time the reality of issues facing Solid Energy was known, they had already spent around $250 million on all these projects, including $146 million on renewable projects and about $80 million on land purchases.[14]

So, what were these new developments?

South Island lignite

New Zealand has 10–15 billion tonnes of lignite resources, mostly located in Southland. Lignite is a very low-quality coal. Solid Energy had been investigating a range of options for the use of lignite. This included use by industrial markets, electricity generation, transport fuels, petrochemicals and coal-to-oil and coal-to-fertilisers.

Solid Energy looked at the viability of reopening Mataura Mine near Gore to serve the South Island's industrial market. The mine operated between 1951 and 2000. It was purchased by Solid Energy in 1996.

Solid Energy faced strong opposition to the projects from environmental groups. The Coal Action Network Aotearoa described them as projects that produced "dirty, low-grade coal being turned into a product nobody wanted, digging up prime Southland farmland for coal".[15]

Solid Energy made significant land purchases and purchased the rights to minerals.

It considered three main technologies: lignite to diesel; lignite to fertiliser; and lignite to briquettes.

The lignite-to-fertiliser concept was pursued with joint venture partners Ravensdown, the New Zealand agricultural company. The venture aimed to produce urea fertiliser that would make New Zealand self-sufficient and potentially an exporter.[16]

The plant to convert the lignite was predicted to cost more than $5 billion, would create about 500 jobs and turn an estimated 2 million tonnes of lignite into 1.2 million tonnes of urea annually. This was a huge investment for any business, let alone a small company like Solid Energy.

Government officials expressed concerns about the project. Solid Energy had already committed large amounts of money without consulting the shareholder. It was also a shift from their core business and strategy.

Solid Energy also pursued a project to convert lignite into higher-energy coal briquettes for local and export markets. It built the $28 million Mataura Briquette Plant in 2011, partnering with an Australian business that had developed its coal-upgrading technology at two demonstration plants in the USA. The Mataura plant was considered a demonstration plant that was unlikely to generate income in the short term, and perhaps ever.

Projects of this size were always going to require external funding. Solid Energy did pursue this.

By 2013, with rising debts and no likely revenue, these projects were abandoned. By 2014, it had sold its 2000 hectares of farmland in Southland.

Solid Energy sold the briquette plant to its Australian partner in 2014, after which it was mothballed awaiting a buyer to operate it locally or dismantle and move the plant.

Renewable energy projects

A move away from thermal fuel into renewable energy options at the time seemed a wise strategic move. Unfortunately, it proved to be very costly and unsuccessful, eventually seeing $146 million being written off these projects.[17]

Every one of these ventures was relatively unproven, was high risk and unlikely to see any return on investment for many years.

These are some of the details.

WOOD PELLETS

Solid energy bought a small business, Nature's Flame, in 2003. This was Solid Energy's way of entering the renewables industry. Nature's Flame operated a small wood pellet plant in Rolleston, near Christchurch.

Solid Energy, through Nature's Flame, built a $34-million plant in Taupo, which opened in 2010. A review of the project by the Auditor-General indicated the project "significantly underachieved".[17] It cost more than expected. It produced less wood pellets than was planned, and the price it received for the pellets was below expectations. It lost money from the day it opened.

Solid Energy sold out of Nature's Flame in 2012. They wrote off almost $30 million in the process.

The Auditor-General's review stated that the decision makers (management and the board) did follow a reasonable process to make the decisions but failed to objectively assess the risks, holding an overly upbeat view of the project's viability.

BIODIESEL

In 2007, Solid Energy purchased Canterbury Biodiesel, which processed waste vegetable oil from various sources.

They were hoping to tap into the government's then biodiesel mandated targets. At the time, Elder stated:

❝ *Increased use of biodiesel will offer greater energy security and, as imported oil prices continue to increase, better affordability while at the same time reducing environmental impacts.*❞[18]

The government was dissatisfied with the level of take-up of the scheme and ended it in 2012. This policy change effectively ended this project — a risk any business should consider when its survival is based on the policies of the government of the day. Solid Energy sold the business back to the managers and a supplier (at an undisclosed price) in early 2013. The business is now called Green Fuels Ltd. Solid Energy wrote off $9 million when it was sold. This excludes the losses running the business leading up to its sale.

Gas production

Solid Energy had been working on pilot processes to produce gas from its underground coal reserves for some years. It was looking at two processes. One extracted gas trapped in the seams of coal reserves (coal seam gas) and the other converted the coal from deep underground seams into a synthetic gas before pumping it to the surface (underground coal gasification, or UCG).

In the 2011 annual report the chairman stated:

❝ *These projects will test the viability of technology to upgrade lower-rank Southland lignites and to access deep un-mineable coal seams in the Waikato and will pave the way for other large-scale and more complex projects in the future. It will take some years to bring these large potential projects to fruition, but they provide real opportunity to deliver value to the business and create significant benefits for New Zealand.* ❞ [19]

Solid Energy built a $22-million gas pilot plant near Huntly in the central North Island. It started producing gas in April 2012.

They had hoped to use this technology to tap into the much larger gas reserves in Taranaki. External expertise from petroleum consultants Netherlands Sewell and Associates, out of the USA, assessed the gas reserves that could be extracted from coal in Taranaki. They believed them to be significant.[20]

Gas reserves looked good and the initial trial plant (at Huntly) showed real promise, but any such exploration involved risks at a time when they did not have the capacity to fund these risks, nor did the plant deliver the level of success first hoped.

In response to the issues in 2012, Solid Energy was forced to scale back operations at the Huntly demonstration plant. The cash required to keep the exploration and research going and the fact the pilot plant produced no sellable gas gave them little choice. They had to write off about $18.5 million on this investment.

By 2013, all activities in gas exploration and production ceased. Gas assets were disposed of in 2014.

National Resources Company — Solid Energy's "audacious" goal

The BHAG

In 1994, Jim Collins and Jerry Porras coined the phrase a "Big Hairy Audacious Goal", or BHAG, in their book *Built to Last: Successful Habits of Visionary Companies.*[21] Developing a BHAG is a technique to drive the leaders of companies to push the boundaries of their thinking. Collins and Porras stated that:

> **"**... *a true BHAG is clear and compelling and serves as a unifying focal point of effort — often creating immense team spirit. It has a clear finish line, so the organisation can know when it has achieved the goal; people like to shoot for the finish lines* ...**"**

They also stated that the BHAG, to be successful, must have a wide level of commitment to the goal and be one that will live on beyond the leader or leaders who created it. Example BHAGs that Collins and Porras gave in their book included Kennedy's goal to reach the moon, Boeing's development of the 747, Ford's democratisation of the motor vehicle, and General Electric's goal to be number one or two in every category it operated in.

Solid Energy's BHAG

Solid Energy's BHAG was to become the National Resources Company, a majority state owned, diversified, natural resources company for New Zealand – a further clear message that the board and CEO did not see the existing operations were sufficient to fulfil Solid Energy's purpose.

Don Elder's vision for the National Resources Company was outlined in a paper he developed in November 2009 titled *"An Export- Led Economic Step Change for New Zealand"*. In that report, he raised concerns about New Zealand's economic future and its opportunities to maximise the use of its resources.[22]

The National Resources Company would see Solid Energy continue with its existing coal mining activities. However, It also sought preferential access to hydrocarbon and mineral resources, absorbing oil and gas exploration and production into the National Resources Company, as well as expanding its lignite conversions projects, iron sands, coal seam gas, underground coal gasification and other renewable projects.

Solid Energy predicted a capital expenditure programme of over $15 billion to develop the projects to 2020. They forecast this would generate positive revenue by 2014, exceeding over $12 billion per year by 2020

The shareholder was not keen — at all

Solid Energy pitched this to their shareholders (the government) in 2010. John Palmer wrote directly to Prime Minister John Key in May 2010 seeking his support for this.[23] This was a clear indication that, while a vision born from Don Elder, it was one that had the board's support.

The shareholders expressed unease about the concept. They felt it was based on aggressive expectations on future resource prices, including coal, oil and gas prices, and would require the government to override the rights of other commercial businesses, not to mention creating very difficult policy changes and the associated political challenges. Solid Energy also looked to the government to support the longer-term funding of these projects.[24]

Advisors to the government cautioned against proceeding without *"heavily testing the strength of the above arguments"*.[25]

A Treasury Report to Solid Energy on behalf of SOE Minister Simon Power and Finance Minister Bill English stated:

> **66***[We don't] support the development of a single National Resources Company as the optimal way (given the potential risk and return) to maximise the value of New Zealand's mineral resources. We consider that Solid Energy should focus on areas where it has specific capability.***99**[26]

Unfortunately, Solid Energy's BHAG had mixed levels of support from within the company and no support from the government who would, as both a policy maker and shareholder, have a significant part to play in its success.

It is also particularly interesting that the board and management wished to change Solid Energy into a business the owners did not want — when it should be the owners' wishes they should have been pursuing.

Shareholder's influence and its impact on Solid Energy

Solid Energy and the shareholder's relationship was always a difficult one. The management and board had a strong appetite for risk and growth. The shareholder, being government, was always going to be conservative, conscious of public perceptions, and careful in the way it used what was, ultimately, taxpayer's money.

Crown Company Monitoring Advisory Unit — the government's watchdog

The performance of all SOEs and the selection of SOE boards, including those for Solid Energy, was overseen by the Crown Company Monitoring Advisory Unit (CCMAU). They acted on behalf of the government. In 2009, CCMAU was absorbed into Treasury, which took over this role.

While Elder had a very close relationship with senior politicians, including the Prime Minister, John Key, and was well regarded by them, he and Palmer always had a mixed and difficult relationship with the officials. When the troubles arrived for Solid Energy, it is not surprising that the senior politicians, who were once supportive and close to Elder, distanced themselves from what had happened, and the officials were never likely to show any empathy for Solid Energy's situation. If anything, the officials showed Solid Energy and particularly Don Elder no sympathy.

Go forth — be commercial

In the years leading up to Solid Energy's demise, CCMAU was putting significant pressure on all SOEs to lift their commercial performance, complete credible valuations of their businesses, take on more debt and deliver higher returns to the shareholder. While not explicitly stated, it appeared the government was preparing its energy-based SOEs for a potential sale and wanted them to reflect performance that would prove attractive to buyers.

These requests were also made to the other energy-based SOEs that were eventually part-sold (Genesis Energy, Meridian, Mighty River Power). The government was comfortable for these businesses to structure themselves in a way that increased their debts, provided greater dividends to government and, as a result, would likely lower their credit ratings.

In May 2009:

> *Officials recommend that Ministers communicate a strong expectation that SOEs increase gearing and dividend yield, in accordance with company-specific targets, in order to increase accountability, discipline and financial outcomes.* [27]

In 2010, correspondence from the government to Solid Energy's board stated:

> *Rather than striking an appropriate balance between the payment of dividends and retaining cash for future investment, the SEL [Solid Energy Limited] Board continues to place capital investment ahead of providing dividends.*

Dividends appear to be treated as a residual item, only to be paid after all capital requirements have been met and subject to maintaining a 35% gearing ratio.[28]

An overvalued business?

This gearing ratio is the ratio of debt to equity. Solid Energy's assessment of the value of the business affected the perceived value of debt to equity. The higher their assessment of the value of the business, the higher the perceived equity in the business. The higher the perceived equity, the greater ease there was in attracting debt. As we will discuss, Solid Energy's view of its value was not agreed by many outside the company.

In the government's defence, they were expecting SOEs to calculate accurate valuations of the business — debate over the credibility of Solid Energy's valuations went on for some time leading up to the failure.

The push to extract more money out of Solid Energy in the form of dividends continued, as in a letter to John Palmer in 2011:

Shareholding Ministers expect that dividends show a degree of consistency across years, and that an appropriate balance between dividends and re-investment in the business is maintained. In addition, shareholding Ministers have asked the COMU [Crown Ownership Monitoring Unit, who replaced CCMAU and oversaw SOEs at that stage] to work with you to determine an appropriate dividend policy.[29]

While SOE boards and management can push back on these requests from government, the pressure can be overwhelming (something I saw first-hand from my time in the executive team of an SOE). While Solid Energy may not have directly responded to these requests, its board could not have ignored them.

Between 2009 and 2012, Solid Energy paid the government $194 million in dividends.[30]

They were lending to the government — or maybe not?

When Solid Energy finally failed, the bulk of the debt owed by Solid Energy was to five banks. These were ANZ, BNZ, the Commonwealth Bank of Australia, Westpac and the Bank of Tokyo. Solid Energy also had other lending arrangements in place with TSB Bank.[31]

This lending was on an unsecured basis, indicating the banks' confidence in the business. It is unlikely this would have happened had the banks done detailed due diligence and understood the real risks of lending to this business.

The banks that lent money to Solid Energy did so with what they believed was an implied guarantee from the government, as the sole shareholder. Basically, many lenders felt that if they were lending to Solid Energy, they were lending to the New Zealand government. As such they saw the risk as being much lower than had Solid Energy been privately owned or listed on a stock exchange, as most mining companies around the world were.

I spoke to the key Treasury officials who were around when Solid Energy failed. They recall speaking at length to the banks on this point and continued to reinforce, as per all the documentation, that the government was not going to guarantee the activities of their SOEs including Solid Energy. This view was highlighted in the comments from Kevin Murphy, the Chief Executive of TSB Bank:

> **❝**I'm sure many people would consider that investment in state owned enterprises provided an implicit guarantee, but clearly the performance of Solid Energy indicates that there are risks associated with SOEs that perhaps were not well understood by people in the market place.**❞**[32]

The banks did not feel the government would allow Solid Energy to fail and would provide a rescue package. They found out the hard way that they would not bail out Solid Energy.

When others were finally able to take a closer look

The mixed ownership model

The New Zealand government went to the 2011 elections with a policy of selling 49% of its four energy SOEs, Meridian Energy, Mighty River Power, Genesis Energy and Solid Energy. This is what the government called its *"mixed ownership model"*.

After winning the election, the government instigated a detailed review of each of these companies to see how ready they were for sale. The three electricity companies were all ready and were subsequently part-sold, but things did not look so good for Solid Energy.

The review of Solid Energy raised some serious concerns for the shareholders, not only of its readiness for sale but the underlying status of the business.

The UBS report

The November 2011 report, completed by UBS, the international financial services business, made several recommendations before a sale could be considered:[33]

- Focus on the core coal-mining business.
- Increase expenditure to prove the current levels of coal reserves were correct *[Note: This would have increased the value of the business in readiness for a sale but would have been unaffordable considering the state of the company.]*
- Downsize the New Development activities particularly around the large-scale projects associated with the Southland lignite resources (coal-to-fertiliser and coal-to liquids for liquid fuels).
- Sell its renewable businesses (biodiesel and wood pellets).
- Repayment of debt before the partial sale.
- Reduce corporate head office and overhead costs.

The report also threw doubts over the ambitious forecasts Solid Energy had on future coal prices.

Solid Energy's board and CEO did not accept these views.

World coal prices and what the business was worth

Figure 2 on the next page shows how coal prices have fluctuated over some 20 years. It shows the prolonged low prices in the late 1990s and early 2000s. From 2007 onwards, prices were highly volatile. The significant rise in price in 2007 followed by the significant crash highlighted the volatility of international coal prices. The three lines superimposed on this figure approximate Don Elder's prediction of future coal prices taken from his 2009 paper

The government noted Solid Energy's response to this price crash in 2008:

> ❝The speed with which Solid Energy responded to the near collapse in global coking coal prices and demand in late 2008 was very pleasing as was the way shareholding Ministers were kept appraised.❞[34]

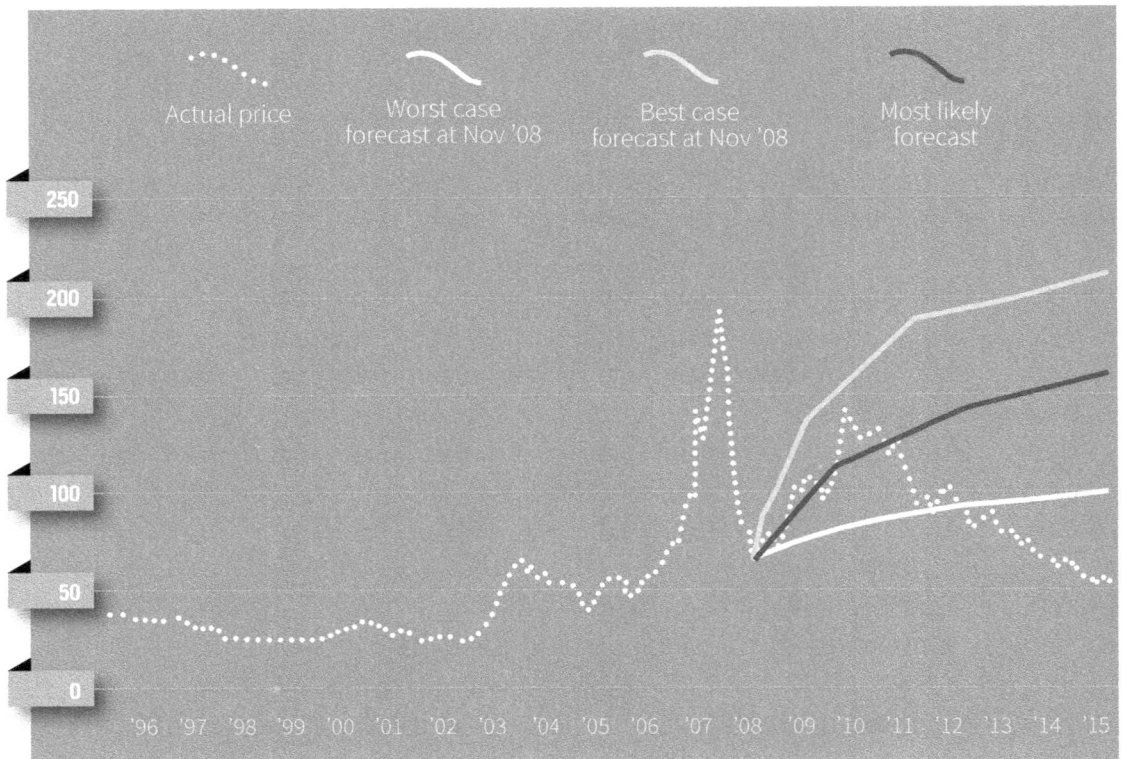

Figure 1. World coal prices 1996 to 2015.

It would seem that Don Elder and Solid Energy were buoyed by the views of others at their ability to predict and act on world coal prices. This level of self-confidence eventually proved fatal.

Were coal prices going only one way?

Don Elder held the view that world energy prices and therefore coal prices were going to increase, especially with the predicted growth in countries like China and India. This was outlined in his 2009 paper where he warned of a possible resource shortage:

> 66 *Prices of most resources will rise to 2008 levels, then eventually pass them and continue rising into the futur.e* 99 [35]

The connection between Solid Energy's performance and coal process was acknowledged. Members of a Select Committee hearing asked:

> 66 *Solid Energy's performance is obviously very susceptible to international coal prices. Are there any options for gaining longer term contracts to smooth out some of the volatility?* 99 [36]

While the answer to this question was "No", it does highlight that even those distant from the business understood the importance of coal prices to Solid Energy.

Was Air New Zealand worried about oil prices?

At the time John Palmer was chair of Solid Energy, he was also chairman of Air New Zealand. A question government officials posed to me after the events of Solid Energy was the inconsistency that appeared to exist in his views. Rapidly rising energy prices, as predicted by Don Elder, would have been a serious risk to Air New Zealand.

It is unclear whether the view held by the Solid Energy board about future energy prices was the same view held by the Air New Zealand board.

It is surprising that a person as experienced as John Palmer was not more vocal in challenging Elder's prediction of future prices. It is unclear why the prices presented to Palmer at Solid Energy did not lead him to apply significant scrutiny considering the information he would also have been receiving about oil process on the Air New Zealand board.

High coal prices meant an over-valued company

The value of the overall business was impacted by the company's assessment of the price of coal and their bullish view of the returns they would get from the new developments.

In 2010, the government expressed concerns about Solid Energy's assessment of how much the business was worth:

> 66 *The most significant issue is the change in the commercial valuation which has increased 60% from $2.5 billion to $3.9 billion.* 99 [37]

In the later stages of 2011 and early into 2012, Solid Energy still valued the business at $2.8 billion, which, at the time, was significantly higher than the $1.7 billion calculated by two separate independent valuations. [38]

The government continued to raise concerns:

> 66 *'Officials recommend that Ministers communicate a strong expectation that*

SOEs conduct credible commercial valuations in accordance with the SOE Act, and transparently report the valuation in their Statement of Corporate Intent' — While Solid Energy did this, in the years soon after it was shown that their valuation was much higher than other people saw it due mainly to the elevated view of future coal prices. [39]

People were starting to raise doubts about Solid Energy's view of coal prices. In the scope of a meeting between Don Elder, his executive and government representatives (COMU) in April 2011, the following was raised:

Although Solid Energy holds its own view on the future oil prices, COMU would like to test the value produced by the New Energy projects based on alternative price paths. [40]

. . . but then coal prices started falling

In late 2010, prices started to turn and drop — and continued to drop. World demand for coal was generally lower, but one of the main reasons for the fall in coal prices at that time was the increased production of gas extracted from shale in the USA (sometimes called shale gas).

In 2000, shale gas provided only 1% of US gas production; by 2010, with advancements in extraction technology, it grew to over 20% and the trend was predicted to increase. This forced the price of gas down and saw a switch from coal to gas in the USA. This in turn saw a glut of good-quality US coal having to be sold on the world market. This forced world coal prices down — and with more shale gas being produced the trend was likely to continue.

As mentioned, UBS did not support Solid Energy's views. Solid Energy's board countered UBS's reports with comments like the following:

UBS have applied their view of future price paths for coal which are at considerable variance to those of Solid Energy. Our historic analysis suggests not only is Solid Energy's track superior in this regard (and the motivation for UBS's low case projections transparent), but a significant element of Solid Energy's competitive advantage in promoting its growth strategy lies in the company's well worked and proven analysis.

and

66 *In summary, the UBS approach runs the significant risk of sub-optimising the future value of Solid Energy.* **99**[41]

We can't always get it right

When enough people make predictions of the future, it is likely some will get it right and some wrong. Those who get it right may be considered enlightened experts. Those who do not may be ignored in future discussions.

Forecasting the future is, at best, an educated guess. It may even be luck. For Solid Energy to imply so boldly that you are wrong as we are always right shows a level of arrogance that was courting danger. It is unclear if anyone at management or board level asked, *"What if we are wrong?"*

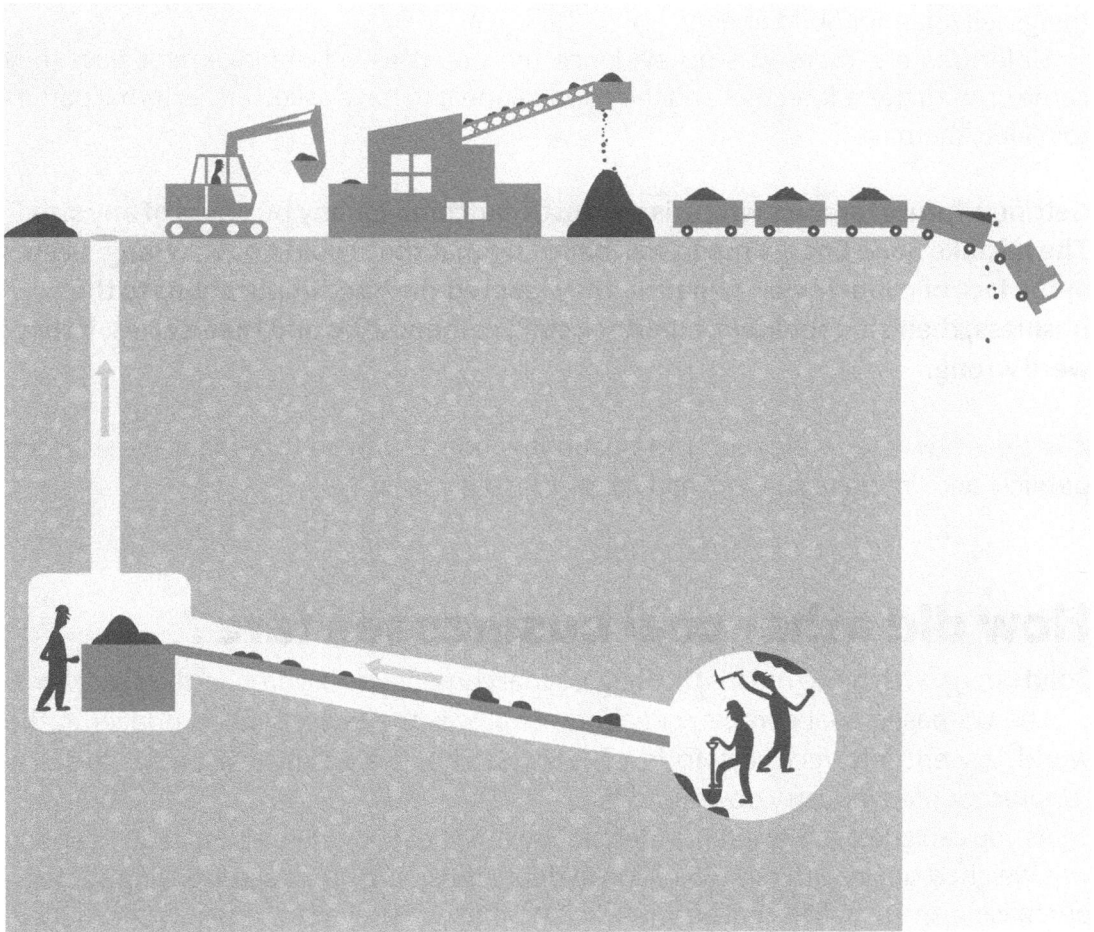

A report by the Auditor-General in 2014 surmised why Solid Energy countered everyone else's views on coal prices:

- Solid Energy considered that it had a better track record than analysts in predicting future price paths. Solid Energy's understanding of the fundamentals of global coal and related markets, its contacts within the industry, and its application to its business, had been accurate in the previous decade;
- Solid Energy believed that few resource companies, at least in the coal sector, rely on market analyst forecasts to make their internal investment decisions.

Solid Energy did have a good track record of forecasting coal prices, relative to market analysts. They had access to industry knowledge not readily available to the investment community.

Other entities like the New Zealand Treasury, Forsyth Barr and Macquarie Equities Research all made more conservative assessments of coal prices some years before things fell apart for Solid Energy.

Unfortunately, there was no evidence the board asked management how they came up with these forecasts and they don't appear to have asked any external parties to review them.

Getting a future forecast wrong is a realistic outcome for any business of any size. The mistake Solid Energy made was believing that they could not be wrong, even in the face of counter views. In turn, they ignored the huge implications to the business, their shareholders, creditors, staff, communities and themselves, if they were wrong.

It is clear now they were very wrong and it is not a surprise that many were saying publicly and I'm quite sure privately that "We told you so!"

How did other coal businesses fare?

Solid Energy was by no means the biggest coal company to fail around the same time.

The US-based coal company Peabody Coal was the largest coal producer in the world. It went into receivership in early 2013. They stated the reason for this was "unprecedented industry downturn".[42]

As you can guess, other internal decisions within Peabody were also at play. Peabody was weighed down with over $5 billion in debt after going on an asset-buying strategy, purchasing an Australian coal business in 2011 that was proven to be highly overvalued.

Alpha Natural Resources, another US coal business, also failed. It too took on significant debt when it bought several other coal businesses, before striking issues in 2012. It had to sell mines and lay off hundreds of staff. After four years of losses it filed for bankruptcy in 2015.[43]

There are numerous other examples of coal-based businesses that struck major issues and losses with the downturn. Others failed. However, many more survived the shock than failed.

What can we learn from the Solid Energy failure?

There is no question that running the Solid Energy business was not an easy task for anyone. Don Elder took a company from the brink and grew it into a very successful business, one that he was completely devoted to. Even in the face of significant challenges faced by Solid Energy, it had demonstrated financial success over many years.

In simple terms, the failure came from business leaders that ultimately made the wrong decisions. While this may appear obvious in hindsight, such decisions did not consider the risks and the signals many others saw, including the owners of the business.

So, what can we learn from the events of Solid Energy's failure?

1. **BE CLEAR ON STRATEGY — AND WHEN TO SAY "NO"**
   Businesses need to be very clear what success means for their business and what its core purpose is. That is, why it exists.

   While Solid Energy's move away from coal mining was a deliberate strategy, it went way beyond its financial capability and competence. It would seem that the ambitions of the company's CEO, supported by the board, meant Solid Energy was living well beyond its means.

   Instead of having a very strong business with many sources of income to back a few high-risk projects, Solid Energy had really only one solid source of funding, Stockton Mine, but many high-cost, high-risk projects that it alone was funding.

2. **ASK "WHAT IF ...?"**
   "What if coal prices don't continue to rise?" If the worst case does happen, how

will it be managed? What signs will be seen that the chosen scenario may be happening and what action can be taken? What are the consequences if the worst case eventuates for this business? It seems, even with hindsight, Solid Energy and especially Don Elder and the board did not ask "What if …?" enough, even when many around them were asking this question of them.

3. WE DO NOT HAVE ALL THE ANSWERS

We should be very wary about past successes leading to the belief that "we know best". No matter how smart or how experienced we feel we are, we can always learn from others. We may not be the smartest people in the room. In Solid Energy's case, there is no questioning their abilities. However, there were many people warning them and whether it was ego, arrogance or some other motive, they seem blinded to this.

4. NO ONE CAN PREDICT THE FUTURE

Anyone who believes they can forecast the future with certainty will be disappointed. If we get it right, it could be foresight or it could also be luck. If we don't, it does not mean we don't know what we are doing. Solid Energy refused to accept they could be wrong in their future forecasts. They got it right more often than they got it wrong, but when they got it wrong the impact was catastrophic for the business. Many good people paid a serious price for this.

We must always consider the flaws in future projections. Even the best-resourced analyst in the world can never predict the future — no one can.

5. IRRATIONAL PEOPLE, IRRATIONAL MARKETS

Economies, markets and therefore the price of products and commodities are determined by people, and people are irrational, as we will discuss in some detail in later chapters. This is the basis of behavioural economics. Even if those in these markets are acting rationally, world markets are unpredictable. Becoming overly confident about future economic or projections of markets is predicting the unpredictable.

6. IF YOU CAN'T AFFORD IT, YOU CAN'T AFFORD IT

Solid Energy needed to spend significant sums on their existing coal assets. To then spend many hundreds of millions on high-risk ventures based on optimistic future forecasts, on the back of large debt, in a relatively small resource business was living beyond their means.

7. HIGH DEBT AND HIGH FIXED COSTS

Unfortunately, high debt and high fixed costs result in a pretty simple challenge — you need lots more cash coming in every month to cover these costs. If your sales fall, for whatever reason, and there is not enough cash each month, things will not end well — no matter how big or small the business is.

8. THE BANKS ARE RUN BY IRRATIONAL PEOPLE ALSO

Sadly, the banks were happy to lend money to Solid Energy on the assumption the government was going to back Solid Energy if it got into trouble; a very flawed and dangerous assumption. Likewise, just because the banks are prepared to lend us money does not mean we should take it.

We will cover the risks of debt, fixed costs and cash in greater detail a little later.

9. LISTEN TO YOUR SHAREHOLDERS

The relationship between Solid Energy and the shareholder was always a strained one. Solid Energy appeared to look upon the government as a hand-brake on their aspirations rather than the owner of the business. When the management and board of a company need to act in the best interests of the company, they can't ignore the interests of the shareholder, even if it is the government.

10. THE ROLE OF GOVERNMENTS IN BUSINESS

The shareholder was by no means blameless in the years leading up to the failure. It put significant pressure on Solid Energy, and all the SOEs that it owned. This was to produce regular and healthy dividends to fund the government's activities and, if necessary, to take on debt to do so. While it might be within the board and management's right to ignore such requests, the pressure to respond can be overwhelming. There is always a danger when the owners of a business who are not involved in the running of that business (as managers or directors) ask for short-term financial benefits that may not be in the business's long-term best interest.

11. NO ONE WINS IN A FAILURE LIKE THIS

The failure has weighed heavily on Don Elder, personally and professionally, and he has suffered from the failure. John Palmer and most board members were replaced. All the executive lost their jobs or faced managing the company as it collapsed. The shareholder saw the end of a business that had delivered significant value to them over many years. Worst of all, many hundreds of good people lost their jobs, and communities, especially on the West Coast of the South Island, have suffered ever since.

Saying sorry is not always enough

Don Elder appeared, at least publicly, to be in denial to the very end and in the years after the failure. One of the few remaining executives present at his farewell speech to staff recalled Don's almost bizarre upbeat hope for Solid Energy's future. And even years after the failure when I met with him, I still fear Don Elder failed to accept the mistakes that were made and his role in the company's demise.

After the events of 2012, the Solid Energy chairman, John Palmer, was quoted as saying:

> **❝** *I'm willing to acknowledge that we made some mistakes, but it's very important for New Zealand that we have a risk culture that says taking risks in business is crucially important. For someone who's been in business, and volatile businesses, for a lifetime, you take risks and they don't always work. But I have no regrets with the path and the strategy we set out and some regrets that we didn't perform as well as we could have.* **❞** [44]

John Palmer might be given some credit for showing the humility to accept some fault, although it is unclear whether he truly believes the statement that he has no regrets. Clearly risks were taken at Solid Energy and these risks were poorly assessed and this misjudgement had serious consequences.

The admission that mistakes were made is also cold comfort for the hundreds of people who lost their jobs, the government whose business had become almost worthless overnight, the creditors who were owed millions of dollars, and the communities impacted by the loss of this large employer.

DEATH OF A KIWI ICON — PUMPKIN PATCH AND THE RISK OF GROWING

A star is born

Pumpkin Patch was started in 1990 by Sally Synnott. It started as a provider of childrenswear, through mail order catalogues, before opening its first retail store in Auckland. It then opened its first retail store in Australia in 1997.

It was listed on the New Zealand stock exchange on 9 June 2004. It continued to grow for the next few years building a presence in Asia, the Arab countries, the USA, the United Kingdom, Ireland, Russia, China, Singapore, Malaysia, Indonesia, South Africa, Pakistan and South America. At its peak, it had over 230 stores in 21 countries and over 2000 employees. It had its peak sales of over $400 million in 2009 and was the Kiwi exporter of the year in 2010.

A talented team

Like Solid Energy, Pumpkin Patch was led by people very experienced in business, governance and retailing. They were talented people.

Founder Sally Synnott remained in the company until 2014. Maurice Prendergast was CEO of Pumpkin Patch for around 18 years until 2011. He was followed by Neil Cowie, who is now the CEO at Mitre 10, and then Di Humphries took over as CEO, who later returned to Glassons as the CEO.

Jane Freeman was a board member from 2004, including the role of Chair. She also held senior roles and directorships in Telecom, Air New Zealand, and Sky City. Peter Schuyt, a Pumpkin Patch board member, also held directorships on multiple boards including Tatua and the Foodstuffs board; Luke Bunt, another board member, was CFO at The Warehouse and board member of other large retailers.

There was no lack of capability at the helm of Pumpkin Patch leading up to its final demise.

Still too raw

I found the longer the time from a failure to now, the more likely it was that people were prepared to talk about it. I found things were still quite raw in the case of Pumpkin Patch. As such, the motives of those at the helm were less clear. The following discussion is based on information in the public domain.

I guess with time, when people can reflect on these events, we might learn more about why things transpired as they did for Pumpkin Patch.

I connected with one former middle manager from Pumpkin Patch, who stated the reason for the failure was:

> **"**Pretty simple really. Upper management got greedy.**"**

When I probed further, her response was:

> **"**I'm really not interested in discussing further — sorry.**"**

Sadly, this is typical of many people I contacted about the Pumpkin Patch failure.

Aggressive growth, debt and decline

The troubles for Pumpkin Patch started to appear with its substantial growth offshore, especially its moves into the USA and the UK. The expansion into the US and the UK was rapid and almost totally funded by debt.

Pumpkin Patch had no debt in 2005, but by 2008 it exceeded $80 million.[1]

We will discuss the role of poorly managed debt in failures in later chapters, but growth requires money. This typically comes in the form of equity — people buying into the business — or debt. For Pumpkin Patch, equity came from the listing on the New Zealand stock exchange.

Expansion seemed an obvious next step for Pumpkin Patch. The brand was hugely successful and it achieved strong support when it listed on the stock exchange. It had achieved great success in New Zealand and Australia. After such a successful listing, the company might well have been criticised had it not expanded — things looked good for Pumpkin Patch.

Following the listing, Pumpkin Patch also borrowed significant funds from the ANZ bank.

Pumpkin Patch had limited experience in the UK and USA markets. It opened over 30 stores across eight states in the USA. This was in addition to some 200 stores in other countries. This growth put significant strain on the business.

With the amount the business had borrowed to support this growth, good sales in these new markets were essential.

Unfortunately, this rapid expansion funded by debt started Pumpkin Patch's path to its eventual failure.

Internal weaknesses become more obvious with growth

If any business has weaknesses prior to its growth, they are likely to be magnified and prove costlier as it grows. Pumpkin Patch underestimated the impact their ambitious growth plans were going to have on their internal operations.

Its internal systems and processes for managing all aspects of the business were adequate for Pumpkin Patch when it was a smaller retailer in Australia and New Zealand. However, they were inadequate for what Pumpkin Patch was becoming. While they were aware of these limitations, as the troubles hit and the money dried up, they did not have the finances to do anything about it.

The company also used regular discounting, which damaged the brand as customers simply waited to buy, knowing sales were coming. This undermined Pumpkin Patch's margins.[2]

Pumpkin Patch was not vertically integrated, relying on a small number of suppliers, and often found they were low on stock when these suppliers could not deliver. The company was often forced to hold excessive stock, which went out of season, devaluing the stock and incurring storage costs. This was an added issue in the US and UK stores, as they were forced to buy in bulk causing the cost of inventory to increase from $86 million in 2007 to $122 million in 2008.

They were also hit by the loss of some large wholesale clients.

Maybe it's best to fold and walk away instead of betting more?

Pumpkin Patch continued to open US stores even though the existing stores were not performing.

The stores in the USA were performing so poorly, the US retail network was placed into "Chapter 11" (effectively voluntary administration) in 2009. All its US stores were closed by January 2012.

The UK stores were also performing poorly. Administrators were appointed for the UK stores on 19 January 2012.

By the time Pumpkin Patch had completely exited the USA and UK markets, it had cost the business almost $100 million, most of which was funded by debt. It left Pumpkin Patch with almost no money to fund a turnaround of the remaining business.

Staying relevant

Pumpkin Patch's time to create designs and get them into stores was slow by industry standards, so they could not keep pace with changing customer needs. This was made worse with the arrival of larger vertically integrated competitors like Cotton On, Zara and H&M.

Many also felt the brand was not keeping up with the market tastes:

> 66 *I thought the brand had lost its way and that its former glory as a beloved New Zealand company founded by Sally Synnott in 1990, was fading. For a long time, Pumpkin Patch has felt like a brand still in the nineties. While parents' tastes changed, Pumpkin Patch designs did not.* 99
>
> — Bella Katz, Melbourne mum and market strategist who met with Pumpkin Patch on this issue in 2014.[3]

The end was nigh

Pumpkin Patch made a small profit in 2010 but saw consistent losses each year thereafter. Pumpkin Patch did not ignore these issues, bringing in external expertise to look for options in 2014. It also disposed of assets and inventory, reduced its running costs, and changed management. Even with these actions, it could not slow the decline. A lack of money and very high debt restricted its options.

The company's directors resolved to put the company into voluntary administration in October 2016. At that time, it owed the ANZ around $60 million. ANZ also called in receivers to recover their money, as a secured creditor.

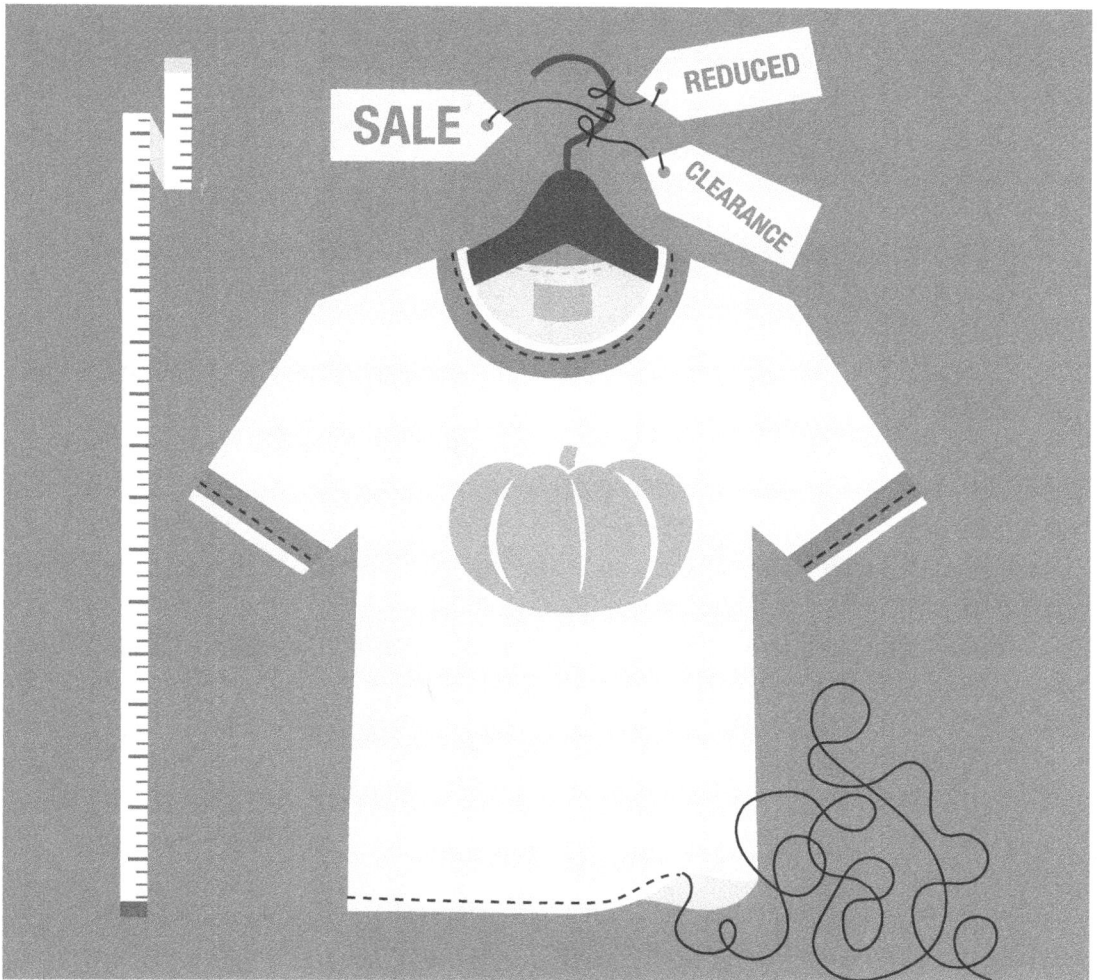

What might Pumpkin Patch have done differently?

Hindsight is always great in a case like Pumpkin Patch.

There is no question the success of Pumpkin Patch would have given everyone confidence that expansion would be a success. Such rapid growth, funded heavily by debt, was always going to be risky. Growth in sales to support the international expansion was essential and any slowing in these sales was always a significant risk — risks that the company failed to identify and then manage quickly enough.

One of the biggest issues was the huge increase in debt. The company raised over $100 million through its Initial Public Offering (IPO) on the stock exchange.

However, over $60 million of this was used to purchase shares from existing shareholders, leaving limited cash to fund the expansion.

Pumpkin Patch took on this growth on the back of inherent operational issues within the business that were magnified during growth. If a business intends growing and it has internal operation problems before the growth, those problems will only magnify and have greater consequences as the growth continues.

If a company wishes to grow, it needs to ensure its internal processes, systems and structures will support that growth. Pumpkin Patch was not ready to grow at the rate it did.

When sales didn't eventuate, the costs of winding back that growth made recovery impossible.

The receivers tried to find a buyer for Pumpkin Patch but this was unsuccessful. They later managed to sell Pumpkin Patch's name and other intellectual property for about $2 million to an online retailer, so the brand name may live on.

Pumpkin Patch Limited was delisted from the New Zealand stock exchange in June 2017, 13 years after its heralded listing in June 2004.

The failure of Pumpkin Patch saw the closure of all its 230 stores and the loss of well over 1400 jobs.[4]

4 WHEN BUSINESSES FAIL, WHO DECIDES THE TRUTH? — SALTHOUSE MARINE

There is a saying about conflict and disputes, whether they be in business or in relationships:

> 66 *There are three sides to every story: your side, my side and the truth. And no one is lying. Memories shared serve each differently.* 99
> — Robert Evans

My research into the Salthouse Marine liquidation brought this view out very clearly. I started looking at this liquidation as I felt it highlighted, from the liquidation reports, what happens when those running the business follow poor management practices.

The Salthouse Marine liquidator, John Price, wrote in his first receivers report about the owner, Julie Salthouse:

> 66 *Ms. Salthouse has taken the opportunity whenever possible to deflect responsibility for the Company's failure to external parties and has blamed those very parties for failing to provide adequate working capital to ensure the Company's survival.* 99[1]

Mr Price went on to say:

> 66 *Over a lengthy period of time and with consistency, the Company under the management of Ms. Salthouse has extinguished the working capital that has been made available to it, primarily as a result of an unsustainable overhead*

*structure, poor management and time controls and an inability to produce a vessel within budget.*99

This appeared to be a simple case of a once-successful business failing due to the actions and inactions of its owner and, therefore, backed a view that the failure of the business fell entirely at the feet of the person making the decisions.

As we will discuss about Salthouse, this was only partly the case.

The failure of Salthouse Marine demonstrated that there are many aspects to any failure, and irrationality can extend to many involved, not just the owner. This in turn results in the real reasons for failures being lost in the perceptions, biases and the inaccuracies of each of our memories — the facts and truths fall somewhere in the middle of all this.

The Salthouse Marine story

The Salthouse name is one that is synonymous with sailing, the marine industry, and boat design and building in New Zealand. Brothers Bob and John Salthouse set up their companies in the 1950s and the Salthouse family have designed and built boats ever since. Their boats are known and admired the world over.

Their family have been actively involved in many America's Cup teams. Rob, Phil and Chris Salthouse were all part of the successful 2017 campaign in Bermuda. Chris Salthouse has been involved in a score of America's Cup events, while Rob Salthouse has also sailed in Sydney to Hobart races and Volvo Ocean races.

The family have, and continue to run, marine brokering, sales and boat-building businesses in New Zealand.

Unfortunately, one of the companies originally set up by Bob Salthouse, and ultimately run by his daughter Julie Salthouse, did not fare so well.

In 1983, Bob left the company he and his brother set up and started his own boat-building company, called Salthouse Marine Limited (SML). Bob Salthouse was a director and designer from the formation of the company.

His daughter Julie joined the business in 1999 as General Manager after a career in human resource management and with a background in information technology and accounting. Julie became a director in 2003 and Bob retired in 2007.

Julie indicated that her goal was to build the Salthouse business and the industry internationally and build a strong work environment and culture for her staff.[2]

This did require changes in the Salthouse way of doing things, a change to a culture that was well embedded and not easy to shift.

SML built large, luxury, multi-million-dollar boats including 57-, 65- and 68-foot vessels. In discussions with Julie, she indicated the goal for SML was to build high-quality vessels to the Lloyd's Register standard for shipping. This did result in higher costs to build and did not meet with uniform agreement from the Salthouse family. The goal was to build no more than five or six boats a year.

The strategy initially proved successful, with demand for the boats building a loyal following in New Zealand and Australia. Prior to SML getting into trouble, Julie indicated the business was delivering good sales and at reasonable margins, especially for the larger vessels.

The business did carry high overheads, with over 50 staff and high rent on the property in Henderson.

Everything about this industry was expensive.

It was typical to present the boats at marine expos like Auckland, and Sanctuary Cove and Perth in Australia. This cost many hundreds of thousands of dollars per expo. Attempts were also made to access the US market, through New Zealand Trade and Enterprise, at some cost, but with little success.

When the wealthy stop spending

When the GFC started taking hold, it saw a fall in demand for luxury items, like pleasure craft, which put significant pressure on the business. Customers, on the brink of settling deals with SML, withdrew their orders either due to an inability to pay or to avoid the perception of luxury spending during troubled economic times.

As the CEO and publisher of the *Club Marine* magazine put it (in a 2011 edition):

> 66 *Ever since the financial tsunami, otherwise known as the GFC, rolled through the world's major economies back in late 2008, marine businesses everywhere have seen sales plummet as buyers held on to whatever money they had. While much of the economy seemed to dodge the more harmful effects of the GFC, sections most dependent on discretionary spending — high on the list being the marine industry — continue to suffer.* 99 [3]

Many boat and yacht builders faced very tough times during this period, with many failing. Sensation Yachts, Vaudrey Miller Yachts, Sovereign Yachts, Calibre Boats, Genesis Marine and Hakes Marine all went into liquidation during 2009 or soon after.

And then their finance company collapsed

During the height of the GFC, SML's finance company, Capital and Merchant Finance, also failed (owing 7500 investors $167 million). All the directors of Capital and Merchant

pleaded guilty to fraud charges related to making untrue statements in the company's offer documents and all spent time in jail.

Capital and Merchant Finance's failure threw doubts over SML's capacity to fund monthly cash requirements. SML had used this funding to support growth and at the time the finance company collapsed, SML owed it $6.1 million. The receivers of Capital and Finance sought repayment of this money. Without an investor, SML would have likely joined the growing list of marine industry failures.

Entry of a new investor

It is worth considering if the business should have made efforts at this point to reduce costs, reshape the business and see if it might survive the downturn. It may also have been appropriate to wind the business up. However, the owners, justifiably, wanted to do all they could to keep the business afloat.

However, without an investor, SML was unlikely to survive.

Chris Norman proved to be that investor. Norman was a West Australian with a lifetime of experience in shipping and boating. He became involved with SML through his business, Yachts West.

He was one of the founders of Austal Limited, a publicly listed builder of very large ships including naval vessels. At one stage, he was a non-executive director and held over 26 million shares, which at that time were worth $95 million.

He had been successful in selling Salthouse boats in Australia. Julie Salthouse came to know Chris Norman through the purchase of a Salthouse 65 yacht by Norman's company, Yachts West, in 2005. Yachts West became a sales agent for SML in Western Australia shortly thereafter.

After Capital and Merchant was placed into receivership, its receiver looked for interested parties to purchase the SML debt. They settled on a deal with Norman, where he paid a fraction of the debt outstanding to gain a stake in SML — less than $700,000 to buy out the $6.1 million.

He became a director of the company in December 2008 and a 50% shareholder in April 2009 (he purchased these shares for one dollar). He also did not charge SML any interest on this debt, which saved SML significant interest charges.[4]

Security agreements and the power they hold

Chris Norman's lending arrangements included a security agreement over the business. Such agreements give the party holding it great power over a business should it get into any trouble and the holder wants to step in.

Norman indicated that he wanted to invest in SML, notwithstanding its level of indebtedness, because he thought SML's designs were outstanding and sales could be improved through better representation in Australia.

Norman became a non-executive director (i.e. he had no role in the management of the business) and remained resident in Perth, while Ms Salthouse became SML's Managing Director. She was previously SML's General Manager as well as a director and shareholder.

Too much money needed — then receivership

Norman continued to offer SML financial support, putting many millions more into the business to keep the business operating from day to day.

Norman continued to advance more cash but, as he indicated in later court proceedings, he had not seen the sales picking up. At that stage he asked his accountant, Staples Rodway, to review the accounts and they recommended appointing a liquidator.

Instead, Norman agreed to appoint a receiver rather than a liquidator, and Mr John Price of HBL Partners was appointed on 4 February 2010.

Norman's lawyers said he *"agonised over the decision and felt physically ill"*, having previously believed the company could return to profitability.[5]

John Price felt there was no hope of recovering any money and dismissed all staff and commenced selling assets (including boat moulds and designs) to recover as much money as possible before handing the business over to a liquidator. Many of these assets were purchased by Chris Norman. There is no indication he used them in any other ventures after purchase.

Being West Australian based, and with the challenges of making Salthouse profitable, it appears that Chris Norman wanted to back out of the business. It also appears that Yachts West started selling competitor boats, such as Maritimo, soon after the receivership of SML. It is likely he lost interest in Salthouse for better prospects closer to home.

Unfortunately, his actions did come as a surprise to the rest of the SML team and left many unanswered questions. It appears to reflect a relationship that was not completely transparent and candid.

Who decides the facts?

The receiver, John Price, placed the blame completely at the feet of Julie Salthouse. He believed she'd managed the business poorly.

Ms Salthouse strongly challenged these assertions and felt Mr Price did not fairly represent the real situation within the business and handled the receivership poorly. While accepting the business was struggling, with the correct approach she felt it was recoverable, or at least the outcome could have been handled very differently. It is not possible, even with hindsight, to assess whether this would have been the case.

Unfortunately, once a receiver is called into a business and the owner loses control, it is very difficult to recover the business, if it was recoverable.

An unfortunate reality when a business goes into receivership or is liquidated is that the owners lose not only control of the business but any influence over the views that are formed and ultimately documented by the receiver or liquidator.

They have no recourse and must accept whatever is documented, which then goes on the Companies Office register forever.

Options available to any receiver or liquidator are to see if the business can continue to be operated to give the creditor under the security agreement the greatest chance of recovering their money. They can also look for buyers to sell the business as a going concern.

Offers were made to buy the business by members of the Salthouse family but were rejected by the receiver, on behalf of Mr Norman. This does raise some questions. It is possible a sale would have left Mr Norman with more money than he gained from the receivership.

In the end, the greatest financial loser in the collapse of SML was Chris Norman. As the later court cases stated:

> **“***He advanced approximately $3.3 million to SML. He also bought the Capital and Merchant debt for $700,000. He lost his total investment.***”**[6]

The courts and the wine tycoon

When businesses fail, there are always innocent casualties.

One of the boats that was incomplete when SML went into receivership had been for Jim Delegat.

Mr Delegat is the chair and majority owner of the Delegat Wine group, which supplies wine brands like Oyster Bay. He is a regular on the New Zealand rich list and an avid sailing and boating enthusiast.

A separate company, called Boat 93 Ltd, was set up by SML to ring-fence all aspects of the build of Delegat's boat. This was the process normally followed by SML when they won an order. They would set up a separate company for the special purpose of completing that vessel. These companies were subsidiaries of SML, with Julie Salthouse the only director. All money related to that project was meant to come in and out of that company.

Ms Salthouse believed this was the best way to protect the owners of the vessel. This is not how things eventuated for the owners, as money was taken from one project to fund others.

While the practice of ring-fencing each boat was a reasonable strategy, for whatever reason money was not always captured within that business. At the time of liquidation, money had moved between the builds. This was described in the courts as borrowing from Peter to pay Paul.

Who was to blame?

The 68-foot Salthouse design was ordered in 2009 following a sale through Chris Norman. When SML went into liquidation in February 2010, Delegat's boat was in its early stages of construction. Delegat had paid $1.23 million, effectively for nothing.

Delegat took Chris Norman to court. In turn, Chris Norman brought Julie Salthouse into the process as he felt that if action was to be targeted at him, she was also accountable.

Delegat believed Chris Norman had deceived him when progressing the sale, believing he was aware of the risk that the boat might not be completed. He felt Norman, while not technically a director of Boat 93, was a de facto director and was responsible. He also pursued other charges such as reckless trading. This in turn implied that Julie Salthouse was also responsible for Delegat's losses.

Unsuccessful in court, but the boat was finished

Jim Delegat was unsuccessful in his case against Chris Norman and, in turn, Julie Salthouse. Mr Delegat also had to pay for legal costs.

In the end, Julie Salthouse, her husband, and former SML staff completed Jim Delegat's boat.

What can we learn — what might the truth be?

There were many factors that contributed to the failure of SML. The GFC was clearly a factor for all luxury boat builders. However, as always, many decisions, perhaps with hindsight, may not have been wise.

- Whether building million-dollar luxury boats for the wealthy or running a small business, high fixed costs and debt can kill a business, especially in a downturn. No one predicted the extent of the GFC and any amount of cost control was unlikely to save SML. There are events that cannot be predicted but they will be made much worse with high costs and debt.
- Partnerships and multiple shareholdings are common in business but do not always work out. They must be built on trust, which includes being honest and candid, especially when times are toughest. The amount of unanswered questions in the failure of SML appears to indicate not all agendas were transparent and the

relationship was doomed from the start.

- As the investor propping up a struggling business, Chris Norman took on significant risk yet had little or no operational involvement in turning the business around. He lost all his money. One would ask whether buying into such a business was a rational decision or an emotional one based on unjustified optimism and his love for Salthouse boats.

- If a business is forced into receivership and/or liquidation, the impacts can be brutal and cause irreversible emotional damage. Receivers are there to act on behalf of the person holding the security. They have no obligation to the business or the staff. The business owners have little or no ability to influence what is written in the reports produced by receivers. In this failure, the owner, Ms Salthouse, had a very different view of the actual events compared with what was documented in the receivers reports.

5 DISHONESTY, FRAUD, AND ROSS ASSET MANAGEMENT

Something I used to say to my kids when they were too little to explain right from wrong was:

> 66 *There is no right or wrong — there are only consequences.* 99

I guess, like most parents, my wife and I tried to instil some measure of right and wrong and a moral compass so that our kids could go out into the world as good, decent people. I was privileged to have two parents who did that for me.

Now that my kids have left home and are at university, I still recite this same quote to them, even though I have less (actually, I have no) ability to impart the same consequences. I am now often faced with the reply from them, *"Yes, Dad, but it's only wrong if you get caught."* While I don't know all that my kids get up to at university (in fact, I know very little — I just kid myself, I know), I do believe my wife and I have brought up two great, well-adjusted kids with a very clear understanding of right and wrong — and when they respond like this I'm pretty sure it's just to tease me.

It would seem self-explanatory that a business is likely to fail, eventually, when the owners resort to dishonest, illegal or fraudulent behaviour. Most businesses that carry on with such activities usually get found out. Unfortunately, many do not, and such behaviour could go on for a long time before it is brought to light. If the behaviour is discovered, it may not be before it has inflicted significant harm on the business and many innocent people.

Before we get into a discussion about the effect of dishonesty in the failure of businesses and we shake our heads in disgust at the foul deeds carried out by some business people, let me state a sobering point:

We all lie, we all cheat and we are all dishonest. The only thing that distinguishes us is the extent of that dishonesty.

I will explore this further shortly, but keep this in mind as you work through the next few paragraphs.

Breaking the law and business

It goes without saying that business owners should always act within the law. Unfortunately, business people breaking laws happens far too often. Many are caught, others are not, and it will continue to happen. There is nothing in any research on business success or failure (or common sense) that would consider illegal behaviour has some place in the running of a business — it never will.

This does not mean all laws serve businesses' best interests. Many do not.

Many can make succeeding in business difficult. However, ignoring the laws within which we must operate or deliberately breaking these laws are never justifiable and are poor business. They are simply dumb. Now, you may well believe the actions of business people in charge of failed companies drifted into a grey area that many may perceive as illegal or at least unethical. Many of us may feel, with good reason, that the actions of some parties should have been punished.

Following the collapse of the banking sector in USA during the GFC, with the resultant eye-watering losses, prosecutions were few and far between. Perhaps what I told my kids about there being no right or wrong, only consequences, may not always apply. What many of these people did was very wrong but they faced little consequences.

> 66 *Tell the truth and you won't have so much to remember.* 99
> — Abraham Lincoln

For the purposes of the discussions that follow, let's simply say that those who lie, cheat, deceive, defraud or break the law will eventually fail. If not in business or in the eyes of the law, then morally. They will also inflict immeasurable pain on others.

Fraudulent behaviour and the Serious Fraud Office

Unfortunately, there are far too many cases where businesses and their owners have fallen due to openly dishonest, illegal and fraudulent behaviour, and usually caused significant collateral damage to other people and businesses.

The work done by the Serious Fraud Office (SFO) is a good place to start in exploring the many cases where business owners have engaged in fraudulent behaviour, and faced the consequences.

The role of the SFO

The SFO exists to provide:

> A productive and prosperous New Zealand safe from financial crime, bribery and corruption.

And:

> The Serious Fraud Office investigates and prosecutes serious and complex fraud so that New Zealand is a safe place to invest and do business.[1]

There are too many examples

The following is but a small sample of the companies, business owners and employees prosecuted by the SFO in the last few years, as detailed on the SFO website.

- The SFO pursued the leaders of 15 finance companies, including Bridgecorp and Hanover Finance, following the collapse of finance companies during the GFC. Around 20 directors faced jail time or home detention for their roles in these collapses. We discuss finance company collapses, including South Canterbury Finance, a little later.
- Mrs Teremoana Kimiangatau, an employee of Auckland International Airport, pleaded guilty to committing fraud against the company. She transferred almost $1.8 million from the company's bank account to her own account by changing client bank account numbers to her own within the airport's accounting system.
- The former chair of the Wellington Tenths Trust, Sir Ralph Heberley Ngatata Love, was jailed for two-and-a-half years after redirecting over $1.6 million from the trust

for a significant commercial property development to himself and his partner.

- Hemant Kumar Maharaj and Suresh Din were sentenced for corruptly obtaining public funds of approximately $849,000 from the North Shore City Council. Mr Maharaj received two years and 10 months' jail and Mr Din home detention. The offending took place over a 10-year period, where they invoiced for work that was never completed.

- Four people involved in an Auckland development were charged by the SFO. The defendants, Timothy Slack, Leonard Ross, Michael Wehipeihana and Vaughn Foster, allegedly made false statements and used forged documents to obtain a credit facility from the ANZ bank. This was to allow their company, Emily Projects Limited, to develop the Waldorf Celestion Apartment Hotel in Auckland. It is alleged that a loan facility of approximately $40 million was obtained.

- Joanne Harrison, a former senior manager at the Ministry of Transport, was sentenced to three years and seven months' jail after the SFO discovered she had stolen hundreds of thousands of dollars over three-and-a-half years to pay off credit cards and her mortgage.

- Wayne Thomas Patterson pleaded guilty to 10 fraud charges after making up over 120 false identities to con $3.4 million out of the Ministry of Social Development. He was jailed in New Zealand but had also been jailed in three other countries prior to this. The judge called him *"a determined recidivist fraudster"*.

Inland Revenue fraud

The Inland Revenue Department (IRD) also prosecutes business owners who defraud the tax system. A few examples that were in mainstream media include the following:

- A former Junior All Black and Taupo bar owner was jailed for defrauding the IRD of nearly $1 million in company tax, GST and PAYE. He knowingly filed tax returns with false information over about six years.

- A Hamilton director was jailed for failing to pay about $500,000 PAYE. He admitted failing to pay the PAYE he had deducted from his employees, who provided construction services. This was for residential and commercial properties around the North Island and in Christchurch, during the rebuild after the earthquakes, between 2011 and 2015. He was jailed because of this fraud and also because he had previously defrauded the IRD in 2009.

- A former Hamilton IRD employee had not paid any tax or PAYE over a five-year period, totalling more than $600,000. She spent most of it at Hamilton's Sky City Casino feeding a gambling addiction, while using the rest on her family's lifestyle and expenses. Her company, Mana Scaffolding Ltd, had earned over $1.6 million over six years but no PAYE tax had been paid.

- The owner of a Wellington-based security company was found guilty of charges stemming from unpaid PAYE and GST of around $740,000. The judge said his evading was inherently premeditated, as the owner had maintained a *"fairly generous lifestyle"*.

- A couple that ran Korean restaurants in Hamilton and Te Awamutu systematically defrauded the IRD for over five years to the tune of more than $230,000. Once one of their companies accumulated significant liabilities, they would be liquidated and a new, almost identical, company formed to take over the running of the business. They also accumulated over $200,000 in cash income that they deliberately hid from their accountant. They were sentenced to home detention and community work.

And, sadly, I could add many, many more examples.

New Zealand's biggest individual fraud — David Ross

One of the largest individual fraud cases in New Zealand history was that of David Ross and his Ross Asset Management business. He was sentenced to 10 years and 10 months' jail in November 2013. The judge said:

> ❝ *The cold, hard reality is that you were a liar and a thief operating on a scale unprecedented in this country. What you have done has wrought misery on hundreds of people, most ruined financially, many elderly and frail, and many suffering far more than simply monetary losses which are bad enough anyway …* ❞

— Judge D. R. W. Barry.[2]

Some history

David Ross was from North Otago, was schooled at Waitaki Boys' High School in Oamaru and graduated from Victoria University in 1977. He was married to Jillian, and had two children, William and Anna.

He had been in the investment business most of his career. He was an investment manager with Leadenhall Investment Management from the early 1980s, which had delivered good returns for its 200 investors, until the 1987 stock market crash. The other owners of Leadenhall bought out Mr Ross before selling Leadenhall to another party.

David Ross then set up his own investment businesses. His time with Leadenhall showed Mr Ross to be a higher-risk investor favouring growth stocks and small and medium-sized Australian mining companies.[3] He set up Ross Asset Management (RAM) in 1989 and several investment businesses in the later years of the 1980s. These were set up at a time when the financial market regulations were much weaker than they are today.

In October 2012, the Financial Markets Authority (FMA) began receiving complaints from investors who wanted to withdraw their funds but were having difficulty contacting Mr Ross. The FMA inspected the offices in Wellington and then froze all assets.[4]

When the liquidators from Price Waterhouse Coopers (PWC) first came in to close RAM, Ross's accounts indicated he had investments of around $450 million. However, the liquidators could only account for a little over $10 million.

PWC quickly established that Mr Ross, through his company RAM, was running a Ponzi investment scheme.

Ponzi schemes — they are nothing new

Ponzi schemes are named after the Italian-American Charles Ponzi who was jailed in the 1920s. Ponzi was not the first to use this scheme to swindle investors. However, the size of his scheme (he lost investors around $US20 million) and the profile it had (the *Boston Post* eventually brought him down), and the luxurious lifestyle it afforded him before it collapsed in August 1920, have linked his name to this type of scheme ever since.

A Ponzi scheme involves the manager, in this case David Ross, taking money from one investor, promising to invest it wisely for good returns, only to use that money to pay the interest to, or the withdrawals by, another investor, and obviously keeping some of the money for himself. This results in the manager appearing to be delivering good returns for his clients. This is all good until people ask for their money — only to find it doesn't exist.

Unfortunately, while David Ross perpetrated the biggest fraud via a Ponzi scheme in New Zealand history, he is by no means alone in recent New Zealand history. All the following were Ponzi schemes:

- In 2018 Paul Clifford Hobbs was sentenced to eight years jail for running a $17.5 million Ponzi scheme through his company Hansa.
- In 2014, 79-year-old Dunedin lawyer John David Milne described in court as *"a*

consummate thief and liar" was jailed for more than eight years.[5]

- In 2012, Aucklander Jacqui Bradley was jailed for seven years and five months for running a Ponzi scheme.
- In 2010, Hawke's Bay accountant Warren Pickett was sentenced to five years' jail for robbing 200 friends and clients of around $20 million.[6,7]
- In 2006, Margarite (Lee) Papple and Tina Marie West of Rotorua were jailed for five years; Bill Papple was jailed for two years. Margarite Papple spent $2 million of money raised from victims of the Ponzi scheme on herself and family before being caught.

The biggest Ponzi scheme in history was that of Bernie Madoff in the United States, who defrauded $US65 billion and was sentenced to 150 years' jail.

It went on for decades

Many close to David Ross that I spoke to, including the liquidators, surmise that David Ross started out the scheme as a legitimate investment business. No one, including the liquidators, could establish when the scheme crossed the line into a fraudulent scheme. He did engage in higher-risk investments and many believe these got into trouble leading to Ross covering losses. I contacted Mr Ross in Rimutaka Prison but he continues to conceal any details about the scheme.

The liquidators found no evidence that Mr Ross conspired with anyone else. He only had two administrative staff in his Wellington office on The Terrace. The courts found they had no idea what Mr Ross was doing, although in the months leading up to the failure they sensed something was wrong as people started chasing their money and Mr Ross was being very aloof.

Prior to 2000, David Ross kept no documented evidence about his activities. The evidence liquidators found starting from 2000 indicated the Ponzi scheme had been operating since then. It is likely it started in the 1990s. No one knows when the scheme shifted from a legitimate investment business to a Ponzi scheme.

His wife was a 50% shareholder in RAM and part-owner in other Ross Group companies but a director of none of them. She was not implicated in the fraud and it is believed his deceit may have extended to his relationship with his wife, who appeared to know little about what Ross was doing.

To maintain a bogus scheme for so long with no one else's knowledge, travelling the world to investment conferences, pursuing legitimate investment opportunities in mining businesses in Australia, Canada and the USA kept David Ross extremely busy. He ran the fraud scheme for well over a decade, alone, and showed no signs he was doing so to even the closest people around him.

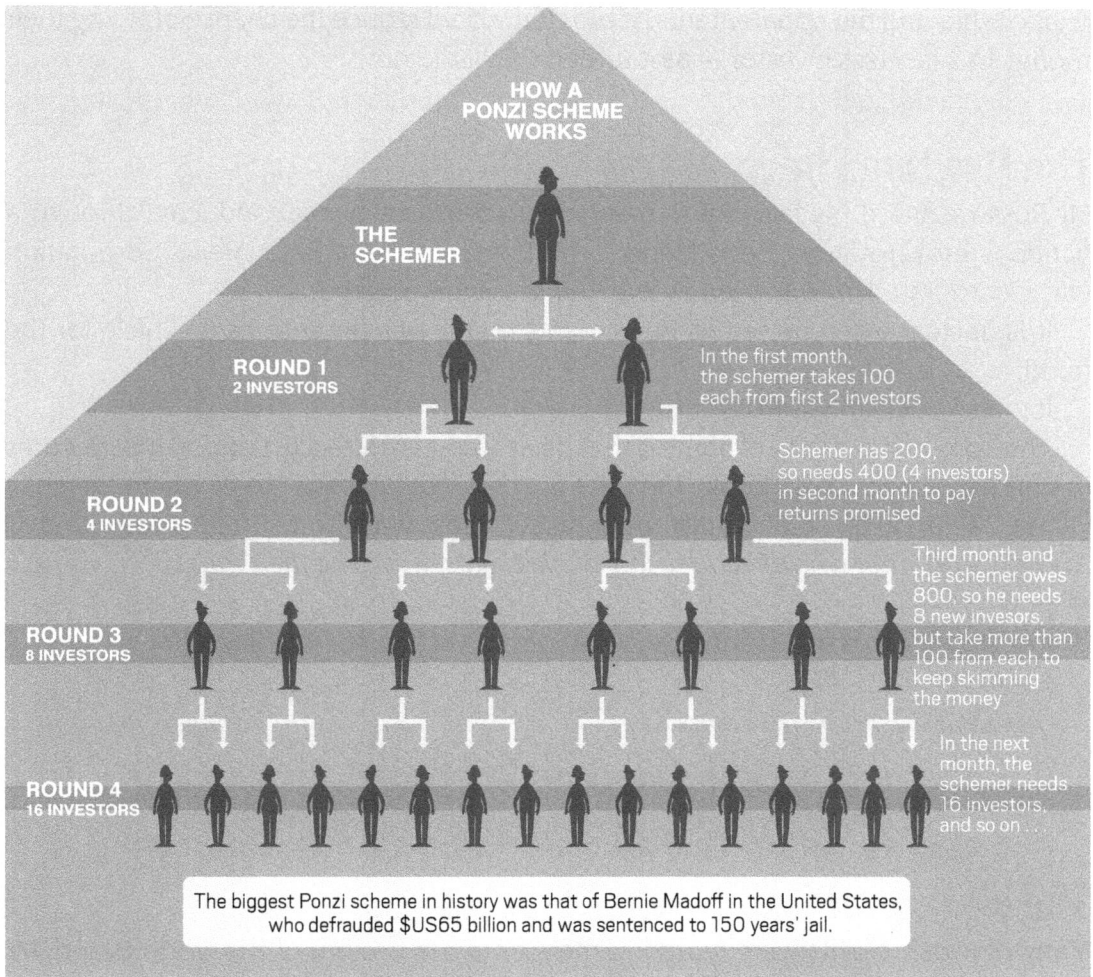

HOW A
PONZI SCHEME
WORKS

THE
SCHEMER

ROUND 1
2 INVESTORS

In the first month,
the schemer takes 100
each from first 2 investors

Schemer has 200,
so needs 400 (4 investors)
in second month to pay
returns promised

ROUND 2
4 INVESTORS

Third month and
the schemer owes
800, so he needs
8 new invesors,
but take more than
100 from each to
keep skimming
the money

ROUND 3
8 INVESTORS

In the next
month, the
schemer needs
16 investors,
and so on . . .

ROUND 4
16 INVESTORS

The biggest Ponzi scheme in history was that of Bernie Madoff in the United States,
who defrauded $US65 billion and was sentenced to 150 years' jail.

Clients started getting suspicious when Mr Ross wouldn't pay them their money when they requested it.

Mr Ross had taken $449 million from 900 clients. When the dust settled on the investigations and court cases, overall losses were calculated at around $115 million.

In sentencing, the judge took account of Mr Ross's remorse, which he accepted was genuine (albeit manifest only after the involvement of the FMA), cooperation with authorities and the nominal reparation.

There was no questioning his abilities. I spoke to victims of Ross's fraud and they indicated that he demonstrated great knowledge of the industry and the markets he was investing in, was pleasant to engage with and very self-confident. One such investor I spoke to chose David Ross only because he wanted to eyeball the person he was entrusting his money to. He, like other investors, felt having a face-to-face relationship and the apparent trust it brought would reduce the chance of losing their money to a faceless investor — as it turned out, it did not.

The fictitious Bevis Marks

Mr Ross recorded his false investment transactions as being conducted through a fictitious broker named Bevis Marks — Mr Ross's creation. Bevis Marks Corporation was incorporated in 1987 even before RAM was incorporated.

It is unclear when he set up Bevis Marks that it was done so as a vehicle for the fraud.

It is also unclear why Ross chose this name.

The irony in the choice of name is that Bevis Marks is a street in London that features in Charles Dickens' 1841 book, *The Old Curiosity Shop*. It is the street where the chief villain, Daniel Quilp, and his attorney Sampson Brass work from. Brass is described as *"a corrupt attorney who affects feeling for his clients, whom he then cheats"*.

> 66 *This Mr. Brass was an attorney of no very good repute, from Bevis Marks in the city of London …*99
> — *The Old Curiosity Shop*, Charles Dickens

While perhaps a coincidence that David Ross chose this name, it is an ironic one.

The victims of fraud — the forgotten suffering

Many of Ross's clients were retired farmers from the bottom of the North Island. Mr Ross was an experienced investor with an outwardly good relationship with clients and a track record of very good returns.

The Financial Markets Authority (FMA) investigators said of the victims that *"If it sounds too good to be true, it probably is."*

Victims found this comment difficult to swallow as they felt Mr Ross's deceit was so well disguised and so sinister that even the most astute investor would have been deceived. The returns most clients gained when the scheme was in operation were healthy but not sufficiently large to trigger suspicion.

Victims I spoke with suspect Ross is aware of who withdrew money closing in on the failure when that money should have been distributed to all investors as part of the liquidation. Victims have redirected their frustration toward the process that has resulted in their recovering very little of their investments.

The liquidator took one such person, Hamish McIntosh, to court arguing the money he took out of Ross was not his to take but should be distributed to all victims. The court decided he could keep the money he invested but the profits he supposedly achieved on top of what he put in were considered to be fictitious.

The court forced McIntosh to repay any money he took out that was above what he put in. There are many others who may be challenged to repay. Ross may well be protecting his knowledge of this.

The greatest injustice in these cases is the lack of exposure given to the victims of the fraud. Focus usually comes to the fraudster. Victims defrauded are too often forgotten. The impact of Mr Ross's fraud was huge. The following is an extract from the victim impact statement of one investor:

> 66 *I am 63 years of age and as at the 2nd of November 2012 I had $1,650,782.57 invested with RAM. As at the 3rd of November 2012 I had nothing invested with RAM. Gone. The lot. Every last cent of our retirement fund had disappeared. The magician was someone who I had trusted unconditionally, who I had regarded as an honest man with real integrity and sincerity.* 99

Victims not only feel the pain from the devastating financial loss but fraud comes with much wider emotional costs. Victims can feel humiliated feeling like they were "taken for fools". It is also the huge undermining of trust. Also, in the David Ross case, victims feel the process of recovering their money seriously let them down, adding a lack of trust in the process to protect victims on top of the pain of the original fraud.

David Ross will be eligible for parole in 2019, after serving half his sentence. It is possible he could be free from jail before the issues surrounding the fraud are resolved.

At the time of writing, an Insolvency Working Group was looking to recommend changes to insolvency practices in New Zealand including Ponzi schemes.

The process continues

It is likely the legal issues surrounding David Ross's fraud will be going on long after he is eligible for parole. Bruce Tichbon, the head of the support group for victims of David Ross's fraud, indicated that many of the victims are quite elderly and may not survive to see resolution.

After the initial liquidation process, the liquidators are now considering those who may have taken money from the scheme that should have been distributed to other victims. This is likely to trigger further legal issues.

This creates many other complications. Was the investor taking the money out, as they had every right to do, for legitimate purposes? Did the investor know RAM was in trouble, and took their money out knowing a collapse was possible, and thus, should have reported it?

Why did David Ross do it?

No one knows why David Ross committed the fraud. Ross accepted his offending and pleaded guilty at an early stage. He read a letter to the court at sentencing expressing his profound sorrow at what he had done. He was suffering severe depression and ill health and spent time in hospital leading up to the trial. The judge considered this in sentencing.

While all Ross's key assets were sold and no other proceeds from the fraud were found, some victims feel that Ross may have other proceeds tied up elsewhere.

David Ross never indicated why he did it and what motivated him to do so. The judge in his sentencing suggesting that it *"seemed to be a twisted form of vanity that led Ross to offending"*.[8]

It is also still unclear how many people really knew things were very wrong before the official complaints were received by the FMA in October 2012.

I contacted David Ross in Rimutaka Prison and asked if I could discuss his side of the story, as no one had heard it. He wrote me a letter. His reply to my request was:

> 66 *I have not spoken to any other parties about the background to the failure of RAM. I intend for this to remain the position for a variety of personal and commercial reasons.* 99
>
> — David Ross

Hamish McNicol, senior business reporter from Fairfax Media, expressed his views to me on Mr Ross from his reporting of the fraud. He, like all observers, could only surmise on Mr Ross's motives, as Ross never spoke about why he did it or gave any indication of his motives in court appearances:

> 66 *My understanding was that Ross Asset Management began as a legitimate business but at some stage turned into a Ponzi, likely when some investments soured and he wanted to hide any losses. RAM is interesting because there were some legitimate investments in there, which also lends to the idea it was at one stage out to do what it did.* 99
>
> — Hamish McNicol, Fairfax Media

Why do people commit fraud?

For those of us who believe we go about business in an honest way, which is the clear majority of people, frauds such as David Ross and the impact they have on people and business seem abhorrent. The question asked is why would they do it?

If David Ross had paused and thought rationally about his actions, even if he had no concern for those he impacted, he must have realised he would eventually be caught. He could never sell RAM, hand it to someone else, or retire from the Ponzi scheme. The charade had to continue if it was to remain undetected — either you die before being caught or you are caught.

Unfortunately, the answer to the question of why people act so dishonestly in business is not an easy one to answer. Victims of fraud, such as those impacted by David Ross, yearn to have this question answered to get some closure, but sadly this is unlikely to occur.

In my correspondence with Mr Ross and in all interactions after his arrest, he has never given an explanation.

While fraud is committed by a wide variety of people, statistically, the person most likely to commit fraud will be male, have been working in the organisation they defraud for some time, be in a managerial role, be between 30 and 45, and be university trained.[9]

In the book *A.B.C.'s of Behavioral Forensics* by Dr Sridhar Ramamoorti et al., the authors try to provide some insight into the question of why people commit fraud.[10] They split fraudsters into two categories.

One they describe as the ***accidental fraudster***. This fraudster doesn't set out to defraud, but sees an opportunity present itself, can't resist, and the fraud may grow over time. The longer the fraud goes on, the bigger it becomes and the harder it is to hide.

The second, and the more sinister, is what they call ***predatory fraud***, where the fraudster decides to coerce and harm others by luring them into the fraud — David Ross may have started as the first but very quickly the fraud fell into this latter category.

The four factors present in fraud

The four factors that typically exist for people to commit fraud are:

1. **Pressure**. There is usually some pressure or incentive the person faces that pushes them toward fraud. In David Ross's case, many believe it was when investments underperformed or failed. For others, it may be financial hardship, gambling or some other financial problem.

2. **Opportunity**. The fraudster sees a way to carry out the fraud without detection. Usually when they get away with it once, the opportunity to grow the fraud further exists.
3. **Capability**. Frauds such as a Ponzi scheme require a level of skill and competency to pull them off. All those who knew David Ross acknowledged his experience and skills. To carry out such a prolonged and complex fraud without any assistance demonstrated the extent of Ross's skills.
4. **Rationalisation**. Fraudsters find a way to rationalise their actions, e.g. "Everyone does it."[11]

There is often a view that the motivator for committing fraud is greed. This is very often not the case.

There could be a variety of other factors motivating the behaviour.[12,13] While David Ross had a comfortable life and travelled extensively, it was not lavish, especially considering the amount of money that passed through his scheme. Liquidators sold his Wellington home for $1.8 million, with buyers describing it as "a bit tired". He had a small section in the Wairarapa and a modest house in Eastbourne. There were also no pots of cash set aside from his activities.[14]

Ramamoorti et al. believe that some fraudsters may be psychopathic. That is, they have little or no empathy when they harm others.

They demonstrate antisocial behaviour and egotistical traits. They are morally disengaged from the impact of their actions. They almost always know right from wrong, and show remorse, however usually only after they are caught.

David Ross sat with his investors, many of them vulnerable people who entrusted him with their life savings. He showed no apparent concern for these people as he took their money in the full knowledge he was defrauding them. Those around Ross believed he craved adulation. Once caught and sentenced, he did show remorse but never publicly before that.

David Ross did slide into depression after being caught and some believe he may have attempted to take his own life. Clearly, he knew what he had done was wrong.

Unfortunately, the irrationality and unpredictability of people means we are unlikely to fully understand why people destroy businesses and the lives of others through fraudulent acts. Sadly, it will happen again and we always need to be prepared for this.

Dishonesty in different cultures

Some countries are more likely to be engaged in dishonest or potentially fraudulent behaviour than others. Dishonesty in business does vary from country to country.

There are several international indices to measure corruption in different countries. Corruption, in case you needed a clearer definition, is:

> **❝** *the abuse of entrusted power for private gain.* **❞**

The World Bank produces the World Governance Index that includes a suite of indicators, including the Control of Corruption Index, which compares the level of corruption in about 200 countries.

On the World Bank index, New Zealand scores first as the least corrupt country in the world. Australia ranks 11th, the United Kingdom 13th, the USA 22nd, South Africa 88th, China 105th, India 117th, and Philippines 122nd.[15]

Transparency International also produces a Corruption Perception Index that includes 176 countries looking at the perceived corruption of each country's public sector. Transparency International is an international non-government organisation that is based in Berlin and was founded in 1993. Its non-profit purpose is to act to combat corruption and prevent criminal activities arising from corruption. New Zealand, along with Denmark, is perceived to be the least corrupt country in the world on this index.[16]

Considering the long list of examples of fraud that are included in this chapter, one could question how New Zealand rated so high on these indices. I guess, sadly, it is all relative and many other countries are much worse. New Zealand may also be better at catching fraudsters, although it is also likely a lot of fraud goes on undetected.

It is almost impossible to assess if greater levels of corruption translate into higher failure rates of businesses. It is also unlikely that comparisons would produce any useful information. Businesses operating in more corrupt countries are in an environment that is more tolerant of such activities and little enforcement takes place — so businesses continue to operate in a business context that they see as normal.

Does corruption travel?

Are business owners who operate in more corrupt countries likely to bring these practices to other countries they immigrate to? In the case of New Zealand, how would a business owner coming from a country where more corrupt behaviours are acceptable adjust to doing business in one of the least corrupt countries on earth?

Raymond Fisman and Edward Miguel attempted to answer this question analytically by looking at parking tickets that international diplomats received when visiting New York. These people enjoyed diplomatic immunity, being free to offend as they wished. The only factor guiding them was their own internal view of right and wrong — their own moral compass.[17]

This research showed that the diplomats most comfortable to breach these laws for private gain were closely correlated with the more corrupt countries on the various corruption indices.

Therefore, it is likely people who are used to social norms that accept dishonest, unethical, even corrupt behaviour, will continue to act in this way no matter where they are. It is also likely if they immigrate to countries with much higher ethical standards, like New Zealand, they may struggle to adapt and adhere to these standards.

> 66 *Norms related to corruption are apparently deeply in-grained, and factors other than legal enforcement are important determinants of corruption behaviour …*99
— Fisman and Miguel.[18]

So, what might this mean for New Zealand?

The top five countries represented in immigration numbers in the three years to 2016 were Australia, the United Kingdom, China, India and South Africa, respectively. While not as good as New Zealand, Australia and the United Kingdom score positively on the corruption index. The other three countries, particularly China and India, score very low on all corruption indices.

As an Australian immigrant to New Zealand, I did not find the transition difficult, and in fact found the New Zealand business culture to be a great place to do business.

There is no means to assess if business failures within New Zealand are in any way related to cultural differences. However, experts within the insolvency industry cite examples of new immigrants who have struggled to adapt to the way of doing business in New Zealand, and get themselves into trouble.

What lessons can we learn from this?

No matter who we are or where we come from, we need to abide by the laws and social norms of the business community we choose to do business in.

In New Zealand, we all need to accept the advantage of doing business here with its relatively high level of transparency, ethical business culture and the lower levels of corruption. This is something to celebrate and protect. While it might explain why business owners from less ethical business cultures struggle to adapt, it is by no means a reason to condone such behaviour.

How honest are we — really?

> 66 *There's one way to find out if a man is honest — ask him. If he says "yes", he is a crook.* 99
> — Groucho Marx

So we have established that illegal behaviour has no place in business and can be a contributor to business failures, both for the fraudulent business and the innocent businesses impacted by them.

We look upon such unethical and fraudulent behaviour with justifiable contempt and possibly anger.

While we should be appalled at such behaviour, I am sure there are many of these people who started out in business with no plan to drift into illegal activities. While we are unable to dig into the motives of these people, many are likely to have started with good intent, were tempted, started small, and continued to justify their behaviour while the level of their fraud grew.

What is honesty in business?

We will discuss the importance of understanding our values in running a business. We have discussed that there is no part in business for fraud or illegal activity.

So, we could assume that running a successful business requires us to do so honestly. Pretty obvious, right?

I would feel reasonably confident most of us consider ourselves to be honest people. But what is honesty and what does it look like in business? Many of us may list "honesty" as a core value — something we would steadfastly hold true no matter the circumstance. Right?

Let's challenge ourselves on this by seeing if we have ever been guilty of any of the following.

Do any of the following circumstances apply?

- We told a customer all is going well when chaos reigns behind the scenes.
- We altered our annual tax return — just a little.

- I spent hours at work doing personal chores.
- We ducked out of the office for extended periods on work time.
- I added a few extra hours on a customer's invoice to be sure there is enough to cover everything.
- We altered details about the business being presented to a potential buyer — to make it a bit more attractive than it is.
- We took cash for that job instead of recording it through the books.

And I'm sure we can think of many more indiscretions.

While the sample of frauds I have mentioned has resulted in huge financial losses, it would not take too much imagination to assess how much in total is lost in all the numerous small amounts of cheating that occur in business that we all believe are socially acceptable.

We all lie and cheat — a little

The key message is we all lie, we all cheat, and we are all dishonest — it's just that most of us stop at a point where little or no harm has been done, and we feel it is socially acceptable.

It is a mistake to assume economies and businesses are run on the back of rational decision making. It is also a mistake to assume that someone deciding to break the law does so after rationally weighing up the costs and benefits before proceeding to do something illegal.

The rational view of cheating would assume people pursue the greatest personal benefit they can and, when faced with the option to cheat, will do so based on a cost benefit analysis.

The cost is being caught and the benefit is the material gain. If there is no chance of being caught, it would be assumed we would cheat as much as we can. However, people more often act honestly every day, showing care and concern for others when they could have cheated them.[7]

But we are imperfect creatures and there is an inbuilt evolutionary tendency for us to act in our own best interest. We neither cheat as much as we could get away with nor act with complete honesty.

“ *Brains evolved to serve the organisms that house them, and so amoral selfishness is normal and natural in the animal kingdom. Social life, however, requires some curtailing of selfishness for the sake of harmony and effective group functioning.* 🙶

— Nicole Mead et al.[19]

Research outlined by Dan Ariely in his book *The (Honest) Truth About Dishonesty* **has shown that if we are all provided with the temptation to cheat, we will — but only a little bit.**[20]

Even if there is absolutely no chance we will get caught, some moral compass within most of us stops us at a level of dishonesty we can live with. We only cheat to the extent that allows us to maintain a positive image of ourselves.

As Ariely describes it, on the one hand we want to benefit from cheating, which is the rational economic motivation, while on the other we want to be able to view ourselves as being good people, which is the psychological motivation. Basically, if we cheat just a little bit, we feel we can have our cake and eat some of it too.

Cash, conflicts of interest, and group temptations

That same research by Ariely also showed that we are more comfortable pushing the boundaries of honesty the further we are away from the cash associated with that dishonesty. For example, how comfortable are we taking a pen from the cupboard for the kids or off someone's desk versus taking money from the petty cash box or money from someone else's top draw?

Another form of cheating "a little bit" is when we have conflicts of interest. We can often be blinded by our own self-interest.

We could suggest that a client does extra work using our services that they could do without. This is particularly likely if we feel under some financial pressure in our business and could really use that extra cash.

There are numerous examples where people were conflicted in the corporate fails that we go through, most notably South Canterbury Finance. Unfortunately, it is an ongoing challenge for all boards in this country.

When we are part of a group, and we see those in our group cheating, especially if we respect them, the temptation to cheat is greater. The temptation is also greater if that group relies on us. This might be a work group, or those relying on us might be our family where we are the main breadwinner.

Giving in when fatigued

If our self-control is compromised, we might give in to the temptation to push the boundaries of what is right and wrong.

When we are stressed and tired and when we are forced to make many decisions, and our willpower is waning, we will be tempted to take the easy path, which may not be the completely honest path.[8] I'm sure you can relate to those cases where your willpower diminished and you gave in to temptation and ate or drank the wrong thing or decided to flop in the chair rather than do some exercise.

We will talk about the importance of wellbeing, health and managing stress as it relates to caring for ourselves and for our business. This same wellbeing also assists in maintaining our self-control and, therefore, avoiding the temptation to drift in to the increasing grey area of right and wrong.

There are those who are prepared to defraud and act corruptly knowing full well it is illegal and wrong but do it anyway. The rest of us are good, honest people doing the best we can to run a successful business. We just need to remember that we are human and can face the temptations to take the easy path and act a little bit dishonestly, especially if stressed, tired or mentally exhausted.

We have so many opportunities every day to cheat and act dishonestly with almost no likelihood we will be caught or suffer any consequence, yet most of us have the moral fortitude not to do this.

How honest should we be in business?

So how honest should we be when running our businesses, considering all the above discussions?

Where is that line between what is right and honest and what is dishonest? If each of us had to draw that line, where would it be? The clear majority of us are honest, hardworking people in business. However, as Groucho Marx put it, it's doubtful we can say with absolute authority that we haven't been at least a bit dishonest at some stage.

66 *Morality, like art, means drawing a line somewhere.* 99
— Oscar Wilde

This is the point where I will abdicate responsibility for offering you, the reader, advice on what honesty in business looks like.

Our values, our view on ethics, conflicts of interest and even the fundamental question of what each of us believes is right and wrong are the basis of our own assessment of honesty.

If values like "honesty", "ethics" and "integrity" are what you decide are your core values, are you clear what that looks like? What behaviours will you and your staff be demonstrating if you are being "honest"? Are there any lines that you will not cross or not tolerate your staff crossing?

These are very important questions that in the end only you can answer.

6 ALLAN HUBBARD AND THE FAILURE OF SOUTH CANTERBURY FINANCE

In August 2010, South Canterbury Finance (SCF) became the biggest corporate failure in New Zealand history, requiring a $1.5 billion bailout by the New Zealand government. It resulted in the attempted prosecutions by the SFO of Hubbard, the former CEO, CFO, accountant and board members. The failure of SCF also resulted in the loss of savings for around 35,000 depositors.

Significant material has been written about the events of SCF, including hundreds of news articles, biographies, Treasury documents released under the Official Information Act, as well as liquidation and receivers reports.

In reading this material, and speaking to former board members, liquidators, receivers, senior managers and others who operated within the inner circle of SCF, my aim was to understand what happened, why it happened, and what we can learn.

My only regret was not being able to speak to Allan Hubbard prior to his sad passing. It is never good to speak of people who are not able to give their side of the story. One thing that has become very clear to me in researching large business failures is that there are always many sides to the story.

Unfortunately, one cannot discuss SCF and learn why it failed without talking about Allan Hubbard. SCF was a business built, owned, led and managed by Allan Hubbard. His influence over the business was far-reaching from the time he acquired it in the 1950s until its final demise. It was also intertwined with many of Hubbard's other businesses and subsidiaries of SCF, of which there were many.

Allan Hubbard was one of the most respected and revered business people in New Zealand, especially in Timaru and the South Island business community. In over half a century in business he owned, led, supported or advised thousands of businesses, many to great success, and to the acclamation of those business people he helped.

The failure of SCF hurt many people, none more so than Allan Hubbard, whose legacy was tarnished by the failure.

Allan Hubbard — the man and the business owner

A tough childhood and the devoted family man

Much of Allan Hubbard's life is detailed in his biography, *A Man out of Time*, written by Virginia Green.[1]

He was born in March 1928 into a very poor family during the Depression years. His father was a violent and abusive man. His grandmother ran a brothel and brought his mother into a life of prostitution. He only discovered this later in life, and that his aunty was in fact a half-sister, the offspring of his mother's prostitution before he was born. As a child, Hubbard was involved in petty crime before his association with the church, and a growing devotion to his newfound Christian values saw him pursue a far more virtuous path. These values would stay with him throughout the remainder of his life.

He was involved in the Scout movement most of his life. He was an active Christian and donated significant amounts of money to charitable and needy causes.

He married Jean in 1952 and they had five daughters. He was devoted to his wife, saying that:

> *She has fed me, counselled me, worked with me, never had illusions of grandeur or sought riches or honour for herself. I thank her for her magnificent contribution to the firm.*[1]

They remained married until his death in a car crash in Oamaru in 2011.

The dedicated, respected and successful businessman

Hubbard worked in his friend's father's small business before taking a job at Craighead School in Timaru in 1953. He then started a humble accounting business in Timaru. He experienced what most small business owners face in their early life — a slow, hard path to build the business he sought.

He earned a reputation as an extremely warm and generous man. He backed many fledgling businesses, gave back significantly to the community, and held on to clients for decades and they remained immensely loyal to him. Even through his most trying days in business, he remained hugely respected and loved in the Timaru region.

In 2009, the then Mayor of Mackenzie John O'Neill said of Hubbard:

> 66 *He's a man of integrity and generosity. There would be few people in business that haven't been affected by him.* 99 [2]

In 2004, he received a Queens Services Order medal for his "valuable voluntary service to the community". In 2009 (in the midst of the SCF's financial crisis), over 1000 people submitted letters supporting a campaign to see him knighted. Hubbard wrote to the *Timaru Herald* thanking his supporters but indicating he was not seeking such honours. Many felt he dearly wanted to accept this accolade, but for the timing.

Hubbard was very open about the desire he had to leave SCF as a charitable trust to serve communities after his death.

Allan Hubbard's business acumen, appetite for risk, hard work and commitment saw him run his business activities for over 60 years. He was also involved in dozens of other successful businesses.

After such humble beginnings in life and business (he made £1600 turnover in 1955 in his new small accountancy business), Hubbard built his personal wealth to some $650 million by 2008, which made him the 13th richest man in New Zealand at that time.

He was involved in a diverse array of business ventures. At the time SCF was on the brink of collapse, Hubbard was a director and/or shareholder of some 500 businesses. [3]

In the 1950s, he was involved in starting Helicopters New Zealand Ltd that saw the introduction of the relatively unknown craft into New Zealand. It set the scene for the widespread and effective use of helicopters in all aspects of New Zealand business and tourism. The company was 100% owned by SCF and was sold to a Canadian company for $160 million in 2011 after 55 years in operation.

His habits of hard work and frugality were well known.

> 66 *His long-time clients and staff tell stories of extraordinary generosity and kindness that go far beyond conventional business practice.* 99
> — Virginia Green

He was a workaholic, known for working all hours. He was well known to work 80-plus-hour weeks and call those working just a 50-hour week lazy.

In the words of another client, Jack Henderson:

66 There is something in the firm that you would have expected to exist several generations ago — a sort of decency, good grace, and good manners that you don't see much of these days. It's been there for the thirty-odd years I've been associated with them. It seems to encompass respect, trust, loyalty — things that aren't bandied around much any more.99[4]

Traditional lending values

Traditionally, his lending activities and the businesses he favoured were local. He kept a close eye on loan quality and would lend to people who showed financial restraint and good management. He would also rely on local word of mouth.

In her book, Virginia Green wrote about the early practices of SCF:

66 Allan liked to see evidence of a borrower's frugal habits, and his technique could get rather personal. He would scrutinise a borrower — and especially his wife — for evidence of extravagant spending. He also relied on small-town word-of-mouth. 'You can't survive in a town like this [Timaru] unless you have integrity, because you soon get found out.' 99

— Virginia Green

Hubbard was the shareholder, director, funder, advisor and accountant to thousands of ventures that, without him, may never have come to life.

66 Those of us who knew Allan can be confident the credits on his life's ledger far outweigh the debits.99

— Duncan Brand, Hubbard's former accountancy partner[5]

Many people saw the man they knew rather than the man at the helm of a failed business, apportioning the blame on others. In his hometown of Timaru, he was seen as a kind, humble and honest man.

... but the failure was significant

Unfortunately, one cannot expect to be at the helm of a business that fails so spectacularly without less favourable views also being formed.

These views included that he acted unethically, even illegally, and not with his investors' needs in mind.

Any business failure where people are financially or emotionally hurt will result in accusations. With the breadth of Hubbard's interests and the people impacted, it is not surprising that accusations of financial impropriety arose.

Many defended Hubbard to the very end. However, as Rebecca Macfie quoted in an October 2010 article in the *New Zealand Listener* magazine on these people's views:

> **❝** *They fail to acknowledge that Hubbard's imploding empire was founded on other people's money, and that kindness and piety are not substitutes for accountability.* **❞**
> — Rebecca Macfie, *New Zealand Listener*[6]

When I spoke to Rebecca Macfie about her interview with Mr Hubbard, she felt he almost had an "evangelic self-belief". She sensed the adulation people had for him, and his philanthropic activities justified his other business activities including those that were later criticised and played a part in the failure of SCF.

The Global Financial Crisis and New Zealand finance companies

The losses in the USA and the failures of companies like Bear Stearns in March 2008, Lehman Brothers in September 2008 and others are now the basis of folklore, with combined losses drifting into trillions of dollars.

The Global Financial Crisis (GFC) also saw significant upheaval in New Zealand's finance sector.

Between 2006 and 2010, 49 finance companies collapsed in New Zealand costing investors over $8 billion. The government stepped in to bail out many of these companies, under the Crown Retail Deposit Guarantee Scheme. It is estimated that between 150,000 and 200,000 deposit holders were impacted.

It is not clear how much of these losses were recovered after liquidation and other recovery processes, but the numbers are significant by New Zealand corporate standards.

The reasons for finance company collapses

A parliamentary investigation found a range of reasons for the finance industry's demise.[7] The findings included criminal misconduct, poor governance and management, poor communication with investors, and weak supervision. The report questioned the values of some of the leaders of these businesses who showed greater self-interest than interest in their customers. They also questioned the ability of the leaders of these businesses to understand the risks their businesses faced.

The customers of these finance companies tended to be individuals and small businesses that wanted more flexibility or more credit than banks at that time were prepared to offer.

In the decade of rapid growth in New Zealand's property sector up to 2007, finance company lending expanded rapidly. They filled the gap of higher-risk lending that the banks wouldn't cover.

This competition also saw banks drifting more into the property sector and taking on higher-risk lending. This in turn saw finance companies having to take even greater risks to maintain their position in the market.

Finance companies were less diligent in understanding the risks faced by those they lent to or their capacity to repay. This was irresponsible to both their businesses and their customers but was accepted practice.

Many companies did not disclose the level of risk adequately, and some sought to deliberately minimise the perceived risk difference between themselves and the banks. This was the environment SCF was operating in during the first decade of the new century.

The rise and fall of an icon and finance giant

South Canterbury Finance started in 1926 as South Canterbury Loan and Finance. It specialised in small loans to local businesses and households in Timaru. Hubbard bought SCF in the late 1950s in response to the need to get finance for a client.

SCF had survived depressions, wars and oil shocks, and had traditionally only held small percentages of its loans in Auckland and Wellington. Apart from some bumpy times in the Depression years of the 1930s, SCF had traded profitably for over 80 years. By any number of measures, it was a very successful business.

Until the early 2000s, SCF had continued to lend to regional areas where the local managers, best placed to assess the risks, made lending decisions. They tended to be smaller loans on physical assets or lower-risk businesses and property.

An experienced and strong voice exits

Hubbard had always kept a very tight hold over the day-to-day running of SCF and all his businesses. He typically surrounded himself with people he could control or agreed with his position. Nigel Gormack, a partner in Allan Hubbard's accountancy business, who had worked with Hubbard for many years, said that Hubbard would often stop talking to him for weeks on end if he challenged him or disagreed with his views.

Humphrey Rolleston was one person who did stand up to Hubbard. The pair first met in the early 1970s and he was part of the business from the late 1980s.

While considered abrasive and not universally liked, he knew the business very well and stood up to Allan Hubbard like few others could.[8]

The exact reasons for Rolleston's departure have not been fully explained although many felt it was a breakdown in his relationship with Hubbard and disagreement about Hubbard's selection of his new management team.

He sold his 23% shares to Hubbard in 2004 (for around $30 million) and departed. His departure saw the loss of a strong, experienced voice within the SCF leadership that could moderate Hubbard's behaviour.

The first CEO and a new management regime

In 2003, shortly before Rolleston's departure, Hubbard employed his first ever CEO, Lachie McLeod. Rolleston was strongly opposed to this appointment and the way it was done.

McLeod was an ex-Westpac banker in Timaru who had worked with Hubbard on various deals in previous years.

Hubbard appointed McLeod without formal approval from his board. Many questioned McLeod's experience going from the tightly managed lending in the banking sector to a loosely governed company lending into a higher-risk market.

He was also inexperienced in what constituted good governance in a large risky business, reporting to a chairman who had no interest in such processes. It is likely any new CEO would have found this position a challenge. Unfortunately, Hubbard was never likely to select a person to the CEO role that he was unable to control.

McLeod selected his own management team including a new Chief Operating Officer in Peter Bosworth. Hubbard never approved of Bosworth and wanted him removed from the day he arrived. Some felt Bosworth's appetite for growth and the incentive schemes he implemented for his lenders contributed to the rapid growth in lending. Unfortunately, many felt he was well out of his depth, especially investing into the property sector.

The company grew rapidly under McLeod and Bosworth's leadership from 2004 to

2008. During this time, SCF's investments more than tripled from $750 million to $2.5 billion. It also purchased a range of smaller finance companies and other businesses throughout New Zealand that were eventually amalgamated into SCF.[9]

Lachie McLeod commented, in hindsight, that this growth was too great and a smaller SCF may have been better placed to survive the pending shock.

The high price of poor health

Hubbard had some extended periods away from the business during this period of growth with health scares.

First, it was cancer in 2006 and 2007, as he approached 80 years of age. This was a life-threatening illness. In the years after this he also suffered severe kidney problems, requiring dialysis.

SCF saw significant growth in the time he was away, particularly into the property market. On his return, he did express concern about the increased risk profile of SCF. Unfortunately, he couldn't resist the increase in profits it attracted, so supported it.

Those close to him felt the setbacks from health and his age did impact on Hubbard's abilities to operate at the levels he once did. It was felt the decisions he started making and the things he allowed to happen may not have occurred in his more recent past.

The GFC — was SCF still a strong investment?

As late as June 2008 during the GFC, when investment companies in the USA were in serious trouble and New Zealand finance companies were failing, SCF was still considered a sound company. It was considered one of a very small handful of non-bank finance companies positioned to survive the shock.

This was the view of the respected *New Zealand Herald* business journalist Bernard Hickey as detailed in his article in *The 5 Survivability Factors for finance companies*.[10]

Hickey pointed to several characteristics that would see a few finance companies survive the financial crisis of that era, including diversification, good access to bank funding, a strong parent and an investment grade credit rating — all which Hickey believed SCF possessed.

At that stage, the only non-bank finance companies he felt would survive the GFC were UDC Finance, SCF and Marac.

The perceived strength of SCF, the view that is was well led and well-run, saw it grow during a period that other finance companies were collapsing.

Some good offers on the business were passed over

In the years leading up to the failure of SCF, it had some healthy offers to buy the business. These included two offers for around $300 million, one from George Kerr of Pyne Gould Corporation, the then owner of Marac Finance.

People like Nigel Gormack, Hubbard's trusted colleague, and long-term accountant with Hubbard Churcher, recommended this transaction occur. If it had occurred, the new buyers would have expected changes in the management and board and it would see Hubbard lose much of his control.

Unfortunately, Hubbard did not proceed with this option, instead listening to his Forsyth Barr advisors to attempt a listing which it was preparing for.

At the very last moment the decision was made not to float the business. Forsyth Barr received a payment of more than $1 million for their work on the failed listing.

Hubbard came back to Nigel Gormack after the listing failed to proceed and indicated that he'd made a mistake and could Gormack try to resurrect the George Kerr deal — it was too late as that opportunity had gone.

Letting go of SCF was always going to be very difficult for Allan Hubbard. The irrationality we now know was that he steadfastly held on to 100% of what became nothing when he could have had a part of something, if he had relinquished control. The sale to these buyers would likely see SCF alive today.

The government to the rescue — sort of

On Sunday, 12 October 2008, the government implemented the Crown Retail Deposit Guarantee Scheme (the Scheme) to avoid a flight of funds from New Zealand institutions to those in Australia that had a guarantee in place and would make investing there safer.

It happened literally overnight. It was designed and then announced on the same day. The Scheme offered a government guarantee over the money that people deposited or invested with financial institutions — specifically banks and non-bank deposit takers, including finance companies like SCF.

The government considered the Crown Retail Deposit Guarantee Scheme necessary to maintain depositor and public confidence in New Zealand's financial markets.[11]

SCF applied to join the Scheme on 14 October 2008.

When the Scheme ended in December 2011, it had stabilised the finance sector, no banks had failed, but nine finance companies covered by the Scheme collapsed, SCF being the largest.

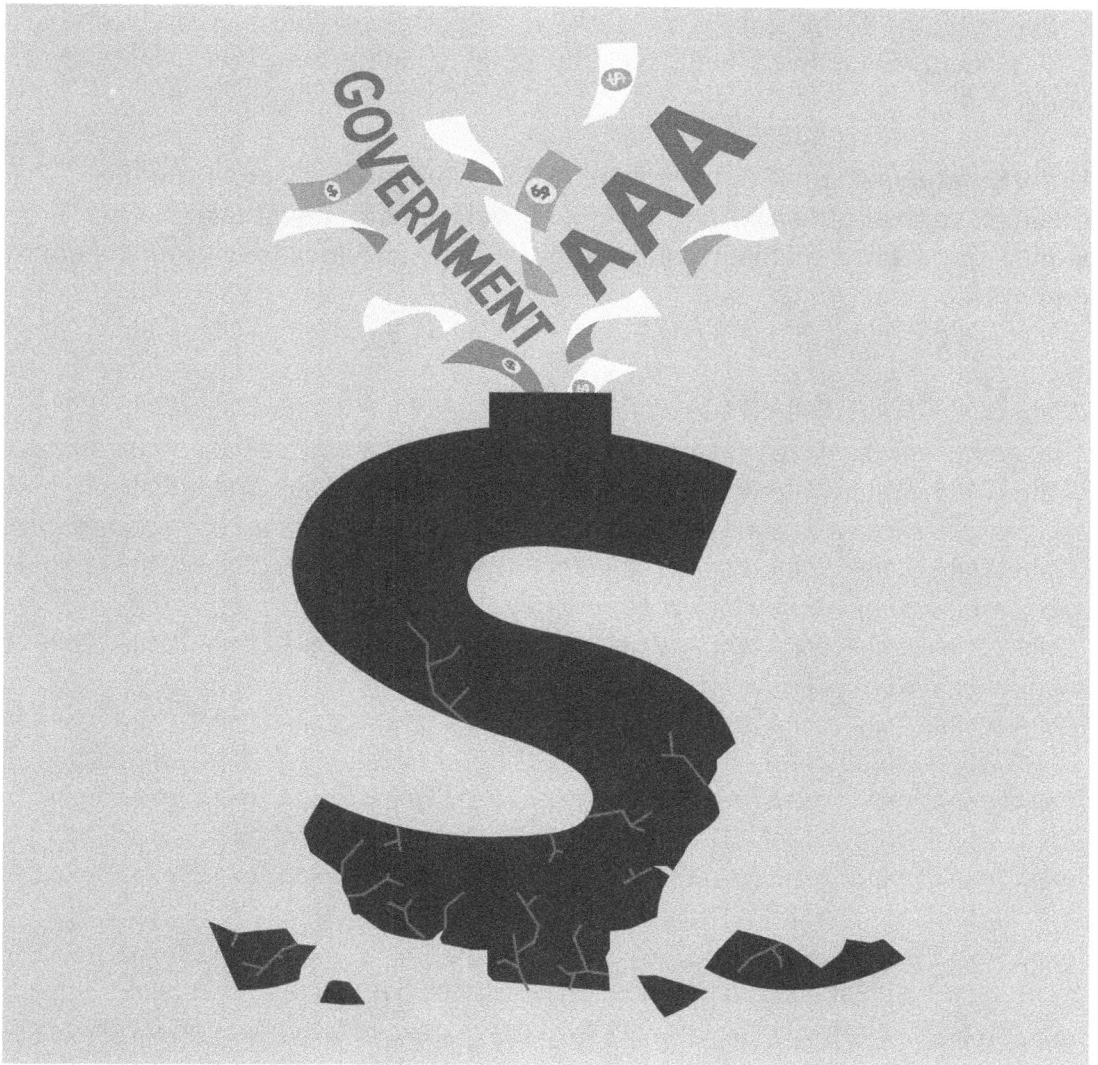

The role of ratings agencies

When SCF was accepted into the Scheme, the Treasury did not know how vulnerable it was. It had a BBB– rating with Standard & Poor's — one it had held since 2006. No one, including the Reserve Bank, expressed concerns.

Much scorn was directed at the ratings agencies for their role in the collapse of the US finance sector during the GFC, the main three being Standard & Poor's, Moody's, and Fitch.

The concern with their practices in the USA was centred on their ratings of complex, and dubious, mortgage-backed securities. This was not the issue in New Zealand. However, their ratings of finance companies, particularly SCF, definitely gave both those within the business and the external marketplace confidence in the business.

SCF openly promoted their BBB– credit rating, including using it on their letterhead and emails.

Unfortunately, when SCF started their slide, Standard & Poor's rode the business to the bottom with many downgrades in quick succession. This would now seem a bit like closing the gate in the paddock long after the horse had bolted.

And the money kept flowing in

The speed with which the Scheme was implemented in the near-panicked environment of the GFC meant the unintended consequences of it were not thought through.

The government was effectively underwriting risky finance companies and unconsciously encouraging even riskier investments into those companies, as people saw them as being backed by a government guarantee.

The Auditor-General, who carried out an audit of the Crown Retail Deposit Guarantee System, stated:

> *Once deposits with these companies were guaranteed, depositors could safely move investments to where they would get the highest return, irrespective of the risk of company failure. During 2009 deposits with finance companies under the Scheme grew. At South Canterbury Finance Limited, the deposits grew 25% after the guarantee was put in place [to February 2009].*[12]

In the growing volatility and failure of many finance companies, brokers like Forsyth Barr and their investors were looking for a safer place to invest their money other than the banks. With a BBB– rating, positive reviews from financial commentators, and now a government guarantee under the Scheme, SCF appeared to be the best option.

No one saw the impact of the GFC on a remote economy like New Zealand being as significant as it was and even fewer felt SCF could fail — it was effectively too big to fail.

This combined sentiment saw more and more money flowing into SCF looking for a place to be invested.

SCF, particularly Hubbard, was reluctant to turn this money away or reduce the interest rates they promised would be delivered. SCF wanted to invest all the money on offer for the best return they could. There was little desire to accept all this money and leave it in the bank. It had to be placed somewhere to attract the high returns investors were looking for.

This saw SCF lending more money to increasingly riskier property developments.

This was at a time when 12 New Zealand finance companies had already failed, Bear Stearns and Lehman Brothers had collapsed, and the US government had bailed out Freddie Mac and Fannie Mae.

I spoke with former board members and executives of SCF. They acknowledge now that they should have closed their doors to this money. Accepting all comers and then investing more and more money in riskier property projects saw more dangerous growth for SCF.

Treasury — were they asleep at the wheel?

The Auditor-General was also critical of Treasury for not stepping in to curb the growing risk it faced as investors and finance companies covered by the Scheme used it to continue engaging in aggressive investment behaviour. As investments grew, the risk to the government underwriting these companies grew as well.

The Auditor-General felt SCF's demise was becoming more obvious and action should have been taken by Treasury. Their report stated:

> *"Effective monitoring of South Canterbury Finance in the months leading up to its eventual failure provided ample warning of the failure and an opportunity to analyse and consider alternative approaches ..."*[13]

The end was nigh

Property values started falling in mid to late 2008 and saw more people unable to meet their commitments to lenders.

In early 2009, the cracks in SCF were starting to show more publicly. The reports reaching Treasury under the Scheme expressed concerns about the governance of SCF, the lower quality of its lending, and related party transactions.

Related party transactions are those where money is passed between the various companies owned by Hubbard. These were not always done transparently, and many later felt they were hiding some of Hubbard's activities.

More loans were looking shaky as developers were defaulting.

The government forced SCF to take on an inspector, KordaMentha, to review what it was doing.

KordaMentha expressed many concerns about SCF's lending practices, the lack of consideration of how they would exit bad loans, how the company was structured and governed, and that loans were being made that were unlikely to be recovered.

This report also highlighted the likely impact on the Scheme should SCF fail — their estimate, at that stage, was approximately $1.85 billion.[14]

SCF challenged this report saying it was misleading and overly pessimistic. Sadly, just as Solid Energy had been in denial when UBS raised concerns, so too was SCF when confronted with KordaMentha's report.

Hubbard wrote a lengthy letter to all the company's investors to reassure them of the finance company's stability and profitability in a volatile environment — clearly concerns existed.

In mid-2009, SCF announced a write-down in assets of over $58 million and announced its first loss since the Depression years in the 1930s.

Leaving the sinking ship

As the troubles started to appear, the once-loyal employees and advocates of SCF started disappearing.

Graeme Brown, the CFO, resigned in May 2009.

General Manager of Funding, Kevin Gloag, with 29 years' service with SCF, resigned in May 2010 because of the risky lending he felt the business was involved in, particularly after receiving a letter from a concerned investor. He said of this investor:

> *Can I honestly tell her we have the business practices in place to protect her money going forward, given our current state of health?* [15]

Gloag stayed on to support his team for what he described to me as the most difficult six months of his career.

A new CEO and new board members

In August 2009, Stuart Nattrass and Bob White left the board.

Under pressure from Forsyth Barr, Hubbard selected three new independent directors, Stuart McLauchlan, Bill Bayliss and Denham Shale. While experienced directors who were unlikely to achieve much this late in the piece, they were Forsyth Barr's choice, and many felt were not the best replacements.

When I spoke to Stuart McLauchlan, he described what he discovered in his initial time on the board:

> *Every rock the new board turned over revealed another problem.*

> *I believe this poor governance contributed to the failure of SCF.*

Lachie McLeod resigned in November 2009, after trying to recover what proved to be an unrecoverable situation. His attempts to hold the team together proved futile, as people saw the issues SCF faced and started leaving.

He accepted that had he not resigned, he would likely have been dismissed.

To maintain his control, Hubbard replaced McLeod with Nigel Gormack.

The new board members opposed this, wanting Sandy Maier. Maier was Harvard law trained, a highly experienced director, and had prior experience with other statutory managements. Hubbard was forced to back down and accepted Maier.

Maier described the lending activities of SCF at the time of his appointment:

> ❝ It might have been cynical, it might have been merely incompetent — it probably violated a lot of prudent lending criteria. I guess the best you could say was it was somebody's idea of aggressive growth. This happens in the lending industry, cyclical excesses and rushes of blood to the head. South Canterbury Finance was poorly controlled and managed for some time. ❞
> — Sandy Maier[16]

By now, finding a way to save SCF was looking increasingly difficult. Not even Allan Hubbard, who many people had been turning to his whole career to save sinking businesses, could do anything to save SCF.

In May 2010, Allan Hubbard was removed from the board.

A government that had lost interest

Sandy Maier indicated that in these latter days, significant effort was made to attract a buyer for what might be recovered from the SCF business.

Maier was confident there was still inherent value in what remained of SCF and that buyers did exist. He felt the government had little appetite to pursue any further efforts to save SCF and just wanted to walk away from it.

On 31 August 2010, the government appointed receivers.

Mr and Mrs Hubbard's businesses — the final straw for SCF

With so many complex connections between Hubbard's business interests, it is not surprising that scrutiny extended beyond SCF into his other businesses.

An unhappy investor and the Securities Commission

In February 2010, an investor in one of Hubbard's other investment businesses, Aorangi Securities, raised concerns with the Securities Commission about an investment where they believed a prospectus should have been provided. Mr and Mrs Hubbard were informed of this by the Securities Commission on 15 March 2010.[17]

The subsequent correspondence between the Securities Commission and Hubbard's lawyers showed an impatient regulator unable to get the answers they wanted. In response, Hubbard's lawyers strongly challenged the validity of the concerns. They also protested the unreasonable expectations the regulator had for providing the extensive information they wanted and the time allowed to collate it.

The Securities Commission handed the issue to the Companies Office in early June 2010, who then commenced their investigation.

The informality of Hubbard's practices, lack of attention to detail, poor documentation, and lack of adherence to acceptable practices, as occurred in SCF, also existed in his other businesses. Some believed it was just Allan Hubbard's honest way of doing things. Some saw it as fraud. These practices did not help his cause.

The Companies Office investigation recommended that the government needed to put these businesses into statutory management. The head of the investigation team stated in the report:

> ❝ We recommend the (Securities) Commission consider whether it is desirable for Aorangi, related corporations and associated persons to be placed into statutory management. I believe decisive and expeditious action is called for to address the perilous governance and management circumstances now facing Aorangi, and to protect the interests of investors. Statutory management is the only remedy which is capable of delivering this outcome. ❞[18]

Too many conflicts of interest — even with the regulator

There were justifiable concerns raised about the independence of the Companies Office investigation team and the Securities Commission.

One of the four members on the Companies Office investigations team was Graeme McGlinn, then of Grant Thornton. In their report, the investigation team recommended that Mr McGlinn and Grant Thornton take on the role of statutory managers, which the

Securities Commission board approved.

It could be perceived that placing Aorangi into statutory management was in Mr McGlinn's interests and removed objectivity. The investigations team should not have made such a recommendation. Once made, the Securities Commission board should have noted this conflict and rejected the recommendation, or chosen a different party to act as statutory manager.[19]

Simon Botherway, a member of the Securities Commission board that made the final decision, was also conflicted. SCF had forced Jonathan Botherway's South Island hospitality businesses into receivership in July 2009, owing SCF more than $10 million. His brother Simon phoned into the meeting where the decision was made to recommend the government put Aorangi into statutory management. Simon Botherway shared many business interests with his brother.

The minutes did show that members had been asked to disclose any interests. None did. While the outcome of this meeting may not have changed for Aorangi, Simon Botherway should have declared his conflict and removed himself from the meeting.

Also, the potential conflict of Mr McGlinn should have been raised by the investigation team, challenged by the board and resolved.[20]

I spoke to other parties who were present at that board meeting. They were not prepared to discuss any of the activities in the boardroom at this meeting, which may be considered good governance but mainly indicated their unease at what had occurred. However, they did say, with hindsight, that they may have acted differently had all the information been available, known and understood at that time. In the end, the statutory management went ahead and soon after SCF went into receivership.

Statutory management — a very blunt axe

The government can appoint outside people to run a company under the Corporations (Investigation and Management) Act 1989. This is known as statutory management. This option was put in place after the share market crash of 1987. The government can instigate statutory management if it believes a company is *"operating fraudulently or recklessly"*.

The then Minister of Commerce, Simon Power, had little choice but to agree with the recommendations of the Securities Commission.

Within a day, on 20 June 2010, Aorangi Securities, Hubbard Managed Funds, and seven charitable trusts of Hubbard's were placed into statutory management, less than two weeks after the Companies Office started its investigation.

This process seemed unnecessarily hasty, poorly thought through, and sloppy. It was also surrounded with conflicts of interest that were not managed. Hubbard's other businesses, including Aorangi, had assets that Hubbard had hoped to use to prop up SCF.

The statutory management, after four years, recovered almost every dollar to investors, so it is questionable it was in the perilous state claimed.

The brutal nature of the statutory management process gave no one an opportunity to do anything to manage the entities into a better position. Hubbard and his wife were banned from going to their offices and accessing any related bank accounts.

It was only the third time statutory management had been placed on individuals, but it was one that was implemented with surprising haste.

When we consider our discussions on decision making and irrationality, it is not unreasonable to question if this decision was well thought through, and whether it was free from many of the biases we discuss later in the book.

The action came under significant criticism. A report instigated by supporters of Hubbard indicated the action may have been unlawful.[21]

Accusations of fraud and failed legal action

In June 2011, the Serious Fraud Office (SFO) laid 50 charges against Allan Hubbard under the Crimes Act. These included *"theft by person in special relationship"*, *"obtaining by deception or causing loss by deception"* and *"false accounting"*.

They were triggered following a complaint being raised with the SFO by the new director, Stuart McLauchlan.

The key basis for the charges was information sent to the government when SCF applied to join the Scheme. A letter was sent by Lachie McLeod applying to join the Scheme on 14 October 2008. Attached to the letter was an audited financial report and a prospectus from the previous year. This letter, the attachments and some further information sent as part of the application were the main basis for the claim that SCF deceived the government in its application, and thus had committed fraud.

Not only was the Scheme set up with some haste, it appears the government's

interest for SCF to join, SCF's application to do so, and Treasury's review of all the documents was also done in haste.

In September 2011, Allan Hubbard's untimely death in a car accident near Oamaru saw all charges dropped. He was 83 years old.

On December 2011, after a 14-month investigation, the SFO laid charges against Graeme Brown (the CFO), Lachie McLeod, Robert White and Edward Sullivan, claiming their behaviour led to losses under the government's Scheme. These charges, if proven, could have led to significant jail time.

Charges against Mr Brown were dropped prior to the court, and McLeod and White were found not guilty by the court.

Ed Sullivan was charged for four out of the nine charges against him, mainly related to supposed misinformation in a prospectus but not the charges related to the Scheme. He received 12 months' home detention and 400 hours of community work.

Timaru — a proud town

An attack on SCF and Allan Hubbard was an attack on Timaru, an immensely proud and tight community, which had seen the work Allan Hubbard and other board members, like Ed Sullivan, had done for them.

They were never going to remain silent while the case played out at the High Court in Timaru. When the legal proceedings started, the community rallied around these people and supported them throughout.

What did the trial achieve?

The court case went for over 60 days. It cost the defendants in excess of $4 million in legal costs (most of which is still being paid off by these people), plus the costs for the prosecution's legal case, the costs of the SFO's 14-month investigation, and other court costs.

All were acquitted on the main charges related to the entry of SCF into the Scheme. Ed Sullivan's charges were related to other matters.

This was a legal process that was likely to have cost well in excess of $10 million, that saw no one charged on the original items that were brought against the accused, and recovered no money for investors or the government.

The judge was very critical of the SFO's investigation. While he said there were grounds for initiating the investigation, he criticised the investigation team's lack of experience and CEO Adam Freeley's premature and public claims of fraud in the media. He also stated the SFO had not collected the critical information they should have (from Treasury) or interviewed all the correct people.[22]

> 66 *Regrettably, I find that the Serious Fraud Office's investigation was deficient in material respects* 99

and

> 66 *In the context of what the director [Feeley] announced publicly to be the 'biggest fraud in New Zealand's history' and one that was the 'most resource intensive and time consuming in recent history' the standard of investigation on this charge fell well below that which the public is entitled to expect …* 99
> — Justice Paul Heath

It proved to be an embarrassment for Adam Feeley and the SFO.

Why did SCF fail and what can businesses learn from this?

The failure of SCF is now a part of New Zealand corporate history and discussion on it is likely to go on for years to come. All the main players have done their best to move on in their lives. There is still a lot of anger and bitterness that may never subside. Many are happy to talk about it, others want to forget it.

The most important thing about a failure of this size and complexity is what we can learn from it. These are what I believe are the reasons SCF failed.

Unprecedented growth

The reason SCF failed was relatively simple. They lent far too much money to the wrong people, and the wrong projects, where the risks were too high, not fully understood nor managed.

They did this at a pace of growth that was unsustainable. This situation was made worse by the property market prices falling during the GFC.

SCF caught the illness that plagued many finance companies of that period —

unmanaged growth in lending and failure to understand and manage the risk during an unprecedented level of volatility.

What requires some deeper consideration is how this came about and what allowed it to go on until it was too late to recover.

What if the GFC hadn't happened?

Most people close to the failure of SCF feel it would still be alive today had the GFC not been such a significant event.

Unfortunately, aggressive growth in property development, rising prices and poor lending practices throughout New Zealand, and the world, were always likely to trigger some form of correction and this should have been considered.

No one expected an event of this size, but the risks were known.

As the statistics showed in Figure 1 from the Companies Office, the GFC had a significant impact on many New Zealand businesses and this external shock cannot be ignored.

Governance and leadership

I have spoken to many people close to the events of SCF and people on all sides of the debate almost universally agree that the governance processes followed by SCF fell well short of what would be expected of a public company of this size. In the end, poor governance allowed the growth and poor lending practices to go on.

The proceedings from the court case triggered by the SFO revealed much about the governance culture that had built up in SCF and contributed to its failure.[23]

While good governance of large organisations does not guarantee success, as the events outlined in Solid Energy's failure attest, poor governance in large organisations will eventually contribute to serious problems.

The company's systems and procedures had not kept pace with its growth and they did not compare well against any standard expected of a business of this size.

There were no strong independent directors. There were very poor processes to approve decisions. Conflicts of interest were everywhere. Many decisions that should have involved all board members were made outside the boardroom, and often by Hubbard alone without anything being documented.

Hubbard did not like board meetings and they occurred sporadically and with

inadequate process for what would be expected for a business of its size and complexity. He was regularly known to agree to motions in the boardroom that were sanctioned by the board, only to change them, and change the board minutes, after the meeting was completed. This behaviour angered and frustrated other board members, who felt helpless to do anything about it.

Allan Hubbard was determined to stay at the helm of SCF, resisting all efforts to build a programme of succession. Succession is considered an essential part of any well-governed business. The success throughout his business career meant he stubbornly held on to old business practices and made him reluctant to embrace new ways of doing things, including succession.

A lot of the accounting and financial record keeping was done manually with the use of handwritten cashbooks, journals and typed ledger cards.

For example, as late as 2006, he wrote a cheque for $25 million for a transaction and everything was recorded manually on paper and in a paper-based cash ledger — something that would have even been out of date 30 years earlier.

When he appointed his first CEO, Lachie McLeod, he did so with little input from other people — in any other similar organization, such a decision would have been heavily scrutinised by its board and gone through a transparent market recruitment process.

Another key role of any board is the selection of the CEO, mentoring guidance and performance management of the CEO, remuneration of the CEO and, in the case of poor performance, removal of the CEO. Lachie McLeod was handpicked by Hubbard without consulting with the board. In his five years in the business, he received no feedback on his performance while still regularly getting pay increases — for reasons that were never explained. If the board was unhappy with his or his team's performance, it was duty bound to do something about it.

Overwhelming complexity, related parties, and conflicts of interest

South Canterbury Finance was a large, complex business. It was 100% owned by the Southbury Group. In turn, the Southbury Group was 75% owned by Allan Hubbard and his wife, with the remaining 25% shared amongst a wide range of people, including directors and managers of SCF. Southbury also owned many other companies.

The appendix shows the complexity of Hubbard's interests. This was developed by the Reserve Bank and was provided to me though an Official Information request.

Allan Hubbard was a director and/or shareholder of some 500 companies. As the majority shareholder of SCF, Hubbard maintained control. Mr Hubbard and a relatively small group of people, many involved in SCF, were also directors and shareholders of most of the subsidiaries of SCF, and in turn the subsidiaries of those companies. Therefore, directors and the managers were not independent, even though, when challenged, Hubbard claimed they were independent.

While this complex structure of companies may have been set up for good reason, what was not good practice was that so few people, especially Hubbard, were in control of all these separate entities. No one, let alone an unwell man in his 80s, could fulfill their obligations in governing such a complex business.

It also created many conflicts of interest. The directors of Hubbard's entities were also shareholders of these entities. It would have been very difficult to separate one's role in the business with one's self-interests. Even if movements of money were for valid and honourable reasons, the perception, and reality, of conflicts was always going to arise.

It was almost impossible to track the movement of money between all these entities, especially with such poor levels of documentation.

The tracking of transactions and money passing between Mr Hubbard's entities and their shareholders (himself included) lacked transparency. These cash movements became central to claims against Hubbard. These transactions may well have been legitimate but the lack of transparency meant those investigating them struggled to understand them.

Hubbard did not see these entities as related parties. From his perspective, entities that he was a shareholder and/or director of, but where he was not involved in their operation, were not related parties, at least in his view. He sought legal advice to confirm this view. Unfortunately, such advice was from a local lawyer who gave him the answer he wanted, rather than the advice he and the board needed on what were related parties and what were appropriate related party transactions.

The courage and capacity to act

Speaking the truth to and challenging people in a position of power require moral courage as well as the professional and technical competence to back the challenge. It also requires other people prepared to support the challenge.

Standing up to someone as respected as Allan Hubbard, with his business pedigree, takes courage and confidence in one's abilities. Those who should have stood up to him, owed him a great deal and had great respect for him.

The board members were immensely loyal to Allan Hubbard and found him to be almost impossible to influence. Those around him tried to change his ways. The loyalty was ultimately so tested that the board took a vote that they no longer had any confidence in him. He stayed on regardless.

These factors were a very dangerous recipe and were a contributor to SCF's demise.

As an independent director of a board, or a member with a small shareholding, there are only a few options that can be pursued to influence change. This includes exerting influence on the major shareholders, other board members, and management, to deliver the change required. Otherwise the only other option is to resign from the board.

In the case of SCF, Hubbard was the chair, the major shareholder, a man loath to relinquish control, someone who hated the formality of governance, and surrounded himself with handpicked directors loyal to him. Those directors also possibly lacked the breadth of skills, experience and capacity to act quickly enough to deal with the risks facing SCF and rein Hubbard in.

Even the most courageous people would have struggled to change this environment — but they should have done more.

Knowing when to let go

Mr Hubbard tended to run SCF in an autocratic manner. Those close to his many ventures indicated he was a man who kept control over all activities.

Allan Hubbard's desire to hang on to the control of SCF was well known and widely documented. His team had on occasions pushed to reduce Hubbard's role in the company. Terms like "The Bank of Allan" and "ungovernable" were used to describe working with Hubbard.[24]

A major challenge for any business, especially small or family-owned businesses, is knowing when to let go and how to do this. Like Hubbard, we can devote our lives to building up our businesses. Few will ever have the passion for it that the original owners do. It becomes like a child the owners have grown

and nurtured. Letting go can be tough.

However, as it grows, the skills needed to maintain its success will change. The capacity of the business owners to cover all activities will reduce, or, if they try to cover everything, they will become overloaded, and make mistakes.

Business owners cannot afford to follow Allan Hubbard's lead. He was a highly experienced businessman but unable to let go and unable to grasp the changing world he operated in. Even if he had trusted his team (which, apparently, he did not), such micromanagement only alienates people and destroys their confidence.

While Hubbard chose the leadership team he decided to delegate to, he ultimately regretted this decision, saying in the later days of his life about Lachie McLeod and Peter Bosworth:

> 66 *When you look back on it, they ruined me. And now I've got to save it.* 99
> — Allan Hubbard[25]

Every small business owner or leader of a large business should consider what their exit plan will be. As time passes, this plan should be reviewed.

Sometimes the toughest part of leadership or business ownership is the self-awareness and humility to accept it's time to move on.

When the cash dries up — capitalised interest

As with all businesses, when the cash runs out, the business dies.

Many second-tier finance companies, like SCF, lent money at an agreed interest rate (above bank rates) but didn't take the cash out to cover interest while the projects were in development. There were also no repayments of the loan principal while the projects were still being completed. Basically, the developers had a loan and interest-free holiday until they finished the projects.

The interest was, as it is described, capitalised. That is, instead of it being paid to the finance companies as the project progressed, it was added to the value of the loan and only paid out when the developers sold the properties once completed.

This put significant cash pressures on the finance companies. As the property market collapsed, developers sold the developments for less than they had lent, or they themselves failed and were unable to pay anything to the finance companies.

The actions of others outside SCF

Failure of businesses ultimately must rest with the leaders of the business, the owners and those governing the business. SCF is no different.

However, when the failure is as large and complex as SCF, other external factors must be considered in the failure.

The government's Crown Retail Deposit Guarantee Scheme proved a double-edged sword. While protecting depositors in SCF, it was not well thought through or overseen, and sped up the failure of SCF.

The Standard & Poor's high credit rating of SCF, which remained in place until well after the worst of SCF's situation was known, and gave everyone an elevated view of its strength. This was further inflamed by respected commentators praising SCF.

The SFO had to pursue the allegations raised against SCF. However, the case was weak and was also poorly investigated.

The hasty and, one would consider, politically motivated statutory management of Hubbard's related businesses removed any residual confidence in SCF and any chance it could be recovered.

A day before the statutory management was ordered, Brian McCulloch (Director of Financial Operations, Treasury) stated:

> **❝** *... even just the action against Mr Hubbard would seem likely to be terminal for SCF.* **❞**[26]

In these highly emotive failures, especially where taxpayers' money is involved, mixing commercial decisions and political decisions is not a particularly good mix. While the failure of SCF was not of the government's making, its role did not help. It became SCF's greatest creditor through the Scheme and appeared to lack the appetite to fight for its survival when buyers showed interest. It also instigated the statutory management, which was the final straw for SCF.

There were no winners from SCF's failure

I spoke to dozens of people close to the SCF failure. Employees, investors, executive managers, CEOs, board members and government representatives. I found no one who benefited from what happened at SCF.

While we want to attribute blame to single individuals, especially Allan Hubbard, such failures have many people who played their part in its demise.

The greatest thing we can hope as an outcome from the failure of SCF, as New Zealand's largest failure, is we all learn from it and work to ensure it never happens again — hopefully.

SECTION 3:

HOW WE MAKE BUSINESS DECISIONS — AND WHY WE GET THEM WRONG

In the early stages of my exploration into business failure, I quickly found myself exploring people more than any other aspect of the business. Businesses are all about people, so I found I could not discuss the failure of businesses without discussing the limitations we all share and how our humanity contributes to failures.

All too often when discussions arise about why businesses or economies do and don't succeed, we try to explain them in terms of factual, rational and even unemotional factors. We need to be able to measure these factors and apportion cause and effect to outcomes. We also strive to blame someone for the events.

Sadly, as businesses are about people working together, making decisions and then acting on those decisions, we cannot discuss business failure without first spending time understanding a little about the mind and the psychology of the business leader, business owner and employee.

Yes, *this is me and it is you too*, so in reading the following chapters we all need to acknowledge that the limitations I will discuss apply to all of us.

From all the examples of failures we discussed in the previous section, there are so many decisions that were misguided and ultimately destroyed these businesses and resulted in pain for so many.

- Why did Don Elder embark on a path of high-risk growth ignoring the impact of others' views on coal prices?
- Why did the Solid Energy board support Elder when clearly it was at odds with the owners of the company?
- Why did the banks lend Solid Energy so much money when it was clear no guarantees existed?
- How could the receiver of Salthouse Marine form such a different view of the reason the business failed to the owner when both had the same information?
- Why did SCF continue to take money from investors under the Retail Guarantee Scheme when they could only invest it in extremely high-risk ventures — which were likely to fail?
- Why did David Ross knowingly defraud so many people, for limited financial gain, knowing it could never last?
- Why did the SFO decide to pursue a flawed prosecution of SCF and so publicly claim it was the country's biggest fraud before the trial had even commenced?
- Why did the Securities Commission accept the views of people who were clearly conflicted and then instigate the statutory management of Hubbard's investment companies — later proven to be healthy businesses?

- Why do many of the decisions makers genuinely believe the failures were not of their making and could never have been foreseen?

And there are so many other decisions that with hindsight make little sense and appear irrational.

The number of decisions made that contributed to these failures and in many cases worsened the impact of them are widespread.

Why do smart people in such positions make the decisions they do? Why do we all make decisions that even we later admit were pretty clueless?

The reason is very simple — we are all human.

So, in exploring the reasons businesses fail, we must explore what it is to be human, how we think, how our brains work and how we decide.

7 THE BRAIN OF THE BUSINESS OWNER

Some basics about our brains

To understand how and why we make the decisions we do, and why we behave the way we do, particularly in running a business, we need to understand how we take information in from the world around us, how we process that information, form judgements about it, and then finally make decisions.

Therefore, we first need to discuss a little bit about how our brains work to understand why we do what we do, how we think what we think, and how our actions contribute to business success or failure.

Only after that can we discuss the processes, systems and rules that businesses need to put in place to bring greater consistency to their decision making. It will also help us understand why the failures we discuss occurred and the role people had in these failures.

Human beings can achieve amazing things — art, poetry, engineering and technology. There are so many examples of amazing businesses that people have started, grown and developed that have changed people's lives and improved the world we live in.

Unfortunately, at times, human beings also do things that seem pretty clueless.

We've all made mistakes, we've made choices we regret. Some we have learned from, some we may still ruminate over.

Our brains are the sum of evolution, genetics, our external environment and all our life experiences. Throughout our lives, we have made choices of where to devote our mental energies, hopefully doing things we loved.

We rarely sit back and think about how we think — we just get on with it. We don't have to over-analyse the inner workings of our brains to succeed at business or life, but a level of understanding may assist in achieving the success we seek — or help us avoid failure.

What this chapter will highlight is that as humans we are up against internal forces within our biology and DNA that will significantly influence the directions we may go in our lives and business. A deeper understanding of these limitations and strengths as humans may greatly increase our chances of making the right choices — rather than being oblivious to the role all these things play in determining who we are, how we behave and what actions we take.

So, let's take a short journey through the workings of the most complex organ known to us — our brains.

The evolving brain

The evolution of the human brain has seen it triple in size over the last two million years. It is still on an evolutionary development journey. While it has evolved, and has become more complex, our brains are far from a perfect creation. They have inherent limitations and inefficiencies.

Our brains are immensely complex and there is still much we do not understand about our brains, even though there is significant expertise devoted to neuroscience and psychological studies across the planet.

As humans, our brains allow us to enjoy many pleasures and joys in life that other animals will never experience. We can create and do things other creatures cannot. We can solve puzzles, talk, sing, feel, and love, grieve, and pursue our passions and dreams. In most cases, creatures with less-developed brains than ours don't even know they exist — they are not even self-aware.

Unfortunately, having an advanced brain also adds significant complexity to our lives — we could say our brain has burdened us with complexities simple creatures do not face.

For example, we can make ourselves sick with worry and stress over things that may never happen and we can ruminate about past events that we can't change.

Our brains can take in huge amounts of information at every moment of our waking lives, beyond what we can ever use or remember.

We have a wide and complex array of emotions depending on who we are and our pasts. We were born with a personality that stays with us throughout our lives.

So, what are some of the inner workings of our brain?

As mentioned, our brain is immensely complex and offering a simple explanation is doing our brains a great disservice. However, going through a few basics is a great start and may be enough to support our conversation on how the brain will play a part in the success or failure of business.

Three brains within one

I will use a simple explanation called the ***Triune or Three-Brain Model*** to describe the physical structure of our brains. The Three-Brain Model is considered an oversimplified interpretation of the brain by many in the field of neuroscience. While technically inaccurate as an explanation for brain activity, it remains a good approximation.

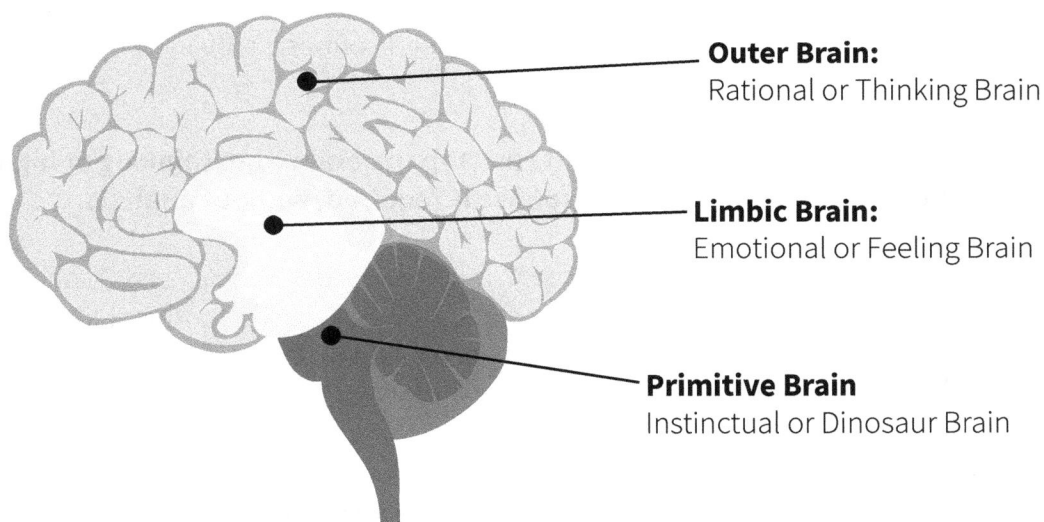

Outer Brain:
Rational or Thinking Brain

Limbic Brain:
Emotional or Feeling Brain

Primitive Brain
Instinctual or Dinosaur Brain

The primitive brain

The ***primitive*** or ***reptilian brain***, in evolutionary terms, is the oldest of the three parts of our brains. It includes the brain stem. This part of the brain controls the body's involuntary, basic and vital functions such as heart rate, breathing, body temperature, balance and sleep patterns, like REM sleep. These are the basic functions that we share with most other animals.

The primitive part of the brain also does an initial amount of filtering of the information that needs to be paid attention to. This part of the brain is called the ***reticular activating*** *system*, or *RAS*.

The RAS is a bridge between the primitive brain, where our automatic functions occur, and our outer brain, where thoughts and analysis occur. It is said to be the gateway between external information and deeper thinking.[1,2]

We are unable to take in all the information from the world around us. The RAS assists with this first level of filtering and it is automatic. Our brains have been trained so when faced with a new situation we scan the environment without even knowing we are doing it.

The limbic system

The *limbic system* includes brain parts like the amygdala, the hippocampus and the thalamus. This part of our brain plays a significant role in regulating our emotions, pain and behaviours related to fear and motivation. Our limbic system can sense danger and start a response even before other senses have had time to allow our brain to analyse it.

The amygdala, lying deep in the centre of the limbic brain, and about the size and shape of an almond, is constantly alert to the needs of basic survival including sex, and emotional reactions such as anger and fear.

The amygdala is an emotional filter. It can stop the brain from thinking at high levels when a quick or emotional response is required, without analysis.

Information stops in the emotional brain if incoming data is too emotional or if the brain already is in an overemotional state. However, such emotional filtering is double-edged. Too little emotion finds the brain dropping some information because of boredom or insignificance, but too much emotion and the brain can't send information to the higher levels of the brain and we can react without thinking — something I am sure all of us have experienced at some stage.

The hippocampus helps form long-term factual memories. Both word-based memories and event-based memories are catalogued here. The hippocampus remembers information, and the amygdala remembers emotional information. For example, the hippocampus knows who your best customer is, and your amygdala knows whether you like them or not.

The thalamus sorts processes, and directs information from the primitive brain to the outer brain where it can be processed. Conversely, it returns information from the outer brain back to the spinal cord. The thalamus is also a relay station for various kinds of memories. It sends visual memories to the visual part of the brain and auditory memories to the auditory section. Because of its role in passing information back and forth within the brain, the thalamus plays a part in many functions like attention, perception, timing and movement.

The outer brain

The **outer brain** or **cortex** is where the functions exist that set us apart from other animals.

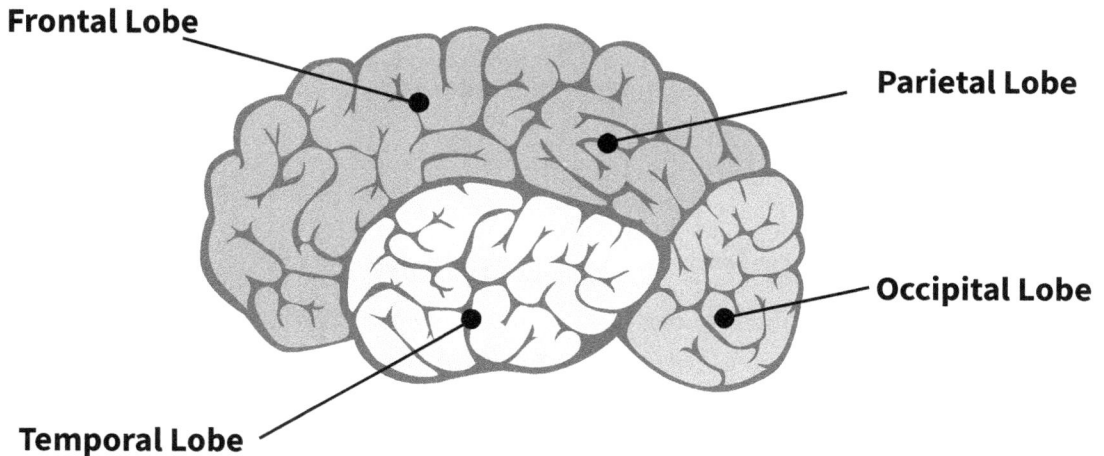

Frontal Lobe

Parietal Lobe

Occipital Lobe

Temporal Lobe

Our outer brain receives and organises incoming messages from our senses. It then manipulates that information along with other related information stored as memories and then sends out commands to our body where we respond, by saying or doing something.

Our outer brain holds our personality. It's where we process language, storytelling, managing motor skills, and involves our reasoning. Our outer brain organises responses to complex problems, plans steps to objectives, searches memory for relevant experience, adapts strategies to accommodate new data, guides behaviour with verbal skills, and houses working memory.

It also helps manage emotional impulses in socially appropriate ways for productive behaviours including empathy, altruism, and interpretation of facial expressions.

The cortex is made up of several lobes that fulfil these higher-level functions.

The temporal lobe is responsible for processing speech and sounds. The occipital lobe processes vision. The parietal lobe processes taste, temperature and touch.

The frontal lobe is the largest of the brain's structures and is where the higher cognitive functions, like thought and decision making, occur. It is also where our personality is formed.

It is the part of our brains that, in evolutionary terms, developed last. It is also the last part of an adolescence's brain to mature, and could still be developing well into our twenties.

Our frontal lobes allow us to consider future events and simulate the outcome before we actually do them — something none of our ancestors or fellow animals, without a developed frontal lobe, could achieve. These functions of decision making and future simulation, as you can imagine, are critical in the running of a business and we will discuss these in greater detail.

The brain basics — a summary

The three parts of our brain do not operate in isolation. Information passes between these parts and across the two hemispheres of the brain. In simple terms, the information from the outside world is processed something like this:

1. New information enters the primitive brain through the senses.
2. The information is received in the brain stem and passes through the reticular activating system (RAS), which is the first filter in the brain looking for danger or important information.
3. If the brain stem accepts the information, it is sent higher in the brain and enters the limbic system, or the emotional brain.
4. The thalamus begins to relay the sensory information, and the amygdala filters the information for emotional content and for emotional memories.
5. Non-emotional information enters the hippocampus, which sends the information to the prefrontal lobe (the thinking brain) to be examined for connections to prior knowledge. If the brain has prior knowledge of the new information, the brain sends it back to the hippocampus, where new and old information are related.
6. Finally, the new memory formed from combining the new information and the old information is sent back to storage areas of the brain.[3]

Keep these processes in mind as you work your way through the book and as you consider why people do the things they do, particularly in the context of running a business.

Facts and myths about our brains

Let's dispel a few of the myths about our brains and provide a few points that may be of interest.[3]

- The brain, while very complex, is not perfect. It is still evolving.
- In two million years, the human brain has nearly tripled in mass, going from about 600 grams to the current brain of about 1.5 kilograms.[4]
- The brain is not an island. While parts of our brains are dedicated to specific functions, the brain is an interconnected organism.
- We use all our brain and even when we are asleep our brain remains active. The various movies and tales about us using only 10% of our brains are a myth. While we may not fully understand exactly what our brains are doing, neuro-imaging has shown that the entire brain is doing something.
- We now know that our brains can continue to change and grow throughout our entire lives (known as **neuroplasticity**). Originally it was thought the growth of our brains stopped at adulthood, like other parts of our bodies.
- The brain is expensive in terms of energy usage. While it makes up only about 2% of the body's weight, 20% of the calories we consume are used to power the brain.
- Considering the complexity of the computations we make every second of our day, our brains are incredibly efficient. A supercomputer racks up enormous energy bills achieving similar computations, but our brains work out what to do with amazing efficiency, using about the energy of a 60-watt light bulb.
- The concept that some of us are left brain and some right brain is flawed. We all use both sides of our brains and both are required to form our personalities.
- While evolution has denied us the attributes that other animals use to survive, like fur for the cold, teeth, speed, strength or size, the growth of our brains, and becoming smarter, has allowed us to become the apex predator.

Test 1

Go through the following list. Read down each column from top left and say out loud (or quietly if in a public place) the **shade** of each word, **not** the word it spells. For example, if the word "GREY" was written in the shade black, you say black.

BLACK	GREY	PALE	**BLACK**	GREY
PALE	PALE	**BLACK**	GREY	PALE
GREY	**BLACK**	GREY	PALE	**BLACK**
PALE	GREY	**BLACK**	**BLACK**	GREY
BLACK	**BLACK**	PALE	GREY	PALE
GREY	PALE	GREY	PALE	**BLACK**
BLACK	GREY	PALE	GREY	PALE
GREY	PALE	**BLACK**	PALE	**BLACK**
PALE	**BLACK**	GREY	**BLACK**	GREY
GREY	PALE	PALE	GREY	PALE
PALE	**BLACK**	GREY	**BLACK**	**BLACK**
BLACK	GREY	**BLACK**	PALE	GREY
PALE	**BLACK**	GREY	**BLACK**	PALE
GREY	GREY	**BLACK**	PALE	**BLACK**
BLACK	PALE	PALE	GREY	GREY

Now calculate the following without writing anything down: **32 x 24**.[5]

(Note: For a colour version of this test, pop onto the website
www.whybusinessesfail.co.nz)

Test 2

Go through the following list using the same procedure as above.
Recite the shade of each word, **not** what the word it spells.

BLACK	GREY	PALE	BLACK	GREY
PALE	PALE	BLACK	GREY	PALE
GREY	BLACK	GREY	PALE	BLACK
PALE	GREY	BLACK	BLACK	GREY
BLACK	BLACK	PALE	GREY	PALE
GREY	PALE	GREY	PALE	BLACK
BLACK	GREY	PALE	GREY	PALE
GREY	PALE	BLACK	PALE	BLACK
PALE	BLACK	GREY	BLACK	GREY
GREY	PALE	PALE	GREY	PALE
PALE	BLACK	GREY	BLACK	BLACK
BLACK	GREY	BLACK	PALE	GREY
PALE	BLACK	GREY	BLACK	PALE
GREY	GREY	BLACK	PALE	BLACK
BLACK	PALE	PALE	GREY	GREY

Now calculate the following without writing anything down: **23 x 41**.

Our inner mental conflicts and mental fatigue

Our brains run on conflict between different possibilities, all of which try to out-compete the others. And there are always multiple options. Even with the simplest task of choosing, say, what flavour of ice cream to get in a dairy, results in a back-and-forth process in our brains. Cookies and cream or hokey pokey?

Tests 1 and 2 highlight this inner conflict and the fatigue battling with it can cause.

The second of the two tests was more difficult, right? Why should this simple task pose any difficulty at all, especially when the instructions are so simple?

David Eagleman in his book *The Brain — The Story of You*[6] explains why the second test is much harder than the first. It's because one network in our brain takes on the task of identifying the colour of the ink and putting a name to it. At the same time, competing networks in our brain are responsible for reading words — and these are so proficient that word reading has become a deeply ingrained, automatic process. The test where the word and the colours are aligned is, therefore, much easier than the test where you fight the word and the colour.

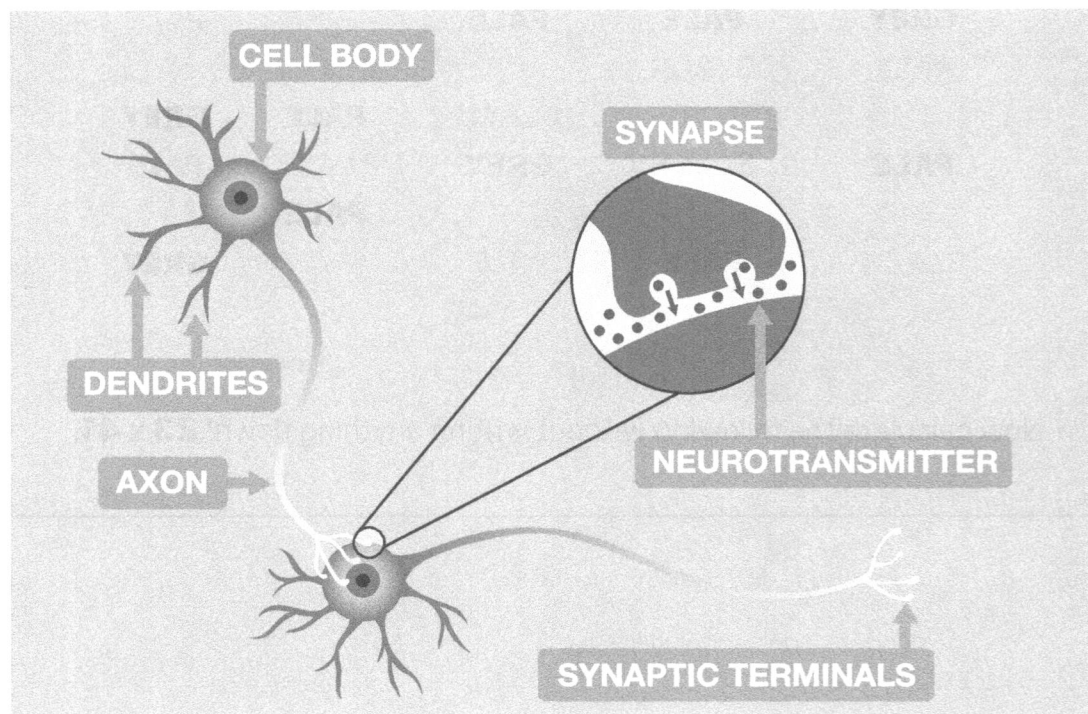

The other point this test draws out, which we discuss in other chapters, is the mental fatigue doing this uncomfortable task can create. By the time you have completed the second more difficult grid of colours, either you struggle to do the mental calculation at the end of the test or you may simply feel like telling me what I can do with my $#$&@#* test as you can't be bothered — your brain is fatigued.

Keep this in mind if you have been straining your brain doing a lot of work. The longer you go on, the more fatigued your brain will become.

Our senses

We take information from the outside world into our brains via our senses.

We assume we have only five senses. While vision, hearing, smell, touch and taste dominate our interaction with the world around us, there are lesser-known senses that are also important to our day-to-day lives.

We can sense where our hands and other body parts are relative to the environment around us, without relying on our sight to establish that. We can move, and accelerate without thinking about it or seeing where our limbs and body parts are. This sense is called *proprioception*.[7]

The balance we gain from our inner ear is another sense. We know how important this sense is if we get a serious ear infection and experience vertigo. In more serious cases, the loss of this sense can be debilitating.

We can sense when we are hungry, thirsty or fatigued. We sense pain in many forms other than through the sense of touch.

As well as the additional senses we rely on to interact with the world are the many crossovers between our senses. We all know the impact of the taste of food when our nose is blocked with a cold and we can't smell.

Practice makes permanent

Each of the billions of neurons within our brain are connected to thousands of other neurons via a junction between the neurons called the *synapse*. Each neuron has thousands of synapses. While we don't know for sure how many neurons make up our brains, there are likely to be somewhere between 80 and 100 billion. Therefore, there are trillions of connections in our brains creating a highly complex network of neuron paths.

Our brain functions by transferring electrochemical signals between neurons. These trigger a series of actions and reactions.

The number of neurons is the same in children as it is in adults. We are born with all the neurons we will ever have.[8]

At birth, our neurons are more sparse and unconnected, and in the first two years of life they begin connecting very rapidly as they take in new information. Every second, as many as two million new connections are formed in an infant's brain. By age two, a child has over one hundred trillion synapses, double the number in an adult.

They then reach a peak and have far more connections than are needed. At this point, the process of creating new connections is replaced by *neural pruning* — unused neuron paths are lost. As we mature, about half of our neural connections will be lost. In simple terms, if we don't use certain neural paths in our brain, we will lose them.[9]

Every time we learn a new fact or skill, we change our brains in small ways, all the time. This process is called *neuroplasticity*.

These chemical reactions or firing of these neurons in our brain are short-lived. To embed these new skills, we need to create structural changes in our brain — this takes much longer. The example of this is doing piano lessons one day and coming back the next day remembering little or nothing about what was learned. To learn the piano and create permanent change, you must repeat the process over and over . . . and over.[10]

As we learn and evolve, change and grow, pathways are forged in our brains where the neurons are connected.

Complex skills are laid down in the brain after countless hours of deliberate training because our brain is a slow learner.[11, 12] Over time, such practice sees these skills become subconscious — we may no longer realise we have such skills, as we take them for granted.

We have effectively built dedicated circuitry in our brains. When a skill is practised enough, it no longer requires conscious thought, being easy and very efficient. This makes more cognitive resources available to us for other types of thinking.

If we stop practising skills, the neuron pathways begin to degrade and this occurs rather quickly. The neurons are eliminated and we lose these skills. It is just like an unused path in a forest. The paths that are not used are disconnected by the forest and disappear. Those things we decided to leave behind and no longer do, like piano practice, French lessons and the things we gave up as we grew and changed, disappear from our brains over time.

We become who we are, not just because of what grows in our brain, but also because of what is removed.[13]

Our brains are creatures of habit. If you do the same thing over and over, the networks of neurons that are involved in that task get strengthened and fire more efficiently. That means that the next time you do that thing, your brain's activity will be slightly more fine-tuned. But it's also more difficult to then take a different path.[14] We can see how this will apply to the skills we had (or didn't have) coming into our life in business and the skills we attain the longer we are in business. The more we use the skills that will help the business be a success, the more they will be embedded in our brains.

This may not be any surprise but at least now I hope we share a greater understanding that the skills we don't work on will disappear and why it takes great effort to attain new skills. We are not slow or stupid — we are human.

Evolution of our brain (and of the modern business)

> 66 *Of all the traits that natural selection has managed to evolve for us, our brains are surely the most valuable.* 99
> — Robin Dunbar, *How Many Friends Does One Person Need?*

As I mentioned in the list of brain myths, the brain has gone through significant evolutionary changes over the life of our ancestors up until the present. Our brains are still evolving and will continue to do so.

In terms of the evolution of the human brain, it is only in the last moment in the evolutionary timeline that the society we now live and run our businesses in came into existence.

> 66 *For more than 2 million years, human neural networks kept growing and growing, but apart from some flint knives and pointed sticks, humans have precious little to show for it.* 99
> — Yuval Harari, *Sapiens*[15]

Therefore, it is only in the last 200 years or so that we have thrust ourselves into a business world that had been essentially foreign to us for the previous 2.5 million years. We could argue that our brains were never given the evolutionary time to cope with the modern business world we now live in.

I guess it's an enthralling thought as to what our mental abilities will be like thousands of years from now if our brains continue to evolve — unfortunately, as intriguing as that thought might be, it is one others will experience.

For now, we must simply accept the limitations evolution has left us with and do the best we can.

There are aspects of the way our brains are wired that are similar in every human being and they can be linked back to our ancestors' battles to survive and carry on the species. Such aspects affect the way we live and operate businesses.

One need evolutionary psychologists believe all human beings have in common is the need to be part of a social group, and not be isolated. Those of our ancestors who were isolated from the protection of a larger group usually succumbed to the environment, and died. Helpless babies needed the undivided attention of their mothers, who could no longer hunt and gather food so others had to do this for them. Raising a human required a tribe of people supporting each other. Today, one of the worst tortures a person can be exposed to is complete isolation from others.[16]

We became smarter and our brains developed more because of our social interactions and the cooperation that came with those interactions. We started working together for a common good and this gave us an evolutionary advantage.

We should not underestimate the contribution our relationships with those around us — our work groups, family groups and the groups we engage with — have on the success of our lives and our businesses. Social interaction is a fundamental part of being human and will contribute to our success or failure in business.

Unfortunately, humans' association with groups has also drawn out one of our greatest failings — when we associate with one group, it can often influence our views of those that are not part of our group. At its worse, over the centuries, we have seen human beings act horrendously toward others simply because they put a label on them as they belonged to a group they did not identify with.

Ethnic cleansing in the Balkans, the Holocaust, the genocide of Tutsis by the Hutu majority in Rwanda are examples of this. One day these peoples were neighbours, the next they were enemies and were brutally killed.

In our work lives we will be impacted by biases based on the groups we associate with and those we don't associate with. We will discuss biases a little later.

Keep in mind the evolutionary tendencies wired within us that we must consider as we go about running our businesses.

Nature versus nurture?

The nature versus nurture debate has gone on for decades. What impacts us most? Is it the genes we are born with (nature) or the environment we were brought up in (nurture)?

The commonly held view now is that both play a part. The evidence to support this view has come mainly from the many extensive studies into identical twins. Twins who have both grown up in the same environments and those who grew up completely distant from each other.[17]

Test 3

Without doing any written calculations, write down your answer to the following:

If a bat and a ball cost $1.10 together, and the bat costs $1.00 more than the ball, how much does the ball cost?

Genetics — what we might attribute to our parents

We are also impacted by *genetics* — the parts of us that were passed down from our parents.

Our parents pass on traits or genetic characteristics to each of us. The term **heritable** applies to traits that are similar in parents and their offspring. We inherit numerous attributes from our parents. The amount a trait can be attributed to a genetic link rather than, say, an external environmental impact, is called **heritability** — the higher the heritability, the greater the trait can be attributed to our parents.

Physical aspects, like our height, have high heritability. Some personality traits and behaviours are passed on genetically. For example, extraversion, openness, agreeableness, and conscientiousness have a high level of heritability.[18]

The environment we grew up in

We are also affected by the unique experiences we all have throughout our lives, the circumstances we were confronted with, and the **environment**. In many cases, the environment we have been exposed to, especially in our younger years, was something we had almost no ability to influence. It is solely by chance we were born to the parents we were, in the country we were born in, and the race we were born as. We had no say in how we were brought up as infants.

As we mentioned already, our brains are remarkably unfinished at birth and in our infancy. This is why we are so helpless at birth. Many animals can function almost immediately after they are born. Their brains are more hardwired with in-built instincts to survive from the moment they are thrust into their environment. A human brain will be shaped by the world around them and their life experiences, and in their early years this will be heavily impacted by our parents.[19]

Therefore, the environment, the care and stimulation offered to our kids as they grow is so important to their development.

Does this all mean that between evolutionary effects, genetics and the luck of who we were born to, we have a predetermined destiny? Clearly, we know that is not the case. There is still so much we can influence in our lives.

Our automatic brain versus our reflective brain

Many neuroscientists and experts have converged on a simple concept of how our brain functions. It describes two distinct kinds of thinking. One that is intuitive or automatic and one that is more analytical or reflective.

The concept was believed to be first considered by William James in his 1890 book *The Principles of Psychology*. It has been advanced and relabelled in many ways ever since.

Nobel laureate Daniel Kahneman called these **System 1 and System 2**, which he described as producing fast and slow thinking, respectively.[20]

Intuition is very fast and takes little mental energy. Analysis is slower and requires more mental energy.

Our intuition allows rapid responses to be made when interpreting information. However, such responses lack any analysis and can very often be incorrect. These are what we often call gut decisions, which we will discuss a little later when talking about decision making in more detail.

At times, we need to pause and analyse the information a little more using our analytical mental processes.

Our intuitive thinking is more influential than we often realise. Intuition is very often what determines our choices and judgements.

We often believe it to be our analytical brain making those choices but we have probably put far less mental processing to it than we realise. Instead it is intuition at play because intuition takes less effort and energy.[21]

Our brains are lazy. When we are faced with problems, our first response is often to respond with what comes easiest to us. These immediate responses help us get through the day. Our intuition comes from the emotional part of our brain. We duck when a bird flies at our windscreen, even though it won't hit us. We feel a little uneasy when the plane we are on shudders in turbulence, even though planes are extremely safe and this is normal.

Analytical or logical processing, usually associated with our outer brain functions, takes much greater effort, more time and more energy. As such, it is also slower. We will discuss in more detail the pros and cons of intuitive and analytical decisions when we discuss business decision making.

In their book *Nudge*, Richard Thaler and Cass Sunstein separated these two different kinds of mental processing as per Table 1.[22]

Automatic (Intuitive)	Reflective (Analytical)
Uncontrolled	Controlled
Effortless	Effortful
Fast	Slow
Unconscious	Self-aware
Skilled	Rule following

Table 1. Our Automatic (Fast) and Reflective (Slow) Brains

With every decision we make, there is a battle in our brains between intuition and logic, and the intuitive part of your mind is a lot more powerful.

Most of us like to think that we can make rational decisions. Very often our decisions are immediate, intuitive and instinctive.

Now for the bat and ball question in Test 3. It has been around a long time and even if we have done it before (and I have done it many times), it's still worth doing it again.

Our intuitive brain jumps to the answer 10 cents. However, it's likely something is telling us that this may not be correct, which is our analytical brain kicking in. If we take enough time we will realise it's not correct, and we may need to grab a pen and paper. Whether we get it right or not will take a little longer. For some, it could take significantly longer.

By the way, the bat is $1.05 and the ball is 5 cents.

Attention — what's important and what is not

We are bombarded with an infinite amount of information every moment of our conscious lives. This has been the case throughout the evolution of us as a species. Our earliest ancestors had to pay attention to those things that posed significant threat to their survival.

In our modern lives, and with every new generation, we are faced with an increasing amount of information to process. The information we face is picked up by our senses, sight, hearing, touch, taste and smell. Our brains simply don't have the capacity to process all the information we are confronted with. Technology has only added to this information and the world is now quite literally at our fingertips. If we were not able to filter this information, we would probably go crazy from the sensory overload.

Likewise, if we are trying to get our business messages out into the world, it has become much easier. However, ensuring that the people we want to appeal to do actually see our message and then pay attention to it is increasingly difficult, as there is an infinite amount of competing information.

When each of us is subjected to the same external information, we are likely to filter it differently. What one pays attention to, another will ignore. Likewise, because our brains are wired differently, once information enters our brains we will process it in dramatically different ways.

We discussed the RAS that forms part of our primitive brain. Our brains have been trained to filter the information it is taking in and the RAS plays a critical role in filtering outside information before passing it through to our outer brain. For example, anything that poses a danger to us will pass through without filtering.

Our brains are wired to respond to **danger**, often even before we are consciously aware that it exists. The fight or flight response is an example of the filtering that occurs in the face of danger and the almost immediate response that follows.

We also filter *important information*. Mothers are attuned to the sounds of their baby crying. The cocktail party effect highlights the importance we place on hearing our name. This was first researched and defined by Colin Cherry in 1953. The effect describes the situation where a person at a noisy cocktail party, who is listening intently to someone in front of them, hears their name mentioned across the room.

Test 4

Look at the following images for 30 seconds. Cover them over, then try to remember as many as you can.

Write them down if you wish. When you can't remember any more, uncover the images and check how you went.

This is because our name is very important to us and when we hear it mentioned, we can't help but pay attention to the person using it.

Even though this filtering is automatic, we can train our brains to let through important information. The first thing to consider is what we believe is important to us and to start focusing on it.

Business owners can believe an opportunity they took up just presented itself and was luck. In some cases, this may have been the case. However, often the business owner had already thought quite a lot about such opportunities. They had discussed them, thought about them, and wrote them down. Some time may have passed, but when something presents itself resembling the opportunity, their brain deems it to be important and does not filter it.

For example, you have decided you want to purchase a new type of vehicle. Once you have decided this, and researched it, you start seeing the vehicle more often — in magazines, on the road, and in newspapers. It is not as though it has started to become more common. It is just that you have trained your brain to look out for it.

If the opportunity we are looking for is a specific type of new employee, a new location for the business, a merger or acquisition, a new partner or anything that is critical to the success of the business, we are far more likely to come across it when it presents itself. If we had not done this, it is likely our brain would have completely ignored it.

The shortcomings of our memory

In business and in day-to-day life, our memory plays a part in everything we do. We all know that our memories do not always serve us well — memory is imperfect. In some situations, this might create minor frustrations. However, if in our business lives the information was critical to the business, failing to pay attention to that information or being unable to recall it could cause us more significant problems.

The steps in forming memories and why we forget

When we pay attention to certain things our senses take in the information and our brain processes that information. The hope is that if we have judged it to be important, we will store it away as a memory for later use.

The first step in creating a memory is ***encoding*** the information. For the information that has come to our attention to be taken in by our senses and then processed by our brains, it must first be converted or encoded into the electrical impulses that our neurons can deal with.

The next step is **storing** that information in our brains.

The third step is **retrieval** of that memory.

All three steps are imperfect. The failure to remember something may be because of a failure at any part of these steps.

The deadly sins of memory

Daniel L. Schacter described the imperfections in our memory in his book *The Seven Sins of Memory*.[23]

If our attention is distracted at the time we are receiving the information, it may not be encoded and never actually end up stored in our brains. Schacter called this **absent-minded memory failure**. Often, failure to remember things may be the result of us not acquiring the information in the first place.

We have all experienced the situation where we are introduced to someone who offers their name — a customer or a person at a networking session. If we are not paying full attention and we don't process the name and then replay it in our mind, it's likely we will forget it almost immediately.

If something is important, and we want to commit it to memory, we must pay attention and then repeat the information to ourselves, increasing the chance it will be retained.

We may have successfully stored a memory but, over time, if we are not recalling it regularly, it weakens. Schacter called this **transience**.

When we recall a memory, it is not like a photo snapshot that is produced in the original form we first stored it, unchanged and accurate. Our memories are not an accurate video recording of a moment in our lives. Every time we recall a memory we reconstruct it again, building it up from scratch. So over time the memory may be altered slightly, even though we do not realise this has occurred. Thinking and talking about past events is one of the best ways to retain them later.[24]

The enemy of our memory is less the passing of time and memories fading but the changes in old memories caused by the introduction of new memories.

We might be supremely confident about the details of a past event, only to find that the facts are very different to what we recall. This imperfection in memory is rather pervasive. Our memories are fading without our realising it is happening.

Examples of this are when people are asked to recall where they were, what they were doing and the specifics of high-profile world events. This could include the 9/11 Twin Towers attack or the death of Diana, Princess of Wales. People asked about the details many months after the event show far less accuracy than they did when asked about it immediately after it occurred. And in many cases these people remain quite adamant that their latter recollection is correct.

Consider this in business when we find ourselves debating with someone over our respective views of a past event. We may well have accurate information but the person in front of us remains adamant they are correct, when our data indicates they are not. They may not be setting out to be difficult or deceitful — they may simply be suffering from the transient nature of their memories. So we need to be patient, as there is every chance the situation will be reversed and we will have the incorrect memory.

An unfortunate counter to transience and the loss of memory are those painful or unhelpful memories or thoughts that we simply cannot forget. In this situation, we continue to recall them, chew over them, and in doing so, keep them fresh and raw. This type of rumination can be very damaging and lead to mental health issues like depression (which I can relate to). Overcoming these may require professional support to develop techniques to accept them rather than fighting them — especially as trying to ignore a thought is a fruitless exercise. It's a bit like being told "Don't think about an elephant" — but I bet you did.[25]

The tip-of-the-tongue phenomenon is a limitation in our ability to retrieve a memory — it is there somewhere, if only we could just extract it. Schacter calls this **blocking**. In this case, we have stored the memory, but we simply can't find it when we need it.

This blocking can sometimes occur due to stress. When the stress goes, the memory might appear. We often remember things much better when they are triggered by something from the time we stored the memory. A piece of music, a smell, or distinctive voice.

False memories

Another failing of our memory is the brain's ability to create false memories. Rather than the inability to save and then accurately recall memories, we can unknowingly combine different but similar events, insert false details or be influenced by other pieces of information that add to what we believe is a memory. We may recall these memories with the genuine belief they are our own, are accurate and represent real events, even though they are completely inaccurate, and even wrong.

Elizabeth Loftus is considered one of the leading researchers and experts in false memory. She changed the way people used eyewitness testimony in legal trials. She regularly argued that witnesses, while genuinely believing their recollections to be correct, were, in fact, very wrong.

Loftus had her own experience of false memories. Her mother drowned in her pool when Loftus was only 14 years old. She had recalled very little about it. Thirty years later at a family function an uncle told her she was the one who had found her mother's body. This triggered a flood of memories of the event, which to Loftus became clear and vivid. She remembered finding her mother. However, some days later the same uncle rang to tell her that he was deeply sorry but he had got the story wrong. It was not Loftus who found her mother but Loftus's aunt. Had the uncle not rung, Loftus would have held on to this false memory from then on.

Loftus has been involved in dozens of legal cases where people were wrongly imprisoned based on false witness testimony from people who genuinely believed their memories to be correct, when DNA evidence later found they were wrong.

Forgetting is to be human

All these limitations in our ability to remember will impact us in our day-to-day lives and in our business. In some cases, the impacts could be trivial, if not a little embarrassing (such as forgetting a name). They could be more damaging.

As with all the limitations around our brains, the challenges with your memory are about accepting the limitations and putting processes in place to manage those limitations.

If we want to ensure we remember critical information, repeat it regularly. Write things down when they are fresh, as they will fade, become inaccurate or even evolve into falsehoods. Be humble enough to accept that someone arguing about a past event may be correct even though we are adamant it is he or she who has it wrong.

Everyone I spoke to about business failures, many who were there at the same time and in the thick of the events, remembered what happened through their own memories. While there were many consistencies, there were often very different recollections of the same events.

It was also clear that memories of past events that should have set off alarm bells in the lead-up to the failures were ignored, forgotten, recollected differently or possibly selectively pushed to the side. I don't feel anyone recollected events and lied about them. Everyone simply remembered events differently. For example, different people within Solid Energy recollect events surrounding the volatility in coal prices in 2008 and subsequent discussions and actions taken as a result of these warning signs. Even those who were in the courtroom for the legal action against the SCF management and board recollected the approach of the judge differently.

You are human — be humble, be kind to yourself

Whether we like it or not, as humans, we have limitations — no surprises there, you might say. Unfortunately, far too often we forget this reality and consider that we should be all things to all people and bulletproof.

We could feel justified in arguing that biology is stacked against us. We are wired by evolution, genetics and the environment we were brought up in. We are who we are and have the skills we have (and don't have) based on everything we have done leading to this point in our lives.

We are effectively wired in ways that we can't control. We do things consciously and subconsciously.

These brutal realities about how we are made up as humans will play a significant part in whether we succeed or fail in business and is the reason that no amount of discussion on the topic will stop further failures occurring — humans will be humans.

However, as we are all aware, there is so much in our lives that we can control, and it is these attributes that we must focus on to achieve the success we seek in our business lives.

8 THE SIMPLE MENTAL SHORTCUTS WE USE TO SURVIVE EACH DAY

In the previous chapter, we explored the basics of how our brains are put together, wired, and the way our brains developed from our ancestors, our parents, our environment, and from the choices we have made throughout our lives.

Our brains are very complex but they are also imperfect. Our brain must filter the infinite amount of information it is confronted with every day, process that information, and deliver the decisions and actions necessary for us to get through each day.

If we stopped to contemplate all this, it is likely we would go a little crazy. We simply get on with things without putting too much focus on how we went about it. To allow us to get on with each day, our brains are continually taking subconscious shortcuts.

Heuristics and biases

The shortcuts our minds take are often called **heuristics**. A heuristic is a mental shortcut that allows us to solve problems and make judgements quickly and efficiently. We could also call them **rules of thumb**.

Because our brains were developed to help us survive, because we must filter information, because we are all wired differently, and because of these shortcuts, our brains will very often get things wrong, and at times we may not even realise we are wrong.

These shortcuts lead to **biases**. Some may be innocent, others more sinister and dangerous.

Our irrational minds are flooded with cultural biases rooted in our tradition, upbringing, and a whole lot of other subconscious factors that assert a powerful but hidden influence over the choices we make.[2]

The importance of understanding our biases is not only to understand ourselves but to understand how those around us may act in certain situations.

The Linda problem

Let's explore the Linda problem from Test 5, which was developed by Kahneman and Tversky.

Many people will choose the second option, that Linda is both a bank teller and a feminist, because of the strong reference to women's rights in the description. But how could the second option be more likely than the first when the first includes all the Lindas that are both feminists and non-feminists?

Linda fits the idea of a "feminist bank teller" better than she fits the stereotype of a bank teller. The stereotypical bank teller is not a feminist activist, and adding that detail to the description makes for a more coherent story. The probability that Linda is a feminist bank teller must be lower than the probability of her being a bank teller. When we specify a possible event in greater detail, we only lower its probability.

This is one simple example of what a very rational answer might be relative to the more likely but less rational answer.

It's intuition

We discussed the way our brain works in the previous chapter. This included our automatic, or intuitive, brain versus our analytical brain (System 1 versus System 2). We more often rely on our intuition, and our "gut" in making decisions — we simply don't have the time, or energy, to analyse everything, every time.

The danger with these shortcuts is they lead to snap judgements that may be incorrect. The shortcuts we take, which lead to the biases we have, are usually our intuitive processes in action.

We must use and, in most cases, rely on our intuition. Just take caution that these mental shortcuts also come with associated risks.

Our blind spots

We have blind spots to the mental shortcuts we take and the biases we form. Blind spots are our tendency to recognise the biases in other people, but not in ourselves.

Unfortunately, we can be guilty of believing that our own view on things is accurate, even enlightened, and therefore the correct view. We may sit in judgement of other people's views, being confident that such views are filtered through their biases and therefore we believe they are incorrect.

Consider this when we get into a debate over politics, religion or sport or in any debate where we stick steadfastly to a viewpoint — we may both be right, and wrong.

Examples of the many biases we suffer

The following are very common biases that could impact any of us at any time and may impact our business. We should be aware that we are all, to different extents, likely to be impacted by these biases. They may seem self-evident when we are reading them, but we may not be aware we are impacted by them when we go about our daily lives.

Attribution error — internal and external

We discussed attribution error in a previous chapter. When things don't go to plan, there are various ways we attribute the reasons for the less-than-adequate outcome.

When we observe others who have got things very wrong (such as the people in the failures we will discuss soon), we usually place the blame squarely with the people at the centre of the problem. This is what is called **internal attribution** — we attribute the problem to the person's internal personality and decision making.

It is too easy for people observing the actions of others to focus on the person more than on the situation they found themselves in, the details of which we may not know. We also assume that these people had greater control over the situation than they did.

We often feel the need to explain world events as though people had far greater control over them than was the case. When bad things happen to people, we tend to assume it's the fault of someone when it may have been out of everyone's control.

At times, we can show little empathy or understanding for the person at the centre of these events. We place almost no emphasis on the other factors that may have contributed to that person's situation.

We don't have to go too far to find examples of this. I am sure we are all guilty of attributing blame for events in public life to politicians or blaming a sporting hero for a result that we were unhappy with.

On the flip side is when things go wrong for us and we are at the centre of the problem. We are tempted to attribute fault to external factors and not our own actions. This is **external attribution**.

After reading through the liquidations of over 1000 businesses, I found very few examples where the owner stated that the reason for the failure was of their own making.

In the case of larger failures, we are unlikely to see leaders of these businesses stumping up and taking accountability for the failures. In the end, these leaders are human and it is possible we would do the same if we were in the same position.

Attribution errors can also occur when assessing things that have gone well.

When we see someone else do well, we may attribute this success to luck, being in the right place at the right time, rather than attributing the success to the person's skills or efforts. However, when we do well, we may attribute that success to our own efforts rather than luck.

Test 6

Look at each face below. Beneath the photo, write one of two words — GOOD or BAD. Do not skip any faces. Apply only these words. By the way, consider that some of these people did do some bad things.

1.

2.

3.

4.

5.

6.

7.

8.

1. Paul Hibbs: A Kiwi businessman under investigation for fraud. (Refer www.stuff.co.nz. Photo by Annette Turnbull.) **2.** Mary Kay Letourneau: A former schoolteacher who pleaded guilty to two counts of second-degree rape of her 12-year-old student. (Photo from http://people.com. Photo by Heidi Guttman/ABC/Getty.) **3.** Maori man: This was used on the Maori media studies website to highlight how Maori are misrepresented in the media. The person's details were not provided. (Refer https://mediastudiesmaoriinthemedia.tumblr.com.) **4.** Chester Turner: A serial killer, convicted of killing 15 people. (Refer Wikipedia.) **5.** David Hobbs: A New Zealander who ran an international Ponzi scheme that fleeced investors of millions. (Refer www.stuff.co.nz, 2013. Photo by Marion van Dijk/Fairfax NZ.) **6.** Salim Joubran: An Arab-born Supreme Court judge at the Supreme Court of Israel. (Refer www.timesofisrael. com, 2014. Photo by Isaac Harari/FLASH90.) **7.** Charles Bolden: Former Marine Corp General and former astronaut and head of NASA. He's upset in this photo because a planned space programme did not go ahead. (Refer www.nbcnews.com, 2010. Photo by Luis Alvarez of AP.) **8.** Brian Stann: A former US Marine, TV commentator and CEO of Hire Heroes USA, a not-for-profit organisation that helps US military veterans. (Refer www.fight-madness.com.)

Representativeness and stereotyping

We would like to consider ourselves to be open-minded people and when we meet new people, or observe those around us, we are not making any pre-judgements about them before we gain greater insight into the person.

Unfortunately, that is not how we are wired. Throughout our evolutionary history, we have had to quickly form views of people, especially strangers, to assess if they may be friend or foe. In doing this we will start to form views about the person without any details about them.[3]

Also, if we are introduced to someone and some pleasantries follow, such as where they are from, the job they have — a doctor, pilot, student, nurse, sportsperson, labourer — our brains will be categorising these people. We form views about them based on a representation we have of them, stored away within our minds — hence the term *representativeness*. We also commonly refer to this as *stereotyping*.

This can lead to some of the more sinister impacts in our society, such as racism, ageism and sexism — we form false impressions of people based on their race, their age and their gender without knowing anything else about them.

This can have major impacts on our business. For example, we may have a view on what the image of a successful business person represents in our minds — large business, lots of staff, expensive possessions and so on. If we are not able to become this in our own business, we may start to see ourselves as failing and pursue goals for the wrong reasons.

When a new customer or potential employee walks through our doors, we may pre-judge them — and get it very wrong.

We would all love to believe we don't suffer from this bias but we do.

The theme that will come out throughout the discussion on our mental limitations is to admit we are vulnerable and then to look at how we might prevent the harmful impacts of theses shortcuts — to just become a little more aware they exist.

As for the faces in our test. How did you decide good from bad? What method did you use to decide good and bad? Did you force yourself to counter any stereotyping and go against your first thoughts? Did you feel I was trying to trick you in some way so you tried to see through my ploy?

Loss aversion and the endowment effect

Test 7

I give you $1,000 on the condition that you must now choose one of these two options:

a. Toss a coin and get a 50% chance to win a further $1,000 or
b. Get a further $500 for sure.

Test 8

I give you $2,000 on the condition that you must now choose one of these two options:

a. Toss a coin and get a 50% chance to lose $1,000 or
b. Lose $500 for sure.[4]

In business, we face risks that might provide the opportunity for us to gain something or to lose something, and we must decide whether to act on these. Unfortunately, when we compare or weigh options, losses loom much larger in our thinking than gains do. We tend to place far more importance and focus on avoiding losses than we do on achieving the equivalent gains.[5]

It is thought that the pain of losing is psychologically far more powerful than the pleasure of gaining the same thing, and since people are more willing to take risks to avoid a loss, loss aversion can explain differences in risk-seeking versus risk aversion.

It may even go back to our evolutionary ancestors — losing a day's food would be considered to have a greater impact than gaining one extra day's food. We are likely to fight harder to keep that day's supply than the fight to gain an extra day's food.

When we buy something, we are more inclined to hang on to it and put more value on it than before we owned it. If you queued for a ticket to a sporting event and paid a price for it that you thought was fair, how much would you turn around and sell it for after you have got it? It's likely it will be significantly higher than when you lined up to pay for it in the first place. We possess the ticket and now put greater value on it.

People place a higher value on a good that they own than on an identical good that they do not own.

This reflects a type of loss aversion. It is called the **endowment effect**. We expect to receive more to give up a possession than what we were initially willing to pay to acquire it in the first place.

Dan Ariely, in his book Predictably Irrational, puts forward the following view of why we exhibit this tendency:

> 66 *Why? Because of three irrational quirks in our human nature. The first quirk is that we fall in love with what we already have … The second quirk is that we focus on what we may lose, rather than what we may gain … The third quirk is that we assume other people will see the transaction from the same perspective as we do.* 99[6]

Let's now discuss Test 7 and Test 8. Again, it was Kahneman and Tversky who used these extensively to establish our aversion to losses. In both cases, you have a choice between the same two options. You can take the certain outcome of ending with $1,500 or take the gamble and end up with either $1,000 if you lose or $2,000 if you win.

Our bias of avoiding losses tends to push us toward the certain outcome in the first Test (option **b.**) but the gamble in the second Test (options **a.**) The certain outcome in the second Test is a Guaranteed loss — which we usually avoid

As with all tests, you may not agree with this — that's fine, but it is an interesting debate all the same.

Test 9

Rate your driving skills on one of the following five levels:

a. Excellent
b. Above average
c. Average
d. Below average
e. Poor.

Test 10

Rate yourself as a friend:

a. Excellent friend
b. Above-average friend
c. Average friend
d. Below-average friend
e. Poor friend.

Optimism bias

We can be afflicted with comparative optimism — the belief that we are less likely to experience negative events and more likely to experience positive events than other people.[7]

We are biased toward more optimistic outcomes for ourselves than others. The *'it will never happen to me'* mentality is one way to describe this thinking, when statistics indicate a quiet different outcome is possible.

When asked how good a driver we are (especially men), most of us believe we are above average — when we can't all be above average. If asked what the chances are

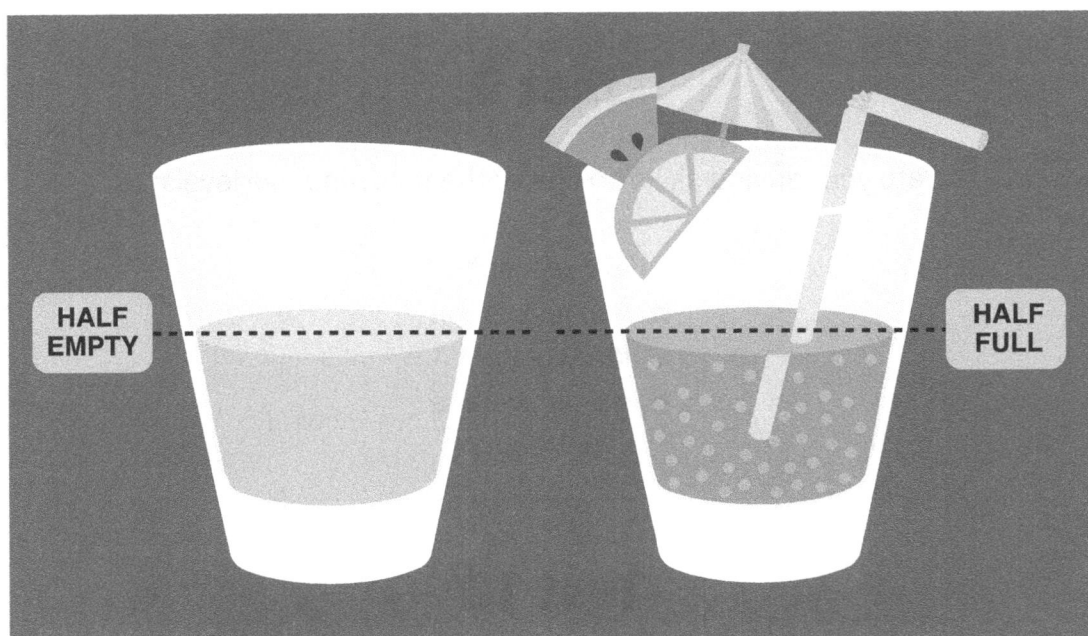

HALF EMPTY   HALF FULL

that we will suffer from cancer, die in a car crash, get hit by lightning, or any number of unpleasant events, we are most likely to underestimate the chances of being impacted by these events.

If you were to ask a couple on their eve of their wedding if their marriage will last, I doubt many will say no. While Statistics New Zealand indicates divorce rates are on the decline, there are still between 8000 and 10,000 divorces happening every year, so divorce is a very possible option.[8]

The leaders of Solid Energy and South Canterbury Finance could both be accused of having an optimism bias. Solid Energy saw future coal prices staying strong indefinitely, and South Canterbury felt the property market would remain strong right up to the very end.

Sometimes this optimism bias might work for us, especially in the decisions to get into small business — a little naive optimism is probably essential.

In entering a new business venture, optimism is important, otherwise it is likely very few businesses would ever come to life. Those outside the business venture are likely to have little optimism of its success, or at least less optimism than the business does.

I have asked many business owners years after starting their ventures whether they would have started had they known what they know now. Many say that it's likely they would have run a mile if they realised how tough it was and the extreme highs and lows that come with it. However, the clear majority are still so glad they did it and would not have it any other way.

Where optimism bias can be dangerous is where we ignore the warning signs about risks that could befall us and we ignore some clear facts or realities that pose sufficient risk for us to stand up and take notice.

Daniel Kahneman described how optimism bias can afflict executives (and yes, I can relate personally to this one):

> ❝ *When forecasting the outcomes of risky projects, executives too easily fall victim to the planning fallacy. In its grip, they make decisions based on delusional optimism rather than on a rational weighting of gains, losses, and probabilities. They overestimate benefits and underestimate costs.* ❞ [9]

Hindsight bias

We are all aware of the saying that hindsight is always 20/20 — basically we can assess events after they happened with complete clarity but not so before they occurred. Unfortunately, this is a common bias that we get trapped by, especially in business.

We are prone to blame decision makers for decisions that worked out badly and to give them too little credit for successful moves that appear obvious only after the fact. When the outcomes are bad, we often blame those who made the decision for not seeing what now seems so very obvious — forgetting that it was far from obvious before the decision was made.

We can also be guilty of chastising ourselves over our decisions after the consequence of those decisions are known, with hindsight. We need to be cautious of this as we can't go back on our decisions. We must make decisions and just deal with the outcomes as best we can.

It can be a fatal flaw that we assume a past success from a decision we made was due entirely to ourselves after the outcome is now well understood. Prior to the decision being made it was anything but certain and a range of factors had to fall into place for the outcome to have come to fruition. Those factors may not have gone as planned and the outcome may well have been different. Don't discount the role luck may have played in the outcome, either good or bad.

We will discuss the role risk, uncertainty and luck play in business in later chapters — and it does play a part.

This was a bias I had to be very careful of when examining the failures of the organisations in this book. It is very easy for someone like me to sit in judgement of the decision makers who led these failed businesses. What I have attempted to do is consider whether at the time the decisions were made, was it reasonable to have seen failure as a possibility and those warning signs were missed or ignored — I'll let you decide for yourself after reading through the failures detailed in this book

Anchoring

Test 11

How many countries are there in Africa? (Hint: Decide if it's more or fewer than 65, and pick a number.)

This was another of the biases identified and researched by Daniel Kahneman and his close colleague Amos Tversky. In their 1974 paper, and through more research thereafter, they described how in many situations people make estimates by starting from an initial value that is adjusted to get the final answer. The initial value, however it comes to us, anchors us and greatly influences the final answer we settle on.

If you knew the answer in Test 11 about Africa, or you had a very strong idea what it was, the hint should have had little impact on you. However, if you had no idea, there is every chance simply presenting you with the hint influenced your choice. There are many similar tests researchers have done that reinforce this bias.

By the way, there are 54 countries in Africa — although you might want to check yourself in case this is not another anchor![10]

We can be greatly influenced by information that we first receive when making decisions, if we feel that information might be valid. The anchor and our intuition can combine to see us accept this information and then we decide based on that information without doing the appropriate analysis.

Let's consider a real business example.

You are looking to buy a small business and you have not done much research into the pricing of the specific businesses you are seeking. A buyer, through a broker, presents you with a business that looks very appealing. They put a price to you of $100,000 for the business. Without your realising it, you are now influenced by the original figure of $100,000 presented to you — it becomes an anchor. You may believe yourself to be a tough negotiator and counter with $70,000 and feel quite happy when the deal settles midway at $85,000. This is cold comfort if you later find, after buying the business, that had you ignored their original offer and done your homework, you would have realised it was worth only about $50,000.

This is a very important bias to consider when going into a negotiation.

If you go in unprepared and have not done your homework, be very careful if the other party puts an offer to you. If it does not scare you away from the negotiation altogether, you may well be subconsciously draw in. All subsequent discussions about the offer will move around the original anchor and that may ultimately be very bad for you.

Availability heuristic

This was another bias originally put forward by Tversky and Kahneman, in 1973.[11]

If we are asked to determine how likely it is for an event to occur, we will dig into our memories and our response will be influenced by the most easily retrieved information rather than what the correct information might be. The easier events spring to mind, or the more mentally available they are to us, the more likely that will be our answer.

After we hear about a series of earthquakes on the news, it reminds us to relook at whether we have fixed objects in our homes to prevent them falling. A friend suffers a heart attack scare so we run off and get that long-overdue check-up. We hear about a spate of shark attacks in Australia and feel more vulnerable when we jump in the sea on our Christmas break. In each case, the risk was no different before or after the information was made available to us — it is simply now more available.

The opposite applies as that same information fades and becomes less available.

For example, as the years pass, our focus on the impacts of events like the Global Financial Crisis and the collapse in the international housing market become less of a worry. Lending becomes easier again. Pressure comes on to relax hard-fought regulations.

The more the availability of the event fades from our collective memories, the more inclined we are to forget it happened and then see it repeated.

In the book *This Time is Different — Eight Centuries of Financial Folly*, Reinhart and Rogoff[12] describe how Greece defaulting on its debts is not a new phenomenon. It seems they have been doing it for centuries. Unfortunately, Greece is not alone in repeating its economic failures. As the availability of the pain diminishes, and old habits come back, we repeat the same mistakes — over and over.

Confirmation bias

We may feel that our opinions are the result of years of rational, objective analysis. Unfortunately, they are really the result of years of paying attention to information that confirms what we believed, while often ignoring information that challenged our preconceived notions.[13]

Over many years, we have formed opinions, views or beliefs about different things. When we come across information that aligns or confirms this view, we can often use it to reinforce an existing view, while ignoring information that may undermine or counter that view. We are basically looking at the world through our internal filters and not with the open mind we would like to think we are using.

Good examples of this include impassioned debates around religion, sport and politics.

For example, during the 2008 presidential election, which Barack Obama won, Valdris Krebs, a researcher in social network analysis, looked at the links between the books people were buying on Amazon and their political affiliations. He found that Democrat voters and those in favour of Obama purchased books that showed Obama and the Democratic movement in a positive light. They purchased almost no books that portrayed a counter view. Likewise, Republican voters, opposed to Obama, purchased books that reflected him in a bad light.[14]

It is not surprising when it comes to our political beliefs that we very often seek out information that confirms that belief rather than looking at information rationally and objectively and voting in this way.

Different people can be confronted with the same information but use that information to confirm or refute a preconceived view of the world.

Like all the biases I have mentioned, confirmation biases are not all bad.

Biases help us cut through the noise and come to more speedy results. In the case of confirmation bias, when we set our efforts toward achieving a goal, we may become almost single-minded in that view. We look to things that confirm what we are pursuing is worth pursuing. It also helps deflect the naysayers who say it will never work.

The key is we are aware of the bias, and are aware that we have decided on a pursuit after considering the views of others, paused to consider them, and then decided to ignore them.

Framing effects

Let's say you are on the operating table about to be anaesthetised for, hopefully, a lifesaving operation. The surgeon leans over, smiles and says:

> 66 *You have nothing to worry about. I have done this simple operation a hundred times and 95% have been completely successful.* 99

A little nervous, I would say? But let's suppose the doctor frames the comment in this way:

> 66 *You have nothing to worry about. I have done this operation a hundred times and, unfortunately, five people died.* 99

More nervous?

Different ways of presenting the same information often evoke different emotions from people. Another common example is how delicatessen products describe something as "95% fat-free" rather than the less-appealing fact that the product contains "5% fat". We know both statements mean the same thing but when information is framed in different ways, it evokes different responses.

This is a regular challenge when responding to news, for example, when an accident is presented in terms of lives saved versus lives lost.

Advertisers regularly use the framing effect to present information in a manner that influences how viewers interpret that information about the products they are promoting.

We can believe that we are too clever to be fooled by such things. However, I'm sure at some point we've all purchased a product that fell short of the expectations as they were presented by the advertiser.

In many cases, having the same information provided to us in different ways may be inconsequential. However, to others it could completely alter the meaning of the information being presented.

We can perceive the same information very differently not only depending on how it is presented, but we can frame it through the internal processing that is influenced from our own life experiences and beliefs.

If we processed information completely rationally, these examples where information is provided to us in different ways should be treated in the same way — but this is not the case.

Unfortunately, the shortcuts our brains take and our inbuilt tendencies to be irrational mean we will continue to misinterpret information depending on how it is framed and how our internal processes interpret the information.

As we discussed in our loss aversion bias, if information is framed to us in a way that implies a loss, we will respond differently to the case where that same information had been presented in terms of a gain.

The danger with our differing frames is that different people receiving the same information may respond differently to it.

Affect heuristic — the emotional response bias

In the context of this bias, affect relates to the affect something has on us — how it triggers emotions. The way information is presented and the content of that information affects different people in different ways — and therefore create biases.

Different words, images or objects will have a different impact on us. If I said "lung cancer", "car crash" or "depression", it will likely produce a response of discomfort or even dread, especially if you or someone close to you were impacted by one of these illnesses.

If, however, I said "hug", "mother's love" or "warmth", these are likely to produce feelings of affection.

This bias is one that is greatly impacted by the emotional responses within us.

This mental shortcut is a bit like our filter on the "goodness" or "badness" of the information we receive and then filter — usually subconsciously, as is the case with most of our mental filters. As with all the mental shortcuts, this emotional filter leads to judgements upon which biased decisions can result.

As Robert Zajonc, the social psychologist, put it:

> ❝There are probably very few perceptions in everyday life that do not have a significant affective component. We do not just see "a house": we see "a handsome house", "an ugly house", or "a pretentious house. ❞[15]

When people are forced to guess why they made a certain decision, they often do not know why. Often, we make these judgements without consciously knowing why we made them. Why did we like that house and not the other house? Why did we feel that way about that stranger? Why did that conversation affect me so much?

Reducing the impact of our biases

The biases detailed above are but a small sample of the many identified shortcuts we take and that have been identified and researched over many years by people like Kahneman, Tversky, Paul Slovic and many more.

We could not survive each day if we did not take these mental shortcuts. We need to take in information and rapidly respond to it, and we do so without being conscious we are doing it.

The examples I've discussed above are typical of those that can impact business leaders and owners in the decisions they make and the impacts they can have on the businesses they own and lead.

The first step in managing the negative impacts of biases and gaining a little more clarity about why we may do certain things, that in retrospect may not be helpful, is to accept that we are imperfect, that we do need to take mental shortcuts. As a result, we have biases that we may not even realise exist.

We need to be aware of these limitations. While we are gifted, innovative, talented and much more, we are still human, we are imperfect, and we need to be cognisant of this. We also need to be kind to ourselves in accepting our humanity. Pretending otherwise is simply being dishonest with ourselves.

When the decisions and implications are significant on the business, on us, or other people, it is worth stepping back and asking ourselves the questions: Are there any biases at play here? Am I being objective? It is also worth deferring to those we trust and whose advice we are comfortable to take. These are people prepared to be honest with us rather than nice to us — remember, **NICE** stands for **Not Interested to Care Enough**.

9 HOW WE DECIDE

We have discussed how our brains work and the shortcuts our brains take in getting through the day. We touched on the impact these biases have on our decisions. We now need to discuss more about how we make decisions.

We take in all sorts of information. We filter most of it, encode it, sleep on it, remember some of it, forget a lot of it, incorrectly recall it, and process it so that we can form judgements and then make decisions.

Remember, the only common factor in all business failures is that people made decisions and those decisions contributed to the failure of the businesses. We cannot discuss business failure without understanding how we make decisions.

All the biases we discussed, what we remember and what we forget, what information we take in and what information we ignore and our personalities all impact on the quality of our decisions. It's not surprising that we get so many decisions wrong.

Let's look further at the way we, as human beings, make decisions to understand why we get them wrong and how we might improve the way we make decisions in our businesses.

Everyday decisions

Every day in our business and our lives, we must make decisions. Most we do without much thought or analysis — we just make them and get on with our day. What to eat for breakfast? What to wear? What route to take to work? Many may be habitual.

Our colleagues, customers, our staff and all those who interact with our business will also be making decisions that may directly impact on us.

We are often faced with decisions that pose far greater impacts and which may require deeper thought. Mergers and acquisitions. Taking on significant debt. Moves into new markets. The decisions may seem small to a larger company, but the impacts could be significant for the small business. Dismissing staff. Buying new assets. Agreeing to a significant job.

Flawed judgement leads to flawed decisions

When we take in information, we will form judgements. They may stay within our minds to no further end. However, we may decide based on that judgement, which may or may not be impacted by our biases. The judgement may be about a person standing in front of us.

We would like to think that if presented with the same situations, facts and circumstances in a business context, we would all assess the situation similarly and arrive at a similar outcome. Unfortunately, we all have our own perspective on the world around us. How we filter the information, run it through our life experiences, will lead us to develop different judgements about that information.

From there we will likely make different judgements and then different decisions. These decisions may not necessarily be good or bad, but they are likely to be different because we are different.

Systems and processes do help

We will discuss all the business systems, processes, risks, good practices and more that, if we follow, will help us succeed in business. However, they will never replace the decisions we must make. They may help us make more consistent decisions but in the end, it is us who make the decisions and it is us who must take accountability for those decisions.

Decisions are made by people, not by companies or businesses.

In large organisations, there may be many layers and process steps that ensure the decisions are well founded and remove the frailties of human beings. Large organisations will apply analytical tools to the data collected, such as Net Present Value calculations, risk analysis, financial modelling or the dozens of other techniques that exist.

Even these do not always guarantee good decisions — as you have seen from the failures of large organisations like Solid Energy, South Canterbury Finance and

Pumpkin Patch, many of the decisions made by CEOs and boards are still made by leaders based on their gut feel and greatly influenced by the experience and personal reputation of the decision maker.

The owners of a small business have less access to data and information and have less capability or capacity to use the analysis larger organisations use.

Also, the decisions are often made by the same person or the same few people and invariably without the processes that would accompany critical decisions in large businesses. This exposes the outcome to the skills, capabilities, limitations and biases of one or a few individuals.

We time travel

Each decision involves our past experiences as well as the present situation. But unlike most other species we make decisions based on predictions of the future. We are effectively time travelling. Before we decide, we consider past experiences, present needs, and jump out in the future to assess what the longer-term impacts of our decision might be. We mentally time travel all the time. We simulate different outcomes to generate a mockup of what our future might be. Mentally, we can disconnect from the present moment and voyage to a world that does not yet exist.[1]

Rational decisions — what are they?

At some point in our business lives we have been told that to make good business decisions we must think rationally and then make rational decisions. We often hear people say, "It's business, it's not personal."

I believe running or leading a business is intensely personal, as our lives, self-esteem, even our families could depend on it. Even the leaders of large organisations find it difficult to separate the business from themselves, as these roles involve a significant level of personal investment.

I am challenging from the outset the view that decision making will be, or even needs to be, rational, especially as we are not wired that way.

But first we should spend some time asking what it is to be rational and ask what a rational decision is and why this has been fundamental to economics, markets and business for centuries.

What is it to be "rational"?

The *Oxford English Dictionary* defines "rational" as:

> 66 *Based on or in accordance with reason or logic. Able to think sensibly or logically. Endowed with the capacity to reason* 99.

A few other definitions from a few quick online searches produced the following additional definitions of "rational":

> 66 *Having or exercising reason, sound judgement, or good sense* 99.

For centuries, economic theory has held the view that businesses, markets and economies operate on the basis that people make rational decisions.

The mathematician Daniel Bernoulli, born in 1700, proposed that business and investment decisions are based on the *utility* associated with the decision. That is, what will be gained or lost in material terms.

Utility has formed the basis of economic and business theory ever since. Basically, the economic utility of a good or service is assumed to influence the demand, and therefore price, of that good or service.

Sounds true and, in the main, is the basis of the economic theory of supply and demand.

At the heart of economics is **Rational Choice Theory**. The central assumption of the rational choice approach is that decision makers have logically consistent goals (whatever they may be), and, given these goals, choose the best available option. It assumes those making decisions are "unboundedly rational".[2]

If people are faced with choices, they will choose what delivers them the greatest benefit (utility) or satisfaction. It also assumes that being rational means decision makers are self-interested individuals.

That is, we will always act in our own interests, making decisions that deliver the greatest self-gain. In business, this is assumed to be in terms of financial gains.[3]

Each of us may have very different views of what rational means.

Who decides what is rational?

I'll use a simple personal example to show how different people see the rationality, or not, of the same decisions. It involved the choices available to my then 16-year-old daughter and her then 50-year-old father — me.

My daughter was (and still is, to some extent) an avid fan of the boy band One Direction. When they came to town they played two concerts on the one day. My daughter had very little money of her own and concerts were one thing she had to pay for herself.

In her mind, seeing One Direction was the most sensible, rational thing to do. Further still, as she was in Auckland all day, why not see them twice?

It's not surprising how totally irrational going once to such an event seemed to me, let alone twice. However, to my daughter the pleasure that investment gave her exceeded all her expectations and was the best money she had ever spent. As such, it seemed perfectly rational.

Economics and human behaviour

In more recent decades there has been a growth in the acceptance of **behavioural economics** or behavioural finance. This brings the irrationality of human beings and our innate psychology into consideration. It challenges past theories that economies, markets and businesses are driven by rational decisions made by rational people.

So, from here on I will be favouring the view that our decisions are not in accordance with historic economic theory. They are based on a wide mix of emotional, irrational, altruistic reasons that may not be aimed at achieving greatest financial return to the person.

> 66 *We usually think of ourselves as sitting in the driver's seat, with ultimate control over the decision we make and the direction our life takes; but, alas, this perception has more to do with our desires — with how we want to view ourselves — than with reality.* 99

— Dan Ariely[4]

When deciding, we compare — it's all relative

When we are making decisions, we more often do it by comparing the relativity of different options. We don't have an absolute view of the value of something in our minds. We tend to compare the relative advantage of one option over another option.[5]

Bread machines and the decoy effect

To give an example of this, let's look at the case study when the homeware company Williams-Sonoma first tried to sell bread-making machines in the early 1990s.

The product was a very new concept but was considered, through research, to have strong sales potential at an original price of $275. However, sales were disappointing. Rather than abandoning the product, they tried a different strategy. They started selling a slightly better bread-maker with more features, priced substantially higher than the $275 model. After this, sales of the original model increased dramatically.

The reason it was believed people were not prepared to buy the original model when in isolation was because they had no other product to compare it with. This marketing technique is called the decoy effect (another bias).

Williams-Sonoma had no desire to sell the more expensive model. It was simply a decoy to get people to buy the $275 model.

We compare — even if it's irrational

Test 12

You are looking for your dream home but the absolute limit on your budget before you start searching is **$700,000**.

After months of searching, you find your dream home — nothing else comes close but the best offer you can get is **$705,000**. Do you pay the extra **$5,000**?

Our decision making is relative and influenced by context. When choosing from alternatives, we can't help but make comparisons between options that are put in front of us. At times, this can be to our detriment.

Our brains are wired to look for change, for patterns, for differences.

In a workplace we will form a view of our value to the business in our office based on our pay packet relative to other employees. We may have no information on what others are earning and feel quite happy. How would we feel if we then found out we were the lowest paid in the office?

Test 13

You promised your teenage son a car for his time at university. You have an absolute budget limit of **$10,000**. He has his heart set on a particular make and model that you support him on. After months of searching, you finally find the car but it is **$15,000**. Do you pay the extra **$5,000**?

This is also why we would add the price of $2,000 to the scope to paint the house we are building for $400,000 but balk at spending $2,000 to paint our existing home — because we are comparing the $2,000 to the $400,000 in one case and $2,000 with spending nothing in the other case.[6]

Another example of relativity in decision making is how we compare the price to acquire something versus the cost to go without.

For example, assume you know the price of a Big Mac is about $5. If I offered you a Big Mac for $10, your decision to buy it is likely to be no. Why would you? Now say you were on a long-haul budget flight for about 15 hours where no food is served, and you arrived on the plane hungry. You had plenty of cash in your pocket and all you could buy were Big Macs and they cost $15 each. I dare say the relative value of the Big Mac has now changed and you probably wouldn't hesitate at paying the money — and you might buy more than one.

In the case of Test 12 and Test 13, most people say yes to the offer on the house but no to the car. If we took a purely rational position we should be indifferent in both cases as the amount involved is the same — $5,000. In both cases the $5,000 we would forgo buys exactly the same. However, we can't help but compare the $5,000 extra to the base price. In the case of the house it's $5,000 compared to $700,000 and the car it's compared to $10,000.

Emotions and business decisions

Normally in business we are made to feel that emotions are something we must manage or control, and where possible should remove emotion from the decisions we make. Many of our decisions are informed by our emotional responses because that is what emotions are designed to do — to appraise and summarise an experience and inform our actions. Emotions are not particularly sophisticated or precise, but their speed make up for what they lack in sophistication and precision.[7]

Our emotions will drive the decisions we make, and our success may depend upon our ability to understand and interpret these emotions.

During critical decisions about the business, we may feel anxious, stressed and uncomfortable. These are signs we need to consider. Emotions can undermine and mislead our decisions as well. Emotions can improve our decision making if we make use of them and consider when the decision is of a critical nature and contemplate if the emotions are helping the decision or undermining it.

> *Emotions powerfully, predictably, and pervasively influence decision making.*
> — Jennifer Lerner et. al.[8]

When a person responds to an emotionally significant event, their brain automatically searches their memory for related events, including the emotions that accompanied those events. If the feelings are pleasant, they motivate actions and thoughts anticipated to reproduce those feelings. If the feelings are unpleasant, they motivate actions and thoughts anticipated to avoid the feelings.[9]

We'd like to think we can divorce ourselves from this process but we can't. Rather, we need to embrace the emotions but caution against spontaneously responding if the decision could have significant ramifications.

Emotions versus being emotional

When I'm discussing emotions here, I'm not implying that it is a good idea to be making critical business decisions if we are experiencing heightened emotions like anger, fear, grief or sadness. If we feel overrun by such emotions, it may be a good idea to pause, calm down and avoid making any significant decisions.

If we are prone to these reactions on a more regular basis, we should consider strategies and the guidance of those we trust to get some distance between the heightened emotion and the decisions we might otherwise make while in that elevated emotional state.

The decisions we make while emotional may have nothing to do with why our emotions are elevated.

For example, in getting ready for work after a bad night's sleep, you have a huge battle getting the kids to school. You leave home angry and frustrated. Traffic is slow and heavy and a few people cut you off in traffic. By the time, you get to work you are not in a very pleasant frame of mind. The first decision you are faced with is dealing with a customer complaint. In your heightened state, you decide to push back. "To hell with them, I'm not going to back down on this as they are wrong." A few days later you regret your actions. Your anger had nothing to do with that important customer you just lost.

Impact of brain traumas on emotions

The neuroscientist Antonio Damasio in his book *Descartes' Error* discussed the role of emotions in decision making, following research with patients who had suffered specific brain traumas.[10]

One was a man Damasio called "Elliot", who had suffered a brain tumour.

Prior to the damage, Elliot was a very intelligent, productive person, a good planner and an effective decision maker. The operation to remove the tumour was a success but damaged some parts of his frontal lobe.

After the operation, Elliot was unable to show the emotions he once did. Even simple emotions like sadness, anger, frustration and impatience that we all experience on a regular basis did not come naturally to him. He maintained much of his pre-injury intelligence — so he might "know" but he could not "feel".

Elliot lacked the ability to balance both knowing and feeling, and his capacity to make decisions almost vanished to an extent he became socially ineffective. He failed to make decisions.

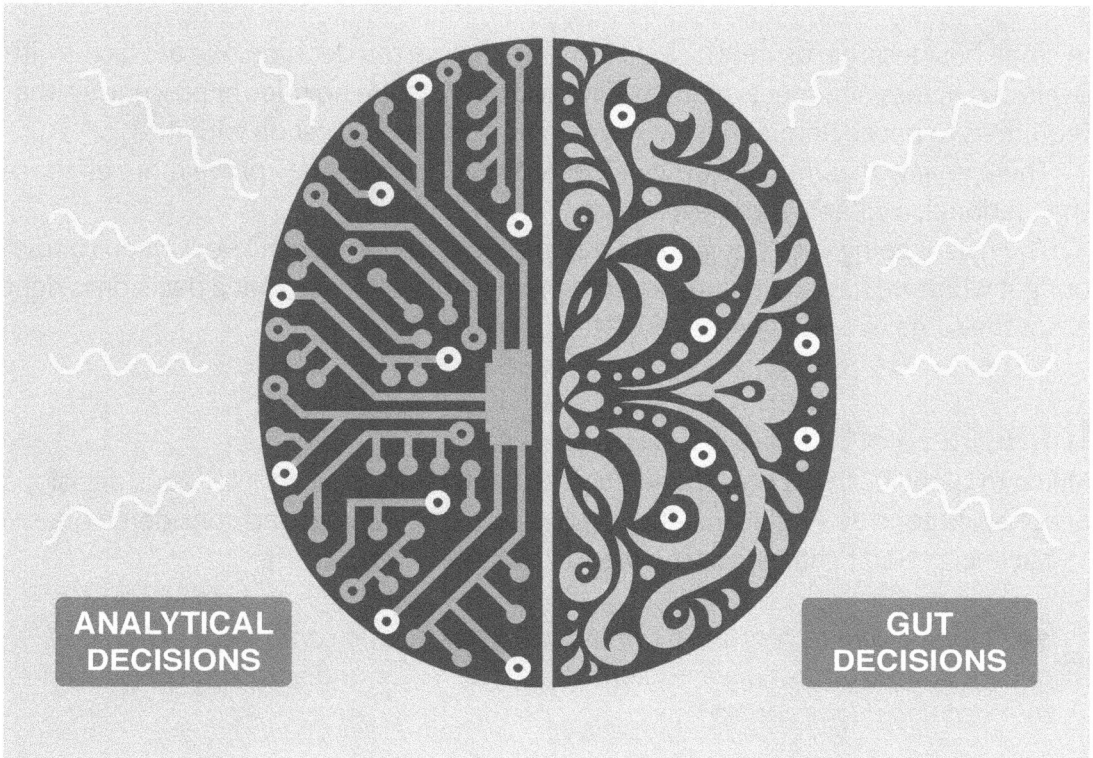

ANALYTICAL DECISIONS

GUT DECISIONS

Normally, for all of us without such injuries, these mistakes will trigger a response — we learn from them. Elliot could not do this.

The science behind, and risk of, going with your gut

In earlier chapters, we discussed how our brains function and the two different types of thinking that we do. One is intuitive or fast thinking and the other is the slower, analytical thinking.

When we make decisions without applying the slower analytical parts of our brain, it's likely we are making what we often called "gut" decisions. They are fast, take less effort, and are usually the most common type of decision business leaders and owners make, especially small businesses.

In small business, we usually lack the time to analyse the decision. We are faced with decisions across all aspects of the business, and there are no rules or procedures that require us to pause before making any decision. We simply get on with it.

There is view that intuitive or "gut" decisions in business may prove more effective than rational, well-analysed decisions.

The risk of going with our gut and our intuition is how we can know when to trust our gut when we have no criteria for determining this. A feeling that a decision is right is not the same as providing evidence that it is right.

It needs more than a Blink

Malcolm Gladwell in his book *Blink* put forward the idea that spontaneous decisions are often as good as — or even better than — carefully planned and considered ones.[11]

Michael LeGault challenged this view in his book *Think*, saying:

> 66 *Critical scientific reasoning almost always involves a component of intuition, and intuition is almost always informed by experience and hard knowledge won by reasoning things out.* 99[12]

Analytical and reasoned decisions require us to look outside ourselves, referring to others or to more information, statistics, data or research. Gut decisions occur within ourselves, so the answers need to be found somewhere from within. We will be guided by our internal knowledge, experience, and past emotional events.

At times, detailed calculations can provide false confidence. If these businesses base this analysis on incorrect assumptions, you may simply get the result you want.

Most CEOs and senior managers are more likely to default to their gut anyway. Research on the decisions of 1000 CEOs and CFOs in large organisations in the USA found that many of even the most critical decisions were made based on the perceived knowledge of the CEO or CFO, their personal reputation and the politics within the business.

In short, there may be far more detailed analysis done in large organisations but when it comes to the final decision, it is very often the gut feeling of the boss that will decide what occurs.[13]

When not to go with your gut

There is a very important caveat on "gut" decisions that we need to consider carefully.

Gut decisions based on deep and detailed experience or extensive training could be better than those based on analysis. However, if we have no experience, we need to be extremely wary about making gut decisions without seeking advice or doing some analysis.

If we have no experience and make a gut decision on a critical issue for the business, it may be no better than a guess. We need to challenge this intuition.

This does not mean procrastinate and do nothing. It means pausing and challenging ourselves before taking the leap.

Making instinctive decisions under pressure

Gary Klein, a research psychologist and critic of Daniel Kahneman's views on biases, did extensive research on the real-life decisions people make in high-pressure situations. He called his work *Naturalistic Decision Making* because it related to observed decisions in natural environments rather than in laboratory tests.[14]

He studied people making critical, even life or death decisions, such as firefighters, military personnel, pilots and astronauts.

These people are making snap or intuitive decisions, with minimal information, with shifting goals, no procedures, under significant time pressure, and with potentially serious consequences.

While there is no question the decisions are made using their intuitive mental processes, and are gut decisions, they are being made based on years of experience and training. These experienced decision makers recognise patterns and they don't compare options. They evaluate an option by imagining how it would play out.

Klein's work demonstrated that expertise primarily depends on tacit knowledge, not on rules and procedures. He challenged that in these situations, gathering more information may not reduce uncertainty. In fact, he found that performance seemed to suffer when too much information was gathered, and that uncertainty can result from inadequate framing of data, not just the absence of data.

So how might this situation relate to running a business and making intuitive decisions?

The critical thing to remember is that gut decisions are fine when a depth of experience and training backs them.

We read literature about high-profile and very successful business people who made snap decisions that proved highly successful. Remember that these people may have had decades of experience doing similar or at least related activities in business and their decisions tapped into that experience.

If we are faced with a serious or critical situation in a business where the stakes are high and we have significant experience, more so than anyone around us, we can trust our gut and make the decision. However, if we have little or no experience, or are feeling uneasy, it is strongly advised that we apply some critical thinking to the problem. Seek out expertise and think the problem through — this may not be a wise time to go with our gut — and then hope for the best.

Fatigue, stress and the impact of wellbeing on decisions

We will spend some time talking about the impact of poor business owner health on business success in later chapters. Many businesses fail due to the ill health of owners.

Even if our wellbeing is not a threat to the business, if we are not at our best, the quality of our decisions will diminish.

If we are stressed, lack sleep or are unwell, the quality of our decisions will diminish.

The more decisions we make, the more energy-depleted our brains become. We become mentally fatigued.

When we do an exercise like that in Tests 1 and 2, we would have found the second test to be particularly draining. Our brain is being asked to complete a task that does not come naturally. When asked to do the mathematical calculation after this, it takes us a little longer or we avoid doing it all together.

We give in to temptation when fatigued

Sometimes the "now" can be very powerful. Good decision making for the future is often compromised by our impulse to pursue instant gratification — at the expense of better long-term outcomes.

We can also suffer from *decision fatigue*. The more decisions we make throughout the day, the harder each one becomes for our brain, and eventually our brain tires and looks for shortcuts.

Our willpower can become depleted and the quality of our decisions will also diminish.

A research project was carried out that observed the decisions made by judges on parole boards.[15] The research reviewed over 1100 parole decisions. The research explored if the decisions had any patterns associated with them. The most striking pattern was the reduction in positive decisions in the latter part of the day after the judges had made many decisions. Basically, the judges were getting tired and the easiest option was rejecting the parole application.

No matter how rational and focused we try to be, we can't make decision after decision without paying a biological price.

It's different from ordinary physical fatigue; we are not as consciously aware of being tired and low on mental energy. The more decisions we make throughout the day, the harder each one becomes for our brain.

We could become more impulsive, lose our self-control, and give in to the easy options. We could also simply avoid making a decision.

It was this latter option that the parole judges defaulted to. The mental effort in deciding to release a prisoner was much greater than the effort to leave the prisoner behind bars.

Our willpower and our self-control are not unlimited resources. The most common life example Is how we more easily give in to temptation, to eat those sweets, to have that extra glass of wine or that ice cream when we are tired.

So how can we make better decisions?

In every business failure I outline in this book, poor decisions led to the failure of the business.

After reading the previous chapters and this chapter on decision making, we should all be able to better accept the limitations that exist with all of us. To be successful in business, it is very important that we accept these limitations and keep them in mind when making the critical decisions that could affect our businesses.

Here is a summary of some of the key things to keep in mind when making decisions:

- Accept our limitations. Our brain cannot process everything. We won't remember everything, and we will take mental shortcuts.
- Consider the implications of the decision. Don't sweat the small stuff but if the implications to the business are significant, pause.
- We should not be afraid to listen to our emotions — how does the decision make us feel?
- Be self-aware about what we are experienced at and what we are not. When we have little or no experience, we need to be careful making important decisions without advice and analysis.
- Don't be too proud to ask for help or at least to have a trusted person challenge our thinking and identify blind spots.
- Apply *Advocatus Diaboli* — the Latin term for Devil's advocate. This was an official role given to people to argue against why a person should be canonised (made a saint). This could be a trusted advisor.
- Accept when we are tired, stressed or have been required to make many decisions. If we start making significant decisions when we are like this, they may prove unsatisfactory — or we may avoid making a decision.
- Build rules, processes and systems into the business that will guide everyone, at least for the repetitive processes that occur.
- Be clear what the strategy is for the business — why does it exist, what does it stand for and what are the goals for the business? We will spend some time a little later on how good strategy guides our critical decisions.

10 EMPLOYEES — THEY ARE IRRATIONAL PEOPLE TOO

While few failures, whether of big businesses or small, are directly linked to the actions or inactions of staff, the success or failure of any business depends on the staff within the business. If a business is successful, it will be the manager or owner's ability to get the most from their staff that will play a significant part.

In all the failures I researched, none could be attributed to the actions or inactions of the employees. Sadly, when things are not going well within a business, staff often bear the brunt of the impact as decisions are made to reverse the impact of the issues. Restructuring and redundancies are common.

If the failures are not caused by staff, it is usually the staff who most suffer from the failures of a business. Even in the small list of examples I've covered in this book, there were thousands of people's lives that were forever impacted by the failures that occurred — many who in no way contributed to the problems the business faced.

From the near 1000 staff who lost their jobs in Solid Energy down to Helena Lintern, David Ross's secretary, who had to defend her innocence in court, many employees suffered greatly as a result of the failure of their employers.

Therefore, not only do the leaders and owners of businesses of all sizes need to get the best from their staff to be successful, they also have a responsibility to these people when making business decisions.

While my research saw little or no connection between the actions or inactions of employees in the ultimate failure of a business, the role of staff in a business

is so fundamental that we need to devote time to it.

Also, the limitations leaders, managers and owners of businesses have — as people — are also the limitations employees have. While understanding employees may not directly prevent failures, it will definitely contribute to achieving success — and probably reduce the frustrations managers and owners of business may face in trying to get the best from staff.

Staff are imperfect. They are irrational, emotional and exhibit all the human frailties we have already discussed.

Good people are hard to find, so when we have them we need to support them and treat them with some patience, care and support.

Caring for our staff, showing humility and self-awareness goes a huge way to keeping great staff. Take time to find the right person. In a small business, it can make a huge difference

Better to have a great vacancy than the wrong employee.

Remember the human in human resources

After many years of managing staff, I've often seen the human resources profession forget the most critical part of what they are meant to do — to look after the people. It's an area of many businesses that can get overrun with the pressures of process. These include employment relations laws, recruitment processes, equal opportunity, remuneration, performance management and payroll. Good human resources practices in any business are very important. Unfortunately, many human resource specialists spend more time in the world of rules and processes than in understanding the people for who they are.

It is so important that we don't lose sight of the most important fact about our staff. They are people with their own weaknesses, strengths, goals and desires. They will have their own life issues. They could bring these issues from home to work. They are likely to have a different temperament to us. They'll have different personalities. Different situations will stress them. Their diversity could be a huge asset or a huge headache.

While we must be conscious of following the right processes, we shouldn't get swamped in them at the expense of treating our staff as human beings.

We must ensure we select the right people, manage our expectations of them, and not tolerate unacceptable behaviours. Get the employment documentation right. If we do get the right person in the business, we need to look after them.

Remember our values. Our staff will scrutinise our behaviours more than anyone. Keep front of mind that we are human too. We don't have to know everything, and we will make mistakes. We need to admit this to our staff, as they are more likely to respect us for this than trying to be all things to all people.

Most of all, we need to be ourselves.

What motivates staff?

As discussed in previous chapters, what motivates each of us may not always appear rational to others. This also applies to staff. To get the best from people in a business, we are looking to motivate them to do the best they can for the business. There are some things that are fundamental in the motives of all people, which we will discuss. However, there are many things that may motivate one person that in no way inspire another and in fact may appear very irrational to others.

> 66 *The term motivation refers to factors that activate, direct, and sustain goal-directed behaviour. Motives are the 'whys' of behaviour — the needs or wants that drive behaviour and explain what we do. We don't actually observe a motive; rather, we infer that one exists based on the behaviour we observe.* 99
>
> — Dr Jeff Nevid, Professor of Psychology, St John's University[1]

As a manager or business owner, we cannot make another human being do anything. We would like to think we can control others but we cannot. We can only control what we do and do this in a way that motivates others to do what we would like them to do.

Motivation is also a very personal thing. We are motivated by both ***extrinsic factors*** and ***intrinsic factors***.

Extrinsic motivators come from things outside ourselves, like rewards, money, trophies, feedback from others, social acknowledgement. Intrinsic motivators are those that come from within us. These are activities we do because they are driven from within. We are not looking for any external recognition for them. They bring us pleasure or contentment in their own right.

The challenge with motivating our staff is that we are all different. Applying pay increases across the board, praise, feedback, or other extrinsic motivators may work for some but not for others. It may be very difficult to assess the intrinsic motivators for staff — they, like many of us, may have difficulty understanding their own motivations.

In his book *What Makes Us Tick*, Hugh Mackay[2] describes the desires or motives that drive all of us. He did not ask people what motivates them to establish this list. Typically, we can't answer the question about our desires or motives. We think we might know but often we can't always explain why we do the things we do. As the theme of this book highlights, we are not always rational so we may say one thing yet do another — and then we may attempt to rationalise why we did what we did.

Let's walk through a few of the key things Hugh Mackay detailed that make each of us tick and are likely to motivate us. It's worth noting that some of these may apply at different times for different people — just another of the complexities of being human that managers and business owners need to contend with.

1. **To be taken seriously** We want to be recognised and acknowledged as a unique individual. We all want our voices to be heard as authentic, legitimate and worthy of attention. We can't bear to be overlooked, dismissed or belittled. Being looked upon as trivial, having our views disregarded or being made to feel our opinion doesn't matter can be very damaging to our self-esteem. Not being taken seriously feels like the ultimate insult, and insults tend to fester and seethe, waiting for a chance to counterattack. Our desire to be valued is universal, but its intensity varies between individuals and at different times of our lives.

2. **To have "my place"** Knowing where we came from, where we belong and places where we feel physically and psychologically safe is important to us. These are places we consider to be our own whether at home or in our work environment. As a person who has travelled and worked in many places, I know the unease and discomfort of confronting a new place. It takes time to be comfortable, to feel safe and then for that place, work or home to draw out the best in us.

3. **To have something to believe in** Over the centuries, what most people on the planet believed in was their god. Over time our beliefs have broadened. We also need to believe in what we do. We might believe in the business we are part of, as it has a deeper purpose. We may simply believe in the team we are a part of. If these beliefs run deep, as can occur with religious belief, it can be immensely powerful — for the good or perhaps not. Such belief need not be rational, if those having that belief see it as fact or knowledge. To the non-believer, the believer looks irrational. If staff genuinely believe in what the business is doing and our actions and behaviours reinforce that, it can be very powerful.

4. **To connect** As we discussed as part of our evolutionary make-up, we are social creatures. We need to engage and communicate with other people. While we need to get on with work and not sit around chatting all day, people need a level of social interaction. This was proven through the Hawthorne experiments, which were carried out at Western Electric's factory at Hawthorne, a suburb of Chicago, in the late 1920s and early 1930s. The experiment was aimed at testing the productivity in a work environment when physical changes in the workplace were made — lighting, working hours and so on. The experimenters concluded that it was not the changes in physical conditions that were affecting the workers' productivity but that someone was actually concerned about their workplace and the opportunities this gave them to discuss changes and the effect that working and communicating in groups had on the individual.

5. **To be useful** We all know how devastating it is to our self-esteem to be called useless, especially by someone whose view we value. All people want to be of use, to add value. Even the laziest person tends to rise to the occasion when there's an opportunity to prove themselves useful. Most people are decent human beings — we want to help others in need. Most of us, when asked, act helpfully; some of us don't even wait to be asked. We often do things for others with no thought of a reward or even recognition for ourselves. Clearly not everyone is like this. Many exist solely to serve themselves, but in the main we are inclined to act to be useful to others.

6 **To belong** There are aspects of what makes us human that are part of all of us that have developed through our evolutionary journey. One is our need and desire to be part of a group. Our ability to socialise, cooperate and use our collective intelligence allowed us to overcome the physical limitations we have that other animals do not.

While the world we live in has changed, this need has not. We are as socially interdependent now as we have ever been. While introverts may gain energy from being alone, our default position, as humans, is still to be together. We love to meet to talk, to work, to eat and drink, to socialise. We love to go to concerts, movies, sporting events or the theatre with someone. We need to belong and a lack of belonging is distressing. Those in our society who are isolated and lonely can find it very distressing and damaging to their mental health.

Therefore, immigrants tend to gravitate toward their fellow expatriates when they arrive in a new town or country. When we moved to New Zealand we congregated with other expatriates from other countries who had no other family, as they shared the same challenges we did. We knew no one and wanted to be able to socialise with others and to feel like we belonged. While we now have a very wide group of friends and colleagues, these original people remain our closest and dearest friends.

This is no different in a business. Staff want to belong. They want to build relationships with the managers, owners and other staff members. If they never develop these relationships and become isolated, they will likely leave or underperform. We need to expect dedication and commitment to the job. However, we also need to provide an environment that allows people to socialise and engage with each other.

7. **To be in control** We like to have or at least feel like we have control over our circumstances. Too often we want to control others, which we can't, and when they fail to do what we want, we can become very frustrated. Rather than trying to control staff, we want to empower them so they feel in control of what they do in their work day. This will build greater ownership for their work.

We also value things we do far more than if they are handed to us. This is sometimes called the IKEA effect — we value things we create and control ourselves, even if the quality of the finished product is lower than that done by an expert. The IKEA effect was first named by Norton, Mochon and Ariely, after the well-known store where we are required to build the items we buy. They cited other researchers' previous work on "effort justification", which had demonstrated that the more effort someone put into something, the more someone will value it. So, empowering staff to have greater control will also see them take ownership over what they do.

8. **To have something happen** We are motivated by seeing things happen, by action rather than words. While we may not always like change and may not agree with the things happening around us, people like to see things getting done — we do not enjoy boredom. We enjoy movies and entertainment because things are happening. There is action and something going on. There is a little tension within us all here. We do like some level of stability and ritual in our lives and we can resist change that is thrust on us (I believe we resist change where we have no control over it). However, we are a species that has continually acted to improve the world we live in, and the pace of the change and the actions we take to bring it about are unending.

Staff within a business will be far more motivated when that business is doing something and achieving results — doing what it says it will do. We all get frustrated when we hear people say they intend to do something then never follow through.

While no workplace, business owner or leader can provide all things to meet a person's needs, we are more likely to achieve it if we understand those who work for us — as people.

Maslow's hierarchy — as relevant now as in 1943

In 1943, Abraham Maslow put forward his famous theory that human beings are motivated based on a hierarchy of needs.[3]

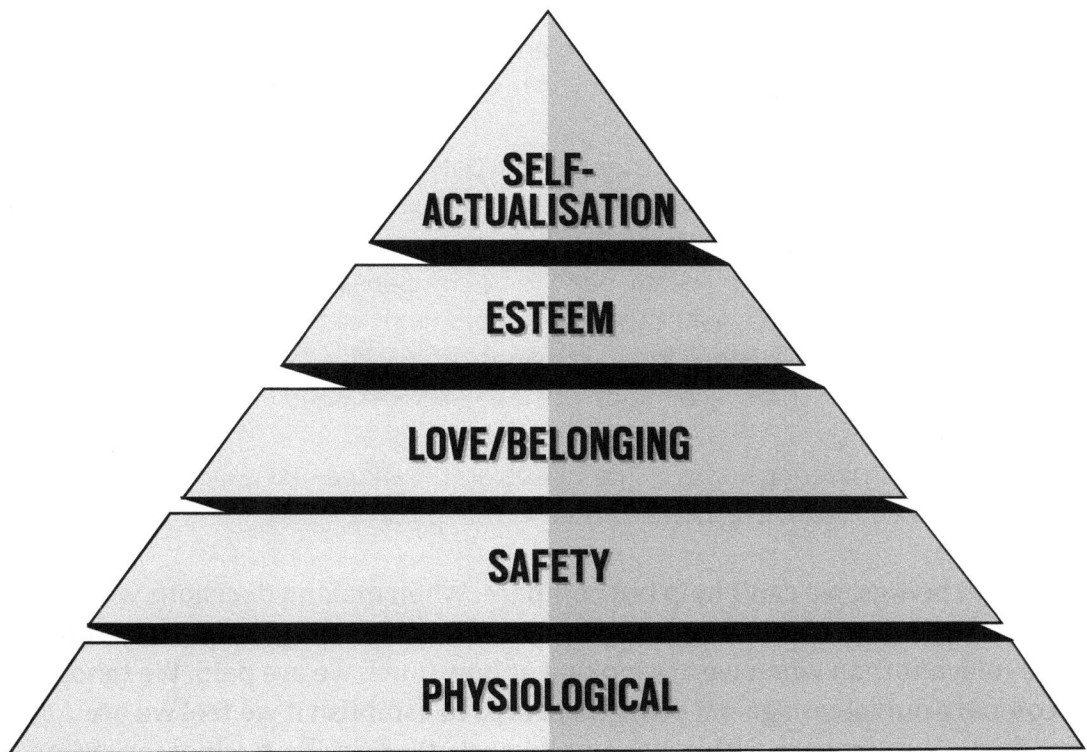

SELF-ACTUALISATION

ESTEEM

LOVE/BELONGING

SAFETY

PHYSIOLOGICAL

We are not likely to be motivated by a higher-level need unless our basic needs are met. The need to be loved and to belong will not be a need if we aren't able to feed ourselves, don't have air to breathe, or believe our lives are in threat. The same applies to the way we remunerate people. If our staff are paid at a level that does not allow them to meet their basic living needs, then they are less likely to be motivated to achieve greater things.

Get to know our staff

Nothing will assist us in finding the best motivators than getting to know as much as we can about our staff. One size will never fit everyone. The more we know about those who work for us, the better will be our chances of finding the motivators that get the best from them for their and our benefit.

Rewards and compensation

While we may be motivated by our work, and extract meaning and pleasure from it, we do still need to make a living, as do our staff. As Maslow put it, we need our basic needs to be met first. We need to be paid enough money to at least lead a basic life, get the kids through school, buy or rent shelter over our heads, and enjoy some basic pleasures in life.

All businesses at some stage struggle with determining how to pay and reward staff. Nothing can bring out irrationality in us than establishing our value in terms of some material measure — namely money. While we may all pursue financial rewards with different levels of vigour, we still need to be compensated for our efforts.

Businesses can only pay what they can afford, with staff wages often being the single biggest financial expense for any business of any size. We also need to ensure we pay fairly and with some recognition of the value society and the marketplace puts on certain positions.

It is worth considering some of the biases and irrationalities that exist within us that will influence how we respond to what we are paid.

As human beings, we can't help but compare. When making decisions we like to compare one option against another before choosing. Nowhere is this more relevant than when we are looking at how much we are paid. We tend to compare ourselves against other measures to establish if we feel we are paid fairly. We compare with other employees, other similar businesses, other professions, and other industries.

The way people's roles are appraised by human resource professionals, and then a salary is attached to that role, is all based on comparisons. We look at the job, compare it with a basket of similar businesses in the same industry and come up with a salary. This process does not consider whether a policeman is more valuable than a doctor, or the CEO of a company, or a person helping the homeless. Unfortunately, society tends to establish the worth of different roles and often, depending on our values, we may believe this to be very wrong.

> ** Thou shalt not covet.

> ** You shall not covet your neighbour's house. You shall not covet your neighbour's wife, or his male or female servant, his ox or donkey, or anything that belongs to your neighbour. **
— Exodus 20:17

If only we all lived by this commandment.

Unfortunately, we can't help but compare. When we make decisions, we are influenced by the bias of relativity.

A pay packet that usually gets significant attention and is compared with many others is the salary of the CEOs of the big companies. While the salary of New Zealand CEOs in large commercial businesses will never match those of countries like the USA, they are still very healthy.

One would think that a CEO making many millions of dollars would feel happy about their salary, considering many of their staff, who contribute to the company's success, earn a fraction of that pay. Our irrationality was demonstrated when CEO salaries were made public in the USA in 1993 by federal securities regulators. It was felt such transparency would make boards think twice about paying excessive amounts to CEOs. Sadly, the opposite occurred. CEOs started comparing their own salaries and bonuses with their counterparts. Before the release of salaries, they were satisfied; however, they demanded increases when they could compare — "Why am I paid less than that CEO?"

Continuing to use money as a motivator can prove very expensive and can often prove rather futile as, in the long run, it is unlikely to change people's behaviours as they will not be driven by cash. No doubt they will take it if offered (most of us would), but whether it changes any behaviour is a very different thing.

If the business can't afford it, it can't afford it

Every business must understand the costs it can afford. If in meeting market wage rates the business starts struggling, and may not be sustainable, then it's likely there are other more fundamental issues the business needs to address.

Often businesses put in incentive schemes, bonuses, commissions or other performance pay processes. If done well they can drive behaviours that support the business — they can benefit the employee and the business.

However, there are many situations where such processes are not implemented well, and they drive perverse behaviours that damage businesses.

A few examples:

- Wells Fargo had a class action taken against it by customers in 2017 to the tune of $US110 million. This was because staff opened about 2 million fake bank accounts in the customers' names. This occurred because staff were set unrealistic performance targets for bringing new clients into the bank, which was only measured by new accounts being opened.
- In 2015, Kathmandu was forced to apologise publicly for mistakes in the CEO's bonus scheme. The company suffered a significant fall in earnings, but the mistake saw the CEO do much better come bonus time.
- Many factors contributed to the demise of Dick Smith. One was the incentive scheme suppliers offered the company. The company was offered very healthy rebates for buying more stock. This saw the business purchase far more stock than it needed. The rebates could be put into the financials to improve the short-term performance of the business, which was the CEO's incentive. Unfortunately, Dick Smith built up huge stock levels that it could not sell.

The danger with rewards is that it shifts from intrinsic to extrinsic rewards. That is, people don't necessarily do their job because they love doing it or believe in it, but because they are motivated by a reward.

We do respond to incentives. The important thing to ensure is that they are the right incentives and drive the right behaviours.

If we feel the pay levels are fair relative to the market, and we have decided not to put in other payment schemes, there are many other non-monetary or social-based factors we can use that could be low cost and extremely supportive. This is where we need to know our staff. All staff members may be at different stages of their lives and be motivated by different things. Some may want more free time. Some may want as many hours' work as we can give them. Some just like to be told they are doing a great job. Some like to be pampered with an occasional gift.

If you consider some form of performance pay, think this through very carefully — these schemes, if poorly designed, could drive the wrong, even perverse, behaviours and we could find we are paying for staff performance when it did not actually deliver what the business wanted.

Some industries have very mature processes (e.g. real estate). If we are new to performance pay processes, we need to do some research before deciding.

Never forget that it is often the little things that can make the difference with staff more so than the large financial incentives.

Managing and supporting your staff's performance

When staff are not fulfilling our expectations, the worst thing we can do is ignore it and do nothing. We will simply be condoning bad behaviours that may become acceptable. Unfortunately, managing performance is something most people do not enjoy doing and we avoid it where we can.

It is very important that we set expectations for all staff early in the relationship and as clearly as possible. We then need to continue reminding the team of our expectations. If people are not fulfilling expectations, do something. If we ignore it, we condone it, and we are likely to have to live with it.

If people are hurting the business and showing no signs of responding to the expectations set out, then we can't allow this to continue. This can be particularly damaging in a small business where there are only a few staff.

Whatever we decide to do, it is always worth seeking advice. Be fair, follow good process and if the staff member must depart the business, do it respectfully. Don't get paralysed by a fear of grievances or possible legal action. Even if we follow the best possible process, we may still face a challenge. This is worth the risk compared to keeping a destructive person who simply doesn't fit.

We don't like the hard conversations

One of the things many business people dislike is having those tough, insightful conversations with an employee when they are not meeting expectations. Unfortunately, it is something that can't be avoided but too often is. We are not good at giving feedback and having the important discussions about what is going well and what is not.

I'm often asked by small business owners what they should do if they see substandard performance. The one thing I say that they should never do is "nothing".

Unfortunately, this can also be the case for very large organisations. People in very senior positions or on boards may be falling well short of what the business needs, may not have the skills required, or may have loyalties that prevent the tough discussions happening. This was the case of the large failures we discuss.

The CEO of South Canterbury Finance, Lachie McLeod, was in the role five years and never had a review of any kind, so this is not just an issue in small businesses.

Therefore, even highly experienced business people may still avoid the tough conversations that need to happen.

The specific actions we take will depend heavily on our style, our relationship with the person, the person's possible responses, and the specifics of the issue.

If the performance issue is minor and just a one-off, we may make a note in case we see it again. If it happens more often, our response could be as simple as a quiet word reminding the person of our expectations. If the issues continue, or worsen, we may need to increase the action required. It's very important to document every stage of this process. It could become vital information if the situation worsens to the point where we may have to let the person go.

If dismissal is starting to look like your only option, it is important we seek advice, especially if we have no prior experience. This is where emotions could be running high, and our intuition is screaming out for us to act — this is definitely the time to pause and seek advice. Reacting prematurely and getting this process wrong could prove very costly, financially, emotionally and on the culture of the business.

The counter to poor performance is how you acknowledge good performance. Business owners can often get so tied up in the day-to-day challenges of the business that they don't stop and simply say, "Thank you, that was great" and "I really appreciate what you did." It can make a huge difference to an employee. This type of reward can often be more powerful than any financial or other material reward.

Our management and leadership skills

Very often the owners of a business or the leaders of large business apportion the difficulties they face to the staff they employ or oversee. There is no question that managing and leading staff is not easy and it is not for everyone. Unfortunately, often the biggest issue for an owner or manager is not the staff but their own style of leading these people — the staff may not be the problem.

> 66 *People will join a company but they leave their boss.* 99
> — Unknown

If your staff are unhappy or leaving, before blaming them we need to look at ourselves. This may be a tough pill to swallow but such self-awareness could be a major contributor in our success as a leader. The humility to accept feedback and then do something about it is a recurring theme in our discussion and applies to our relationship with staff.

As managers and owners, we need to create a work environment of care, not fear. If people fear us or are scared to make mistakes, they will perform to the bare minimum to get through the day. They will also avoid doing anything more for the business than they must — and many will simply leave.

We can be guilty of over-complicating the management and leadership of staff. We need to be ourselves, show interest in our staff, care for them, set and adhere to standards and communicate often with them. People tend to fill in the gaps when there is a lack of information and it's usually filled with unproductive or incorrect information.

Explain to people what you want them to do but more importantly why you need it done. They may not agree but at least they know.

> 66 *People will do almost any WHAT if you give them a good WHY.* 99
> — Friedrich Nietzsche

Know yourself; accept yourself; forget yourself

Consider this statement about what makes a good leader: "Know yourself; accept yourself; forget yourself." It's about being self-aware and accepting what we do well and not so well. We then need to accept our limitations and play to our strengths. And finally, and most importantly, we need to park our immediate self-interests and do what is best for the business.

Leadership is often about being selfless. If we put our staff and the business before our own needs, it will build loyalty and the rewards will be returned to us in many forms in the long run.

Sadly, there are too many cases of business failures where the leaders and owners were overtaken with self-interest. The extent of these examples range from business people who simply cared little about their staff, to those taking significant funds out of the business for personal use, to those like the failed finance company directors who were jailed for fraud in the fallout from the GFC. Many were widely criticised for putting their own interests ahead of the interests of employees and investors.

Leading a successful business requires humility and self-awareness and often means we must put our own immediate interests to one side for the benefit of the business. The clear majority of business owners and leaders do this. Unfortunately, many don't, and the impacts of such self-interest are usually not good for anyone — including the business owner or leader.

We will now devote a chapter to the processes we might follow to become a little more self-aware.

SELF–AWARENESS, PERSONALITY, AND WHAT WE STAND FOR

When I met with those directly responsible for failures or were present when they happened, some were very aware why the events occurred, with the time to reflect, and showed a high level of self-awareness of their role, while others were still in some level of denial. For instance, Lachie McLeod of SCF was very open about the things he and others could have done differently that may have either prevented the failure or at least reduced its impact. McLeod was also very open in his desire to reflect on this and avoid letting it overwhelm him.

The consistent theme throughout this book is the part the owners and leaders have in the failure of businesses. This is perhaps self-evident when, as humans, we make mistakes — we are imperfect. The discussion on our brains, biases and the limitations associated with how we make decisions should reinforce this. This then, in turn, will impact on our staff — for good or bad.

Why is it that we all know we make mistakes, we all know we are imperfect, we all know we could be better, yet we spend so little time truly understanding ourselves?

Most animals have no awareness they exist — they are not self-aware. We, as humans, are self-aware yet we are amazingly blind to who we really are.

We must come to the realisation that no matter our past, we are who we are now, and there is nothing we can do to change that. In the running of businesses and living our lives, we must accept this.

If we devote time to learn about ourselves, the good, the great, the unsure, and the limitations that go with being human, we are in a much better position to accept who we are, play to our strengths and look to others to fill the gaps. This is instead of blindly going forward thinking we are somehow more able than every other human.

Even when we spend all our efforts to become more self-aware, we may be unable to consciously understand our limitations — and accept them.

Self-awareness can take us a lifetime — if we ever truly achieve it.

Let's devote a few paragraphs to this complex topic and how it may assist in the survival of the businesses that depend on it.

Know thyself

Aristotle (384–322 BC) was one of the three great Greek philosophers, the others being Plato and Socrates. They all discussed, to some extent, the role self-awareness, self-knowledge and the awareness of our external environment played in wisdom, our lives, and in our happiness. Aristotle said:

> 66*Knowing yourself is the beginning of all wisdom.*99

After 2400 years, the theme remains as relevant as ever. Knowledge and success in life and in our businesses will be influenced by awareness of ourselves.

We have come to this point in our lives and as business owners, managers or leaders after all our prior years of experience, our education, family, genetics, personality and all those things that make us who we are. We can spend our entire lives learning who we are, what we are good at, what we are weak at, what stresses us and what motivates us. The more we know about ourselves, the better will be our decisions.

We will all make errors of judgement and mistakes. If you aren't, it's likely you aren't doing very much. The aim is to be honest and humble enough to accept we got it wrong and learn from the mistakes.

The Johari Window

The concept of self-knowledge is simply represented by the Johari Window

The American psychologists Joseph Luft and Harrington Ingham created the Johari Window in 1955. (The name is a combination of the two men's first names.) It is also referred to as the Johari House, with four rooms. It represents a simple perspective on self-knowledge. Ask yourself which "rooms" you have never been in or the "rooms" that others close to you may never have had access to. How might that be impacting you, your business and your life?

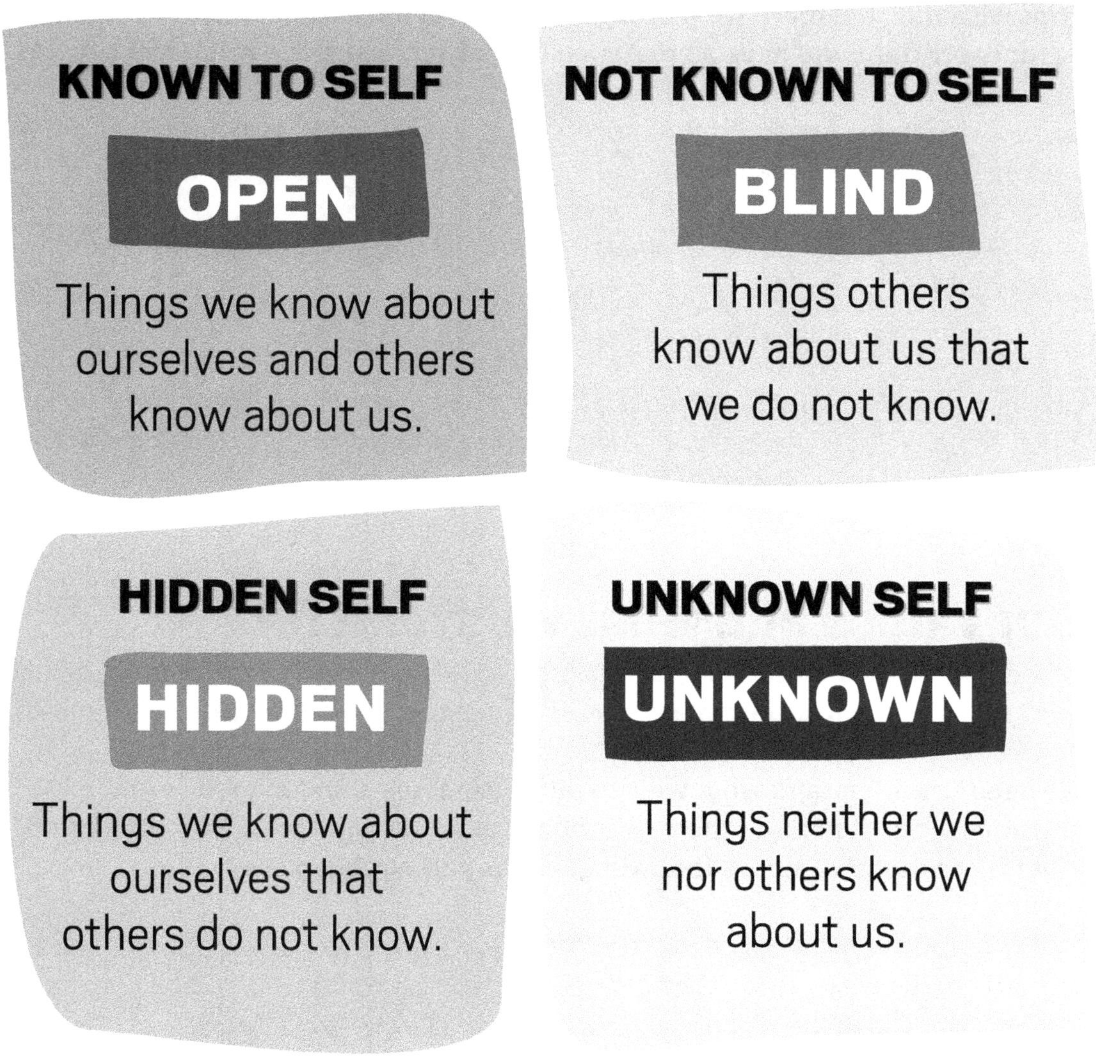

KNOWN TO SELF	**NOT KNOWN TO SELF**
OPEN Things we know about ourselves and others know about us.	**BLIND** Things others know about us that we do not know.
HIDDEN SELF	**UNKNOWN SELF**
HIDDEN Things we know about ourselves that others do not know.	**UNKNOWN** Things neither we nor others know about us.

Figure 3. The Johari Window. Luft and Harrington.

How blind are we to things others see of us? What might we be hiding from others that we know may be impacting on us? How might we learn about our unknown self for the benefit of our lives and our businesses and those who rely on us?

Self-knowledge is a lifetime journey. As we age and are exposed to different challenges and events, we learn more about ourselves. Self-knowledge is a powerful tool that all too many people disregard because it's difficult, uncomfortable or inconvenient to devote time to. The more we can come to

grips with this, the more we will enjoy working in our businesses. We will also be more efficient and have a greater chance of achieving our version of success.

So how might you speed up the process of achieving self-knowledge? After all, we don't have a lifetime to achieve this.

> 66 *Learn from the mistakes of others. You can't live long enough to make them all yourself.* 99
> — Eleanor Roosevelt

Like all attempts to be self-aware, it's about being honest with ourselves and seeking and listening to the feedback of others. We can also learn a great deal from being humble enough to realise we all have much to learn from others.

Our values and what we stand for

A fundamental part of operating in our business lives is being clear on what we do and don't stand for. What are our values, and do we behave consistently with these values?

We need to understand what we and our businesses stand for. When our customers, our staff and others hear about us, what will spring into their mind? What is the moral compass that will guide us and our business?

> 66 *The greatest help in meeting any problem with whatever courage is demanded is to know where you yourself stand. That is to have in words what you believe and are acting from.* 99
> — William Faulkner, American writer and Nobel laureate

What we and our businesses stand for is often described in our values. We observe the values of others in their actions and their behaviours not in what they have written on a wall or describe their values to be. Values are the standards or principles that have a major influence on our thinking and behaviours.

The *Oxford English Dictionary* defines "values" as:

> 66 *Principles or standards of behaviour; one's judgement of what is important in life.* 99

Every person, even the most evil people throughout history, lived by a set of values.

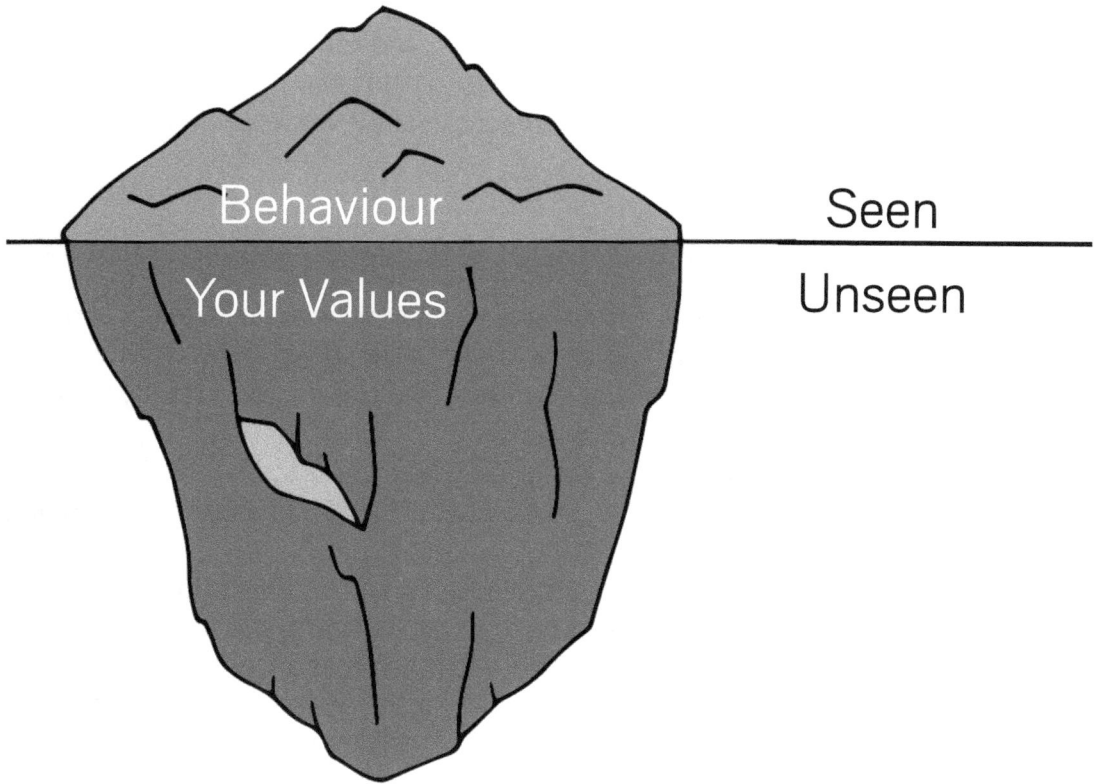

Behaviour — Seen
Your Values — Unseen

The hope is the values we have, result in actions that help the businesses we are involved in and the people impacted by these businesses.

Values are not goals. The goals of a business can change throughout the life of the business. Goals are things that are reached, completed, ticked off, and then new goals are set. These goals may or may not be consistent with our values. For example, "to be loved" is a goal, yet "to be a loving person" is a value. Goals are time-bound, whereas values are ongoing.

We could have a very wide range of values that we fall back on in different situations. Our values can evolve and change as we grow. Our values as a preschool child are likely to be different from those we would have as a parent.

What you need to do is narrow in on your *core values*. These are the three to five values that stand out from all others. They are what you will never waver from no matter the circumstance. We may not know what they are, but they exist within us, even if we have not established them yet.

Often, the times we feel at our best are the times when we are living and working in accordance with our values.

When someone has compromised his or her values, and especially if this has caused harm to others, there is a price to pay. For the person who becomes conscious of what he or she has done, it can be agony, and others can see it written on the face and in the body language of that person.[1]

The cost of forgoing our values — and ENRON

Andrew Fastow was the Chief Financial Officer who, along with Jeff Skilling and Ken Lay, led the process that saw the collapse of the US energy giant ENRON in 2001. Fastow received five years' prison, Skilling 24 years, and Lay was found guilty but died before being sentenced.

Arthur Anderson who, at that stage, was one of the biggest accounting firms in the USA, also failed as it too was complicit in the failure of ENRON because of its auditing practices.

Fastow spoke about his actions after his release from prison. He said he was given the go-ahead and cleared to do the things he did. He felt what he was doing was within the rules even though he knew it was wrong — but he did it anyway. The actions of Fastow and the other key players in ENRON's collapse cost 20,000 employees their jobs not to mention the huge financial losses to so many people.

Fastow said of his actions after his release from prison:

> *I lost my moral compass and I have done terrible things that I very much regret.*

and

> *The question I should have asked is not what is the rule, but what is the principle.*

Our moral compass is determined by a clear set of values that we hold unconditionally. Too often we can lose our way and blur what is right from wrong.

Unfortunately, forgoing our values can not only compromise the success of a business but may cause lasting internal damage for us and those dear to us.

Is it easier for small business?

A small business owner will find it much easier to define values and behaviours and enforce them than the leader of a large organisation — staff and customers will observe how the owner acts and behaves and this is the window into their values and those of their business. It is very difficult to maintain a single set of business values in a large organisation. Even the most charismatic and devout leader at the helm of a large organisation may find embedding his or her values across all levels of a large corporate to be very difficult, if not impossible.

It is much easier to define and embed values in a smaller business as they are invariably the values of the owner who has a more direct impact on all aspects of the business.

> *"Values aren't buses. They're not supposed to get you anywhere. They're supposed to define who you are."*
>
> *— Jennifer Crusie, author*

Our personality

Personality is the combination of characteristics or qualities that form our distinctive character. Parents will see their children develop very different characteristics from a very early stage that remain with them — it is their personality.

Is our personality determined by how we were brought up and the environment we grew up in or were they the result of genetics and what we inherited from our parents?

This is the basis of the **nature versus nurture** debate that has raged on for centuries and the effect these forces have on our personalities.

The over-riding current thinking is that we are who we are due to the intertwined combination of both nature and nurture.[2]

This was not always the accepted view, as highlighted by the psychologist John Watson in the 1930s:

> 66 *Give me a dozen healthy infants, well-formed, and my own specified world to bring them up in and I'll guarantee to take any one at random and train him to become any type of specialist I might select — doctor, lawyer, artist, merchant-chief and, yes, even beggar-man and thief, regardless of his talents, penchants, tendencies, abilities, vocations, and race of his ancestors.* 99
>
> — John Watson[3]

Carl Jung — psychological types and personality

Personality theories have been around for almost 100 years.

The father of the personality theories is Carl Jung, a Swiss psychiatrist who released his work *Psychological Types* in 1921.

Jung observed that when people's minds are active, they are involved in one of two mental activities. These are:

1. How they take in information (how they perceive things).
2. How they organise that information to make decisions (how they judge things).

He observed two opposite ways we can perceive things: either by using our five senses or by using our intuition. He also described the different ways we prefer to make decisions based on this information. We do this either through thinking or through feeling, i.e. using our head or our heart.

He defined the concepts of extroversion and introversion. These describe how we are energised, either from the outside world or internally. The extrovert gains energy from the people around them, from events, activities and the outside world. The introvert gains energy from being by himself or herself, reflecting on their thoughts, feelings and impressions.

> 66 *Everything that irritates us about others can lead us to a better understanding of ourselves.* 99
> — Carl Gustav Jung

Carl Jung's concepts are now regularly used in mainstream conversation when we describe other people, and have formed the basis of almost every personality profiling technique since then.

Plenty of personality tests exist

There are a wide range of tests available that you may wish to complete to gain greater insight into your personality. These tests involve answering questions that have been refined over many decades to now produce reasonably consistent results. Tests are widely used by businesses of all sizes throughout the world and may be of interest to you in better understanding how you tick. Such tests have been the source of debate within the academic and psychological community, so you need to be cautious how you interpret and use these tests. They are a guide but not a complete insight into you or the people around you.

Intelligence

What part does intelligence play in the success of a business or the prevention of business failures?

The Greek philosopher Socrates (circa 470–399 BC) believed his wisdom and intelligence came *"because I know that I know nothing"*. He felt that ultimate wisdom came from knowing yourself and the more a person knows, the greater his or her ability is to reason and make choices that will bring happiness.

Malcolm Gladwell, in his book *Outliers*,[4] discussed the success of students from minority groups who were accepted into universities even though their entry grades were much lower than their peers. Even though they were not as intellectually capable as their fellow students, their success in later life was found to be as good, if not better, than their peers.

As Gladwell described it, we don't have to be smart to be successful, we just must be smart *enough*.

The bigger challenge when discussing the intelligence required to succeed at anything, let alone business, is the conflicting views of how to measure and define intelligence.

The Frenchman Alfred Binet was commissioned in 1903 by the French government to identify students who needed special educational assistance. School had not long become compulsory in France. He developed a questionnaire that would assist in distinguishing children considered to have normal intelligence and those with learning disabilities. It was the first test developed to identify intelligence.

When the idea made its way to the USA, it created great interest beyond just that of children. Stanford University took Binet's test, refined it and developed the Stanford-Binet Intelligence Test, which delivered a single number, what we now know as the Intelligence Quotient, or IQ.

Since its development, debate over the accuracy, benefit, even relevance of IQ tests as a measure of intelligence has raged on.

Even Binet cautioned against using his scale as an absolute measure of intelligence, believing there were limitations with the scale and intelligence was far more diverse than any score could measure.

These tests try to measure general intelligence. But what is general intelligence?

Is a person brilliant on the piano more intelligent than a person expert in mathematics? An engineer versus a doctor? A highly skilled tradesman versus an artist? A business owner with no academic qualifications who has run many businesses versus an MBA graduate?

There is really no such thing as general intelligence. Each person's result in an IQ test represents a level of achievement produced by that person's collection of different talents and skills and each talent is relevant to different parts of the test. There may also be skills or talents not measured.[5]

There is a view that the variability in IQ tests is not a reflection of variability in one's IQ but the variability in one's skill at completing the test.[6]

Nowhere in my research into business failures did I find evidence that intelligence (however you decide to define it) was a factor that would have delivered business success or prevented business failure. You don't have to be really smart. You just need to be smart *enough*.

Even the smartest people get it wrong

There is no greater example of intellect failing to prevent the demise of a business than the collapse of the company Long-Term Capital Management in the USA in the late 1990s.[7]

This investment company was set up and run by people with serious credibility, credentials and expertise in financial markets. It was almost the who's who in financial markets and academia in the USA at that time.

The team included:

1. **John Meriwether** — the founder of Long-Term Capital, former head of trading at Salomon Brothers, university qualified with an MBA
2. **Myron Scholes** — PhD and professor, developed the "Black-Scholes" method for pricing share options (used worldwide) and won the Nobel prize in Economics
3. **Robert Merton** — PhD and professor, joint Nobel laureate with Myron Scholes
4. **David Mullins** — Vice Chairman of the United States Federal Reserve, with a PhD from MIT and a professor at Harvard
5. **Eric Rosenfeld** — arbitrage group at Salomon, PhD from MIT and former Harvard Business School professor
6. **William Krasker** — arbitrage group at Salomon, PhD from MIT and former Harvard Business School professor
7. **Gregory Hawkins** — arbitrage group at Salomon, PhD from MIT and worked on Bill Clinton's campaign for Arkansas

and the list went on.

So impressive was the group that it attracted serious interest from funders. On the day it started trading, in 1994, it had already raised over $US1 billion, which grew rapidly thereafter. This was mainly from large institutional funders, high-net-worth individuals and celebrities, as the minimum level of investment was set at $US10 million. When the world economic situation turned against them and they collapsed, their losses exceeded $US4.5 billion. They were deemed too big to fail and were bailed out.

Being really smart didn't prevent the failure. This loss in 1998 was substantial but nothing compared to what would follow some 10 years later when a whole market of really smart people failed to predict the collapse of the housing market and the resultant Global Financial Crisis (GFC). The combined losses from the top 10 US business failures triggered by the GFC exceeded $US1,300 billion, with Lehman Brothers topping the list with losses of over $690 billion. To give you some idea of how wrong these smart guys got it, $US1,300 billion exceeds the entire GDP of Russia.

The examples of New Zealand business failures we discuss in this book further reinforce this. The leaders of these Kiwi businesses were very smart, highly educated and experienced people. Yet they made decisions that ultimately saw the demise of their businesses.

So, having a degree, a high IQ, an MBA or worldly experience will not prevent the demise of a business nor ensure its success. We should not despair if we do not have these qualifications or academic attributes, or decades of experience. While they may help, they may also lead to arrogance and have no bearing on whether we succeed or fail in business.

Arrogance, stubbornness and the Dark Triad

We discuss the failure of several companies in this book and these are but a small sample of the many failures that have occurred in New Zealand. While it is not possible to assess with any accuracy what attributes these leaders and business owners possessed that may have contributed to the failure, it is likely that they, like all of us, are imperfect and their personal attributes contributed, in some way, to the failure.

There are attributes that as business owners and leaders we need to be wary of. They can be very dangerous in business if they go unchecked. These include arrogance and stubbornness and, to a worse degree, what is described as the Dark Triad of personalities — Machiavellianism, narcissism and psychopathy.

Arrogance and hubris

The *Cambridge Dictionary* definition of "arrogance" is:

> 66 *Unpleasantly proud and behaving as if you are more important than, or know more than, other people.* 99

Another word that came up regularly when I read about and discussed failures was hubris. When pride becomes excessive, even foolish, it is described as hubris.

> 66 *I always knew when a partner was about to get in trouble . . . it was when they started to believe their own bull***t.* 99
>
> — Duane Kullberg, the former managing partner of the failed accounting firm Arthur Andersen

Hubris is from Ancient Greek where people's self-belief passed from a human perception to feeling they were godlike. It was a character flaw often seen in the heroes of classical Greek tragedy, like Oedipus and Achilles.

These Greek heroes achieve unparalleled success, which bred overconfidence, pride and, ultimately, hubris. They felt they had become godlike and invincible. This contributed to their downfall. The familiar saying "Pride goeth before a fall" is basically talking about hubris.

Conor McElhinney is a partner of McGrathNicol, with many years in the forensic and insolvency industry. He was involved in the insolvency process for Pumpkin Patch, TOP Retail and many more. When I asked him what his thoughts were on the reasons businesses fail, from his work, he said:

> 66 *In my experience, the primary cause of business failure is hubris. Time and again we work with businesses unwilling to listen to advice, or incapable of making hard decisions, leading to substantially greater losses to stakeholders (including business owners).* 99
>
> — Conor McElhinney, McGrathNicol

I doubt there is anyone who could say they want to be around anyone who fits these descriptions. Unfortunately, it defines far too many people in business.

The business world is full of cases where owners or managers of businesses allow success and overconfidence to turn into arrogance, even hubris, often without the person even recognising it.

Arrogance can be very dangerous in any business, especially small business. If a business owner starts to think they know it all, and are unable to see fault in themselves, or no longer look to the advice of others, then they could be in very serious strife.

Stubbornness — the good and the bad

Likewise, stubbornness can also be dangerous, as the definition would highlight:

> 66 *Having or showing dogged determination not to change one's attitude or position on something especially despite good reasons to do so.* 99

Sometimes we need to stand our ground and remain steadfast in our views, especially when they relate to our core values.

Business owners and leaders need to stand their ground against naysayers. When we truly believe in the path our business is taking, we have done our research, questioned our biases and irrationalities, sought good advice, and assessed the worst-case scenarios, then we need to hold firm of the path we wish to take.

We just need to be careful it is not drifting into a situation where we are refusing to give ground when the advice we are receiving may be unpleasant but helpful, or even essential, and the stubbornness is blinding us to important feedback.

We need to be self-confident, not arrogant

Self-confidence, however, is important and very different to arrogance or stubbornness. The *Oxford* dictionary defines "self-confidence" as:

> 66 *A feeling of trust in one's abilities, qualities, and judgement.* 99

This is a very different character trait to find yourself with as a business owner than arrogance and stubbornness.

There are many business owners and business leaders who have collected many years of experience. This can be a fundamental ingredient in contributing to a business's success. This breeds self-confidence.

However, when does this self-confidence become arrogance? How might you identify arrogance — or is the essence of arrogance such that someone is blind to this limitation in their character?

Arrogance is characterised not only by having a high opinion of one's talents, which also characterises self-confidence, but that the opinion is based on false beliefs about one's skills and abilities.

Having low to moderate business skills in running a business but believing one's skills are much greater is extremely dangerous for that business.

Another perspective is that one may have high skill levels and having a high opinion of oneself is warranted. It becomes arrogance when one shifts the view to one's skills and oneself as a person, i.e. "I am better than they are".

An overinflated view of one's skills and/or oneself will lead to a business owner failing to listen to people the owner or leader feels are beneath them. They will fail to see the things they could learn from others.

The Dark Triad

Arrogance and stubbornness may well be subsets of deeper issues within the business owner or leader, which may include Machiavellianism, narcissism and psychopathy.

These are socially unacceptable personality traits but still stay within what is considered a normal range of functioning. They are often distinguished as subclinical personality disorders.[8]

Clinical personality disorders are usually those that have been diagnosed by an expert and been supported with medical supervision. People with subclinical personality disorders just go about daily life.

Sadly, a quick search of Google Scholar will show how widely studied the Dark Triad is in business and the impacts it has on business. That is, it's real and an unpleasant part of business life.

1. **Psychopathy**

   In a *New Zealand Herald* article in December 2015 titled "The Everyday Psychopath", clinical psychologist Dr Armon Tamatea, of Waikato University, described the reality that our stereotype of psychopaths from film and media may not represent the reality and is exaggerated. He states that the truth is frighteningly more ordinary. People with personality disorders may well be operating in our everyday lives, or running businesses.[9]

   Tamatea says part of the definition of mental illness is "personal distress" — such as the case with depression.

But psychopaths are set apart by the fact they tend not to suffer, even if those around them do, making them unlikely to seek help.

2. Narcissism

A more common personality disorder that does, unfortunately, describe the personality of some leaders in business is narcissism. The American Psychological Association's *Diagnostic and Statistical Manual of Mental Disorders* defines narcissism as:

"a pervasive pattern of grandiosity, need for admiration, and a lack of empathy beginning by early adulthood and present in various contexts".

It further goes on to describe narcissists as having a sense of entitlement and preoccupied with fantasies of power. They can be envious of others and, while exuding self-confidence, can have fragile self-esteems.

The name comes from Greek mythology and Narcissus who fell in love with his reflection in a pool of water.

Research has found that narcissism is an attribute of many powerful leaders.[10] Along with these negative and damaging attributes, these people do possess charisma and a grand vision and people do follow such leaders.

Like most mental disorders, narcissism exists on a scale. While statistics are inconsistent, people who fit the true definition of narcissism may be as little as 1–2% of the population. Unfortunately, they may be over-represented in leadership roles.[11, 12]

You may well know of people who fit these descriptions either fully or in part. Unfortunately, apart from psychologists expert in the field, few can assess whether someone is a narcissist. Also, narcissists are very unlikely to seek help — considering the nature of the illness, that is not a surprise.[13]

It is likely we have all worked with (or for) people who demonstrate some of these attributes.

From my years operating as a senior and executive manager in large companies, I came across, and worked for, people who showed very strong narcissistic characteristics. They were not dishonest people and were successful in business. However, they had very serious impacts on the people who worked with them and their behaviour did damage the businesses they ran.

3. **Machiavellianism**

    Machiavellianism is named after Niccolò Machiavelli, a political advisor to the Medici family in the 1500s, who wrote about some of the unsavoury behaviours creeping into business and politics at his time.

    People who demonstrate Machiavellianism are cynical, unprincipled, use interpersonal manipulation and are duplicitous.

    Such personalities mean the person is unemotional and able to detach themselves from conventional morality, making deception and manipulation an easy choice to achieve what they want.

Leave diagnosis to the experts, but . . .

We cannot, and should not, make an assessment that someone we work with fits these characteristics and label them as such. Even trained psychologists are unable to diagnose these personalities without extensive work, which is often very difficult as these people rarely submit themselves for analysis. Most don't see there are any issues in their behaviours.

However, this does not mean we should tolerate such behaviour or allow it to go on.

❝ *No one can make you feel inferior without your consent.* **❞**
— Eleanor Roosevelt

All of us should step in and act against people in businesses who demonstrate the behaviours consistent with the Dark Triad. If we are in a position of influence or power and could stop such behaviour but do not, we are as complicit as the person carrying this out.

If we allow it to continue, we are giving consent to it. It can cause immeasurable damage to us, in turn those around us, and the business.

If we are the victim of this from a person in power, it is far more difficult. Seeking help and advice is a good step. In the end if there is no one in a position to stop the behaviour, we may have no choice but to walk away from the business.

These traits hurt people and kill businesses

There is no way to know how personality flaws like arrogance, hubris, stubbornness or even borderline personality disorders contributed to business failures in New Zealand.

However, it is clear, especially in the large corporate failures, that the actions and behaviours of the leaders of these businesses contributed to the failure, no matter how those behaviours and actions are described or categorised.

I will leave you to assess if the actions of the leaders of the failed businesses I use as examples in this book showed any of these attributes. I was in no position to do so.

In large organisations, it is hoped that there will be sufficient processes in place, including the governance and oversight by boards, regulations and compliance, policies or processes, and staff support, to keep such leaders in check. It is not always easy to hold these people to account, as I can confess, having worked for such people. However, if not managed they can cause significant damage to the people who rely on them.

Unfortunately, in smaller businesses these checks and processes do not exist for owners who may demonstrate these attributes. There may be no one to challenge them, so the consequences for the small business could be significant.

SECTION 4:

WHAT WE NEED TO DO DIFFERENTLY

It's more than our irrationality we need to address

While irrationality is engrained within us all and, sadly, we will continue to repeat the same mistakes in businesses over and **over** again, there are many things we can do to manage our fallibility, our limitations, our irrationality that may prevent these events being repeated — or at least reduce their likelihood.

There are consistent patterns that continue to repeat in failures. There are characteristics that continue to arise that reflect businesses that achieve the success they seek. In turn, the absence of these characteristics contributes to failure — over and over again.

Our irrationality results in our continuing to ignore history and failing to accept the basic characteristics that make businesses successful.

The following chapters outline many of the key characteristics that were ignored or compromised in the businesses that ultimately failed.

If we accept our limitations as owners and leaders and heed the messages within these chapters, the hope is we will reduce the number of business failures, or at least reduce their impact.

12 KNOW WHY THE BUSINESS EXISTS, WHERE IT IS HEADING — ITS STRATEGY

As business owners, managers and leaders, we must make choices in our efforts to achieve the goals we seek. We must form judgements based on the information available to us, and then we must make decisions. No business can function without this.

When we discuss the wide range of business failures, we can do this with the complete clarity that comes with hindsight — we are impacted by hindsight bias. Every one of the businesses that failed, like Solid Energy, SCF and Pumpkin Patch, made choices, some of which proved fatal for the business.

In each case, they made conscious strategic choices that ultimately contributed to their failure. In each of these three cases they ventured away from the strategies that had made them successful: Solid Energy growth into non-coal-based ventures; SCF into high-risk property investments in Auckland; and with Pumpkin Patch it was growth into many other countries, most notably the USA and the UK.

Choosing the correct strategy for a business, whether a solo or a multinational, is fundamental to its success (or failure). As with all our decisions, they are impacted by our limitations.

The reason any business must have a strategy is that it has limited resources — limited time, skills, people and money. It can't do everything. It must make choices.

Strategy and too many choices

In her book *The Art of Choosing*, Sheêna Iyengar outlined her research on how people make choices and what impacts on the quality of those choices.[1]

The jam experiment

One of her simplest yet most compelling experiments was carried out in a large US-based delicatessen store. The store had outlets in several US cities and offered a huge variety of products. It offered 15 types of bottled water, 150 types of vinegar, 250 types of cheeses, 300 flavours of jam, and much more.

Such choice was one of their points of difference, of which they were very proud. This created a lot of consumer interest and attracted a lot of people to their stores. Iyengar's research set out to determine whether this level of choice translated into sales.

Iyengar instructed her team to set up a tasting stall for the jams near the storefront as people entered the store.

In the first test, there were almost 30 flavours of jam that customers could choose to sample. This large selection attracted most of the people before they entered the store. They were asked to taste as many jams as they could. They typically stopped tasting after, on average, only two jams. If they liked a jam they could go to the store shelves and buy their selection from the 300 flavours at a healthy discount.

Unfortunately, most got to the jam shelves, became confused, and debated the merits of their choice for up to 10 minutes. Less than 5% ended up buying anything.

In the second test, there were only six jams that customers could choose to taste. In this case, customers again still tasted only two jams. However, when confronted with the large selection, they were far more confident in their final choice, selecting it almost immediately. Of the customers who had to choose from six, 30% made a purchase and were also completely comfortable with that choice when interviewed later.

While the store continued with their strategy of a wide choice of products for customers because it attracted huge numbers of people, they had to assist customers in narrowing their choices to convert the browsing into sales.

This demonstrated that we love to be offered choice; in fact, we find it fascinating. However, if confronted with too much choice, we feel obliged to devote greater time to the choice, and either fail to decide because it's too hard, or are left with an uneasy feeling that we made the wrong choice, even if the choice met our needs.

> ❝ *When people are given a moderate number of options (4 to 6) rather than a large number (20 to 30), they are more likely to make a choice, are more confident*

in their decisions, and are happier with what they choose. **99**

— Sheena Iyengar, *The Art of Choosing*

Too many options — and donkeys

We are naturally reluctant to close off our options. We often hang on to too many options usually for much longer than we need to, reluctant to let them go.

A lack of choice in business is usually not our issue. The issue is selecting from the list of options, and quickly leaving behind those options that we decided to forgo — and hopefully not chastise ourselves afterward about our decision or what we gave up.

There is a fable called Buridan's Ass that attempted to highlight the challenge we face in having free will and the ability to choose.

Jean Buridan, a 14th-century French priest, scientist and philosopher, used the example of a donkey that is both thirsty and hungry to highlight how our freedom to choose can be problematic. If this donkey is placed the exact same distance between water and hay, it can't decide which to choose, as it would normally go to the nearest option. Instead, it sits helplessly where it is, and dies.

> **66** *Should two courses be judged equal, then the will cannot break the deadlock, all it can do is to suspend judgement until the circumstances change, and the right course of action is clear.* **99**
>
> — Jean Buridan

Even though this may seem a little unfair on the donkey, which I'm quite sure would have made some choice and lived on, we can relate to the underlying meaning of the quandary of being stuck between two difficult and competing options.

Our fascination with the challenge to make a choice goes back much further than Buridan. Aristotle raised a similar concept over a thousand years prior when he stated:

> **66** *A man being just as hungry as thirsty, and placed in between food and drink, must necessarily remain where he is and starve to death.* **99**
>
> — Aristotle

So, we have been aware for thousands of years that with the freedom to choose comes the frustration that we can be torn, confused, and potentially take no action at all.

In business, we will regularly face choices where we can't make the call on which option to take. We might become paralysed, procrastinate, and fail to

make any decision. This may mean we end up in a worse position than if we had just chosen something, no matter the option, and got on with things.

Every business will have an infinite selection of opportunities and paths it could take. Markets to sell in; staff to employ; products and services to develop; places to locate; priorities to pursue; systems to buy and implement.

Any business of any size will always have more choices for the future of their business than they have the resources to deliver. Every business must make choices.

The most difficult choice is when to say "NO".

Saying yes to a potential opportunity is easy. Being presented with challenges or opportunities, considering the possibilities, but then deciding not to proceed, is far more difficult.

To achieve this, every business must have a strategy to guide it.

What is business strategy?

The concept of strategy was born out of the military. The word comes from its French (*stratégie*) and Greek (*stratēgia*) origins, meaning "lead" or "generalship".

The word "strategy" became commonly used during the Napoleonic Wars. People like Carl von Clausewitz, who studied Napoleon and his strategies of war, are often credited with its use. The concept has been around for much longer if one considers Sun Tzu's 500 BC *The Art of War*. It only became common in the language of business in the 1950s and '60s.

Willie Pietersen's definition of strategy, as it relates to business, is one of the simplest and most compelling I have come across:

> 66 *What gave birth to strategy was the need to respond to two inescapable realities: the fact that we have limited resources, and the inevitability of competition.* 99
> — Willie Pietersen, Columbia University

No matter how big a business is, it will never have unlimited resources. It must make choices: firstly, what it **will do** to be successful; and even more importantly, what it **won't do**.

Every business exists to meet the needs of someone. If they don't meet these needs as well as an alternative option or a competitor, those they serve will go elsewhere.

Who is responsible for the business's strategy?

Small businesses owners often don't take a long-term view of their business; they have no strategy, no business plan, no exit or succession plan, and no long-term goals. Those running a small business need to set aside time to assess how their business is going and, more importantly, where it is heading. Far too few small businesses do this.

In larger organisations, like Solid Energy, SCF and Pumpkin Patch, the board and senior management set and oversee the business's strategy. In each case, and for different reasons, these boards and management did not do this as well as they should have.

Strategy need not be complex

Strategy need not be complex or long-winded.

Strategy should address some simple questions:

- "Why does this business exist?" (Its core purpose.)
- "Where does the business want to be in the years ahead?" (Its goals.)

While large business failures do occur, small businesses are far more likely to fail or simply disappear. Small businesses don't set aside enough time or put enough priority on their future. They lose sight of why they got into business or of external pressures that may shut them down.

While larger businesses have the resources to monitor the external world, develop and then execute strategy, it is no less critical for a small business. It could be argued that it is even more critical to a small business as they are less able to survive the external shocks that a large business can tolerate.

Why does your business exist?

The reasons each business, large or small, exists will be varied. Whether the CEO or general manager of a large corporate or the owner of a small business, we need to be very clear why the business exists.

What is its core purpose?

66 Purpose is what gives life meaning. 99

— C. H. Parkhurst, American clergyman and social reformer

A small business's purpose often overlaps with the owner's personal purpose. This might be to gain freedom, to pursue an idea they are passionate about. In big business, the leader may have to accept the purpose as part of their role. Hopefully that purpose brings meaning and aligns with the individual leader. It is even more important that the purpose the business exists resonates with the customer.

> 66 *People don't buy what you do; they buy why you do it. And what you do simply proves what you believe.* 99
> — Simon Sinek

If it's to make money, then the business is already in trouble. Money is an outcome.

Examples:

TOURISM NEW ZEALAND

👉 "100% pure New Zealand"

DISNEY

👉 "To make people happy"

XERO

👉 "To make small businesses more productive"

WORLD VISION

👉 "Our vision for every child — life in all its fullness": Our prayer for every heart — the will to make it so."

Figure 4. Examples of purpose statements of some well-known companies

Our ability to prosper in business is not just determined by what we sell. It is far more about what we believe, how our customers look upon the business, and what value it will bring them. If we are unable to establish our core purpose, it's unlikely customers will understand it either.

The long-surviving businesses

Arie de Geus, the author of the book *The Living Company*, researched why some large corporations lasted for decades, even centuries, and others did not.[2] He found many examples in family-run businesses in Japan, like Mitsubishi (founded 1870), Sumitomo (founded in 1919), and the department store Daimaru (1920).

One characteristic of all long-lived companies was that they had a very strong sense of identity. No matter how diverse they were, their employees felt part of one entity, and customers understood what the business was about.

De Geus further found that the ability to produce a return on investment to shareholders had nothing to do with longevity.

This is worth remembering for any business. If making a living or just creating a job for the owner or solely meeting shareholder needs are the only purposes for the business, it is not likely to resonate with customers, and the business is unlikely to live for long.

De Geus indicated that the longest-standing businesses were very conservative in their financing activities, especially around debt. We will discuss the impact of debt a little later, but for now remember that a strategy involving significant debt is not one to rush into lightly.

Your business goals

We discussed the concept of a business's BHAG, Big Hairy Audacious Goal, in earlier chapters. Whether the goal is humble or audacious, every successful business will have one it is pursuing. That goal might be over a short time frame, which is more common with small businesses, or one that extends over decades, even beyond the life of the decision makers, as in a very large corporation.

A critical part of a business's strategy is being clear on what the goals are for the business. Goals are targets that can be measured. They are deliverable and we can say they have been achieved or not achieved. If we have a clear view of

what our goals are, and we are clear why our business exists, we will be much better placed to assess how to make those critical business choices.

Basically, we should always ask when faced with important strategic decisions for the business:

"If I make this decision, am I acting consistently with the purpose of this business and will it get the business closer to its long-term goals?"

Once a longer-term goal is clear, the business can work back to a one-year and then even closer to, say, the next three months to define shorter-term targets and goals. This will further assist in the decisions the business makes on a day-to-day basis.

Without a longer-term goal, we will simply be drifting along as the years fly past.

In a rapidly moving world, goals will need to be reviewed and strategic shifts may be required as the years pass. This can be assessed throughout the journey as part of future strategy development and goal-setting, which are never static processes.

13 HEALTH, WELLBEING, AND THEIR IMPACT ON BUSINESS

When Allan Hubbard fell ill in the latter years of SCF's life, it was a critical time for SCF. While he had a CEO and a team of managers to run the business in his absence, this was not a situation that SCF was used to.

On his return, he was not the strong, young, healthy businessman he once was. He was unwell and a man in his 80s but still insisted on running SCF.

No one should be irreplaceable

No one knows that we are all irreplaceable better than I do. When I fell ill with depression, I was told to take three months off work, immediately — one day I was at work, the next day I was told not to return. In the eight months after I returned to work I went through an emotional roller-coaster and my performance fell well below my self-imposed high standards.

Throughout this time, the large organisation I was an executive of didn't miss a beat. Some great people stepped up and filled the hole I'd left, and the business just kept going, as though nothing had happened.

If this situation had occurred when I was at the helm of the small businesses I now run, the outcome would have been very different. It is very likely these businesses would have collapsed.

We need to take care of ourselves

Sadly, illness hits too many of us far too often. We should all spend far more time caring for our wellbeing, both physical and mental.

From the long list of liquidations I reviewed, there were many situations where the reports indicated that the ill health of the owner played a key part in causing the business to slide into liquidation.

The tragic outcome of ill health of a business owner is not only the difficulty it causes for the business, but the emotional and financial pressure it will put on the family.

Many business owners, especially younger people, or those who have never had health issues can be impacted by an **optimism bias** — the view that *"it will never happen to me"*.

Too often, when discussing how best to run a business, we spend little or no time on our wellbeing as business owners or business leaders. We need to consider if we are sleeping well, managing our time with loved ones, managing stress, considering what makes us happy, and looking to build our resilience.

Many people are on ACC claims

The Accident Compensation Corporation (ACC) provided me with information on the number of self-employed people with active claims, to give some indication of the impact of health on small businesses.

Their data showed that from 2011 to 2015 there were, on average, almost 33,000 self-employed people on some form of claim in any year. This cost on average $66 million per year.[1]

This is only part of the picture. There are many self-employed people on private benefits or income protection plans and many people suffer ill health and don't report it — they just tough it out.

We all get sick and when small business owners get sick it can seriously impact, even destroy, their businesses.

Therefore, we cannot discuss business failures and, therefore, how to achieve success in business, without discussing how we can better look after ourselves.

A few sad examples

From the review of over 1000 liquidations, these are some examples of the real stories where the reason given for the liquidation of the business was failure due to the health of the owner.

1. **DUTCH HOMES LIMITED.** The director advised that the reason for insolvency was due to cash flow difficulties with slow/non-paying debtors and the illness of the director. Total losses were $915,000.

2. **KIWI PANEL & PAINT LIMITED.** The sole shareholder and director, who was principally engaged in operating the business, had a stroke and was partly paralysed on his left side. He also had a hernia surgery. The company director claimed that the company got into financial difficulty due to his ill health. Total losses were $153,000.

3. **RAUMATI PROPERTY HOLDINGS MANAGEMENT LIMITED.** Receivership was instigated by the ANZ Bank. The owner's health declined, and he couldn't operate further. The properties were sold. Total losses were $1,590,000.

4. **GRTNZ LIMITED.** The director and sole shareholder had health problems. On top of this were falling sales, which put a strain on cash flow and added to the stress. Because of the cash flow problems, the company could not purchase enough stock to ensure that budgeted sales could be achieved. The business was liquidated. Total losses were $423,000.

5. **MACSON TRADING LIMITED.** The company operated a specialty grocery store in a mall. An illness in the family overseas put considerable financial strain on the business. Concerned with the position of the company with respect to its debts, the shareholder tried selling the business but was unable to find a buyer. So, the shareholder placed the company into liquidation. Total losses were $8,500.

6. **HIGHBROOK TRUCK & VEHICLE WASH LIMITED.** One of its largest clients was placed into receivership. While the director attempted to mitigate this loss, his personal health prevented his ability to do so. The business began to experience cash flow issues, which ultimately led to the sale of the business. Total losses were $65,000.

So, what to do?

At the risk of being flippant, the best way to avoid a business getting into trouble due to poor health is for the people involved to look after themselves better.

We are irrational. We do dumb things. We do the things that aren't good for us, even though we fully accept we shouldn't do them. We work too hard and too long. We get stressed. We don't sleep well enough. We exercise too little, eat too much and eat the wrong things and we probably drink more than we should. We are all bombarded with these messages daily. The irrational part of all this is that we know what we should do but we don't do it.

It is not my intention to write a book lecturing you on diet or exercise and your wellbeing. However, it would be remiss of me if I didn't cover some of the things we should all do to assist in staying well, enjoying our work and hopefully helping us succeed at our business ventures.

Sleep

We are a society that has become very sleep-deprived. There is a range of scientific views on why the body needs sleep. Russell Foster, Oxford professor and sleep specialist, states that sleep has a vital role in restoration, energy conservation and, most importantly, consolidation of memories and boosting of creativity, areas which are busier when we sleep. Our ability to be more creative and come up with new ideas is enhanced after we have slept compared with when we are tired.

> 66 *Sleep is for wimps.* 99
> — Margaret Thatcher

> 66 *Sleep is a criminal waste of time and a heritage from our cave days.* 99
> — Thomas Edison

Unfortunately, there is an almost perverse view and bravado from people like Thomas Edison and Margaret Thatcher that surviving on little sleep shows great strength. It would seem these people succeeded on very little sleep. Even if that was the case for them, the scientific evidence very clearly disputes this view for most of us.

Sleep is not an indulgence. It is critical for our ability to function, our mental wellbeing and our management of stress. The more tired we are, the more stressed we get.

Harvard and Berkeley universities carried out a study in 2007 in which two groups were tested over a two-day period, one with and one without sleep, using fMRI (functional Magnetic Resonance Imaging) scans to see the impact on the brain. The results showed that sleep deprivation affects our emotional state, can make us more irrational (than we already are), and leads to poor decision making.

A lack of sleep will directly affect our performance in business. It's very closely correlated to the same fall in performance we get with alcohol consumption. This was proven in studies almost 20 years ago at the Centre for Sleep Research in Australia.

So how much sleep is enough sleep? The Centre for Sleep Research in Australia states that there are individual differences in each of our responses to sleep loss. It may even be genetic. However, if sleep is restricted to fewer than seven hours per night, the Centre for Sleep Research believes this will impact function for over 80% of us. Unless we are confident that genetics puts us in the 20% group, we should aim for seven or more hours sleep every night.

What is critical is that we listen to our bodies. It is likely we will know when we are getting insufficient sleep, whether that's seven or more hours per night. If we have the luxury, we should try to go to sleep when we are tired and not wake up to an alarm clock but when our body allows us to wake up. Over time we will start to establish what sleep we need. Unfortunately, with early starts at work, allowing for traffic, getting kids to school, and more, this is a luxury for most of us.

Stress

The World Health Organization (WHO) defines stress relating to our work environment as:

> 66*The response we may have when presented with work demands and pressures that are not matched to our knowledge and abilities, and that challenges our ability to cope.*99[2]

Pressure in business will be unavoidable. This pressure may keep us alert, motivated, able to work and learn, and lift our performance, depending on our available resources and personal characteristics. However, if that pressure becomes excessive or otherwise unmanageable, it may lead to stress.

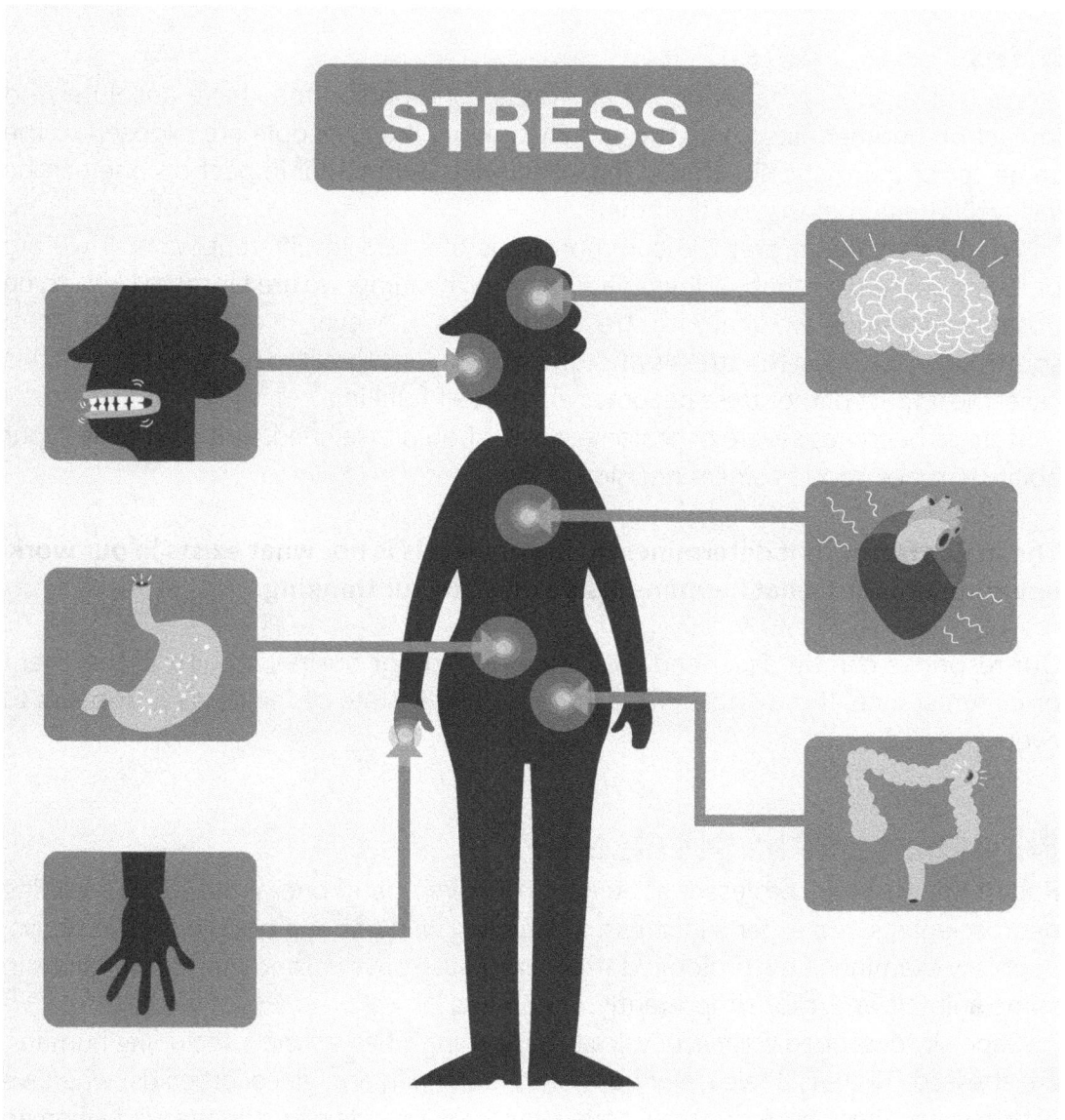

Prolonged and severe stress can damage our health, relationships and the performance of our business. Yet, the right amount of stress is quite stimulating. We experience this with those events that we're sometimes crazy enough to do, like bungy jumping, parachuting, or a roller-coaster ride. I'm sure we can think of similar situations in our business life that gave us this same buzz. In these cases, the stress is transient, or we may frame the stress in a positive way.

Stress — it's personal

Stress is a very personal thing. What stresses one person may have absolutely no impact on another faced with the same situation. If two people are exposed to the same set of traumatic situations, the emotional and mental impact on one can be vastly different from that on the other.

We may each interpret the common signs of stress in different ways. If we are pursuing something that we love that brings us meaning, we are far more likely to be positive about how we deal with stress symptoms. However, in other circumstances, some of us look upon the stress symptoms as a serious threat to our wellbeing. In this case, the impact of the stress becomes almost self-fulfilling.

If stress becomes severe or prolonged, you should take heed, as it diminishes your ability to make good business decisions.

The major factor that determines our stress levels is not what exists in our work environment, but what happens inside of us, in our thinking.

Our response can be described as a state of mind or our perception of the event or circumstance. It may not reflect in any way the state of reality as it appears to everyone else.

Why don't zebras get ulcers?

Robert Sapolsky is a professor at Stanford University, and one of the world's leading neuroscientists and experts in stress. In studying wild baboon populations in Kenya, Sapolsky examined how prolonged stress can cause physical and mental afflictions in some animals and, more importantly, in humans.

Sapolsky described what is physically happening when animals, including humans, are stressed. There is a release of hormones (adrenalin and glucocorticoids) when we get stressed. These hormones can have a range of impacts on us. In the wild when an animal is faced with real stress (that is, being eaten), its attention is focused entirely on survival. In his book *Why Zebras Don't Get Ulcers*,[3] Sapolsky discussed his view that animals such as zebras stress for short periods of time, then recover back to their normal state almost immediately (after running away from a lion). However, in more advanced animal structures, like baboons, where there is a natural pecking order in the group and the animals have too much time on their hands, they can suffer ongoing levels of stress.

Sapolsky speaks of the stress humans suffer, which is often created from our own interpretation of reality. He calls it ***psychological stress,*** or stress that is the invention of our minds, which may not come from a genuine threat.

Stress is irrational — but real

Often, our stress responses seem, and in most cases probably are, very irrational. Not only do we get stressed during actual events, but we also get stressed about the possibility that we *may be* confronted by events — however unlikely.

We spend a lot of our time ruminating about what we did or didn't do in the past and we worry about what might befall us in the future. Humans face severe and prolonged stress caused by psychological or social factors that in no way pose any actual threat to our lives, as would be the case in the wild.

We worry about future possibilities, whether real or imagined (e.g. "My business might fail" or "I might stuff up badly"). This is where the power of our mind overwhelms rational thought. We all know we can't change the past; we can only learn from it. We also know that we can't predict the future and have only a very limited ability to affect it. Yet we expend huge amounts of energy thinking about it anyway.

Robert Sapolsky believes we have evolved to be intelligent enough to make ourselves sick with stress. The most control we have is usually only what we are doing in the exact moment we are doing it. As we use up mental energy ruminating or worrying, we miss what's in front of us. In our business, that could be a solution, an idea, a chance to help a customer or employee, or just enjoying the moment for no other reason than we are alive, well and doing what we love.

How can we better manage stress?

Knowing what we now know about stress, how might we better manage stress as we work in our business? The key to this is resilience. No single 'cure' is applicable when it comes to stress. Stress management is a whole-of-life issue and needs to be approached holistically. Stress is also a very individual experience, stemming from past learning, genetics, personality, temperament, our social standing, and our environment. As a result, quick fixes are hard to find.

There are a few simple things that will help manage short term stress while you chip away at longer-term solutions to problems while building up resilience. We discuss resilience shortly.

Firstly, we must start by accepting that we will get stressed. Rather than considering it to be a weakness, we need to spend time becoming comfortable with the idea it will happen and understanding it. We may then be in a better position to manage it.

Here are some questions to reflect upon in times when we feel stressed:

- Do you recognise when you are stressed?
- How do you feel when you are stressed?
- What triggered that episode of stress?

If the stress comes and goes and we can recognise it, there are some important steps to take to manage it in the short term.

We need to breathe.

We need to stop and take note of the things around us. Take some slow, deep breaths and exhale. We need to refocus our minds back to the present moment. These steps can alleviate short-term stressors.

Happiness

> 66 *We hold these truths to be self-evident, that all men are created equal, that they are endowed by their Creator with certain unalienable Rights, that among these are Life, Liberty and the pursuit of Happiness.* 99
> — from the Declaration of Independence, Thomas Jefferson

The pursuit of happiness would seem a lofty goal for any business. However, if our time in business is not contributing to our happiness, then we may question why we are doing it. It is also unlikely for the business to reach its potential if we are not enjoying it.

Thomas Jefferson stated that happiness is an 'unalienable right', but it is by no means guaranteed. Achieving happiness through our business (and life) is a process, a journey or a 'pursuit', not a goal or set of goals to be sought out and then ticked off as they are achieved.

What is happiness?

So, what is it to be 'happy'? How might we achieve greater happiness as the owner, leading or working in a business?

The *Oxford English Dictionary* defines "happy" as:

> **66** *Feeling or showing pleasure or contentment.* **99**

To me, this seems a rather superficial definition of happiness.

Russ Harris, in his book *The Happiness Trap*, has a much more appropriate definition of happiness:

> **66** *To live a rich, full, and meaningful life.* **99**[4]

Happiness is not a continual state of contentment or feeling good. That is simply an unrealistic situation. In life and business, we will meet challenges; we will suffer inevitable hardships, self-doubt, and grief that business and life can throw at us. We are vulnerable to a fear of shame, failure, rejection or loss.

Those who accept this vulnerability as a normal part of a rich and meaningful life are more likely to be happier in their business and take the risks that may be required.

We can blame our parents — to a point

There is evidence that happiness is influenced by genetics.[5] There have been many studies carried out on identical and fraternal twins. These studies showed that twins reported similar levels of happiness even when they had lived through very different life experiences. These studies indicate that no matter what the circumstances, we are born with a happiness baseline that originates from our parents. Therefore, some of us will find happiness comes more naturally than it does for others. Genetics is only part of the story. There is a great deal more that will contribute to our happiness.

In her book *The How of Happiness*, Sonja Lyubomirsky states that about 50% of our happiness baseline is determined by genetics with only 10% determined by differences in life experiences and circumstances. The remaining 40% comes from our intentional behaviours. Therefore, the key to our happiness is not necessarily in changing our circumstances, nor our genetic make-up (which is beyond our control), but in the intentional day-to-day choices we make and actions we take.

It's about our attitude

Leading a truly rich life is more about the attitudes within us than the circumstances around us. If the circumstances surrounding our business are making us miserable, changing them may help. Yet, that alone may not be enough. We may need to look to our attitude toward the business.

We all know what the elation of a personal or business success feels like, just as we know the feeling of bitter disappointment. The danger of seeking the continual highs is that it is unsustainable, and we will almost always fall back to a baseline of happiness that defines us. We don't want to find ourselves on a happiness treadmill.

Our happiness baseline

When a joyous or pleasurable event occurs, our happiness goes up for a short period, but soon returns to a baseline.[6] Likewise, if we are faced with a traumatic event, we will feel unhappy, but again, with time, we will return to that same baseline. There can be circumstances where a traumatic event is of such significance that when we do return from the trauma, our baseline is at a lower level of happiness than before the event.

The challenge is to build our resilience so we can reduce the number, the depth and the duration of these drops. Most importantly, if a severe event occurs, we can get back on our feet and move on in our business lives.

Resilience should also help us lift our happiness baseline over time. While some of us are wired genetically to be a little happier and more optimistic than others, we can all build our resilience and with it, our ability to live a little happier than we otherwise would.

Our discussions on how our brains work highlighted that we are wired to take the easiest mental path. Changing how we behave and approach issues will not come easily and takes a lot of energy. So, we need to be kind with ourselves.

To achieve greater resilience, we need to take small, measured steps. Be selective on the changes we can realistically make. We should reward ourselves for small gains and not set ourselves up to fail by attempting too many changes at once.

Building resilience

Building resilience is a life journey and involves doing a lot of small things better. The factors that can build our inner strength, to help raise our happiness baseline, and put us in a much better position to manage our business include the following.[7]

1. **Relationships**

   Relationships are vital to our fulfilment and happiness. People who have one or more close friendships are normally happier.

We don't just need relationships; we need close relationships. It's not about the quantity of social relationships. Lots of Facebook friends will not bring greater happiness. It's about quality, open, caring, and candid relationships.

During the times we face significant pressures in our business, we often put our key relationships on hold thinking that we don't have the time to devote to them.

2. Caring for others

Most people who care for others in a selfless manner do so because of a genuine desire to help and improve the world around them. Whether this is volunteer work or simply giving a little extra, the act of caring for others will bring rewards for us.

A study by the University of Exeter Medical School in the UK compared the physical and mental health of a large group of people who volunteered with a group that did no volunteering. The results showed that the volunteers had fewer instances of depression, greater life satisfaction and a longer life expectancy.[8]

In their research and book *Happy Money*, Elizabeth Dunn and Michael Norton showed that the more money people could give away to others, the happier they became.[9]

3. Exercise and diet

It goes without saying that you are healthier and feel better when you look after your body physically. Healthier people are happier people. There are people far more qualified than me to explain how you might go about this. Simply put, we know it to be true; it's just putting priority on it.

4. Meaningful work and meaningful goals

Viktor Frankl, in his book *Man's Search for Meaning* about his time in a Jewish concentration camp, put forward a simple but very powerful message. A person can survive almost any situation if they can find meaning in what they do. While we will never see anything as extreme as Frankl experienced, it highlights the importance of finding greater meaning in our business lives.

> **❝** *Everything can be taken from a man but one thing: the last of the human freedoms — to choose one's attitude in any given set of circumstances, to choose one's own way.* **❞**
> — Viktor E. Frankl[10]

5. **Staying present — being in the moment**

   We have discussed how we might manage stress and those paralysing thoughts by pausing and refocusing on the present. This is known as being mindful which will also help build our resilience.

   For those of us who have done meditation, or some form of yoga, we will have a strong understanding of the concept of being mindful. However, these pastimes are not everyone's cup of tea.

   If we don't have the desire, time or inclination to meditate, then at least breathe. Nothing assists us more in becoming mindful than breathing.

   When we find our minds drifting, or being consumed with negative thoughts, a simple technique is to pause, and take five slow, deep breaths, focusing on exhaling. While doing this, focus on each breath. The oxygen this brings into our bodies, and the focus our minds has on those breaths, will, hopefully, refocus our minds on what is in front of us.

My brutal lesson — and advice

I guess as a person who can relate to the price we can pay for not caring for ourselves, I am able to speak with some authority on the topic of caring for our wellbeing. While the business I was the manager of kept going without a hitch, my poor mental health stopped me in my tracks. I was lucky. I was insured, had some money behind me and was at a stage in my life where I was free from major debt.

Had this event occurred when I was a small business owner, had I been uninsured, with a young family and debts to manage, the outcome could have been catastrophic.

So PLEASE take care of yourself!

14 CONTROLLING THE CONTROLLABLE, RISK, UNCERTAINTY AND LUCK

While I have placed the greatest responsibility for business failures at the feet of its leaders and owners, we cannot ignore the reality that businesses operate in an uncertain world that involves risks, and luck.

> 66 *If no one ever took risks, Michelangelo would have painted the Sistine floor.* 99
> — Neil Simon

We have already discussed in the early stages of our journey in this book that achieving success in our business, no matter how we define it, involves taking risks. The extent, size and consequences of the risk each of us takes will depend on our appetite for risk.

Let's spend a little time understanding the concept of risk, as it is not as clear a concept as we might think.

What is risk?

The *Oxford* dictionary defines "risk" as:

> 66 *A situation involving exposure to danger.*
> *The possibility that something unpleasant or unwelcome will happen.* 99

The *Oxford* dictionary defines "uncertain" as:

> ❝ *Not able to be relied on; not known or definite.*
> *Not completely confident or sure of something.* ❞

The reason risk exists is because we cannot predict the future. While our pre-frontal cortex allows us to develop possible future scenarios in our minds and play out possibilities before we embark on a path, this will never provide the certainty we might seek.

Accompanying this uncertainty in business is the consequences of different futures eventuating. If things go to plan, that is great — our view of the future came to pass. However, other outcomes, more positive than expected or much worse than expected, could also eventuate.

Our challenge in business is to make efforts to consider the level of uncertainty, the consequences if we are wrong, and the likelihood of different futures occurring. While we can never predict the future with certainty, we can consider what scenarios might eventuate and what we might do in each of these circumstances.

Already we have discussed Solid Energy's mistaken view of future coal prices and what SCF's underestimation, like the whole finance sector, of a collapse in property prices might do. We also discussed Pumpkin Patch's liquidation after its failed moves into the USA and the UK. In New Zealand one of our biggest industries, dairy, is impacted by two things over which it has almost no control — the weather and world milk solid prices.

Large organisations and boards devote significant time and effort to identifying and then managing risks. It has become accepted best practice on the boards of New Zealand businesses — assuming those boards follow best practice.

Boards must manage risks

Deloitte discusses the role of boards in managing risk as follows:

> ❝ *An effective risk oversight process helps the board determine that the organisation has a system in place for identifying, evaluating, prioritising, managing, and adapting to critical risks.* ❞ [1]

Most boards follow defined standards that are widely used and applied in boards across the country.

Such processes assist in guiding boards and large organisations in identifying and managing risks. Some may say these processes tie businesses down and kill innovation. Having developed such processes and worked under them for many years, I can say there is some truth in that. They can become very bureaucratic if driven by evangelistic risk managers.

However, they force individuals to stay within some framework, which assists in removing dangerous, gut decisions or the impulsive decisions of misguided business leaders.

What about small business risks?

Unfortunately, it is impractical and excessive for a smaller business to go to the same level of detail of identifying all the risks as a large business.

However, small businesses face significant risks from, potentially, a wide variety of factors they have little control over. Small business owners need to pause and consider the risks that could seriously hurt them.

Typical risks that led to many of the small business owners I reviewed included:

- the loss of a major client
- poorly managed growth
- the loss of a major contract
- loss of key staff
- health of the owners
- changes in external market conditions, especially the property market
- failure of a large client to pay
- disputes between shareholders or partners
- marriage break-ups

and more.

No one, even those using the most sophisticated risk management process, can predict the future. We will be wrong most of the time and when we are right it might well have been luck, which we will discuss shortly.

We can, however, consider credible events that could seriously damage or end our businesses, and do what we can to reduce those risks.

Sticking our heads in the sand and hoping everything will work out is not a particularly effective risk management strategy — unfortunately it is a little too

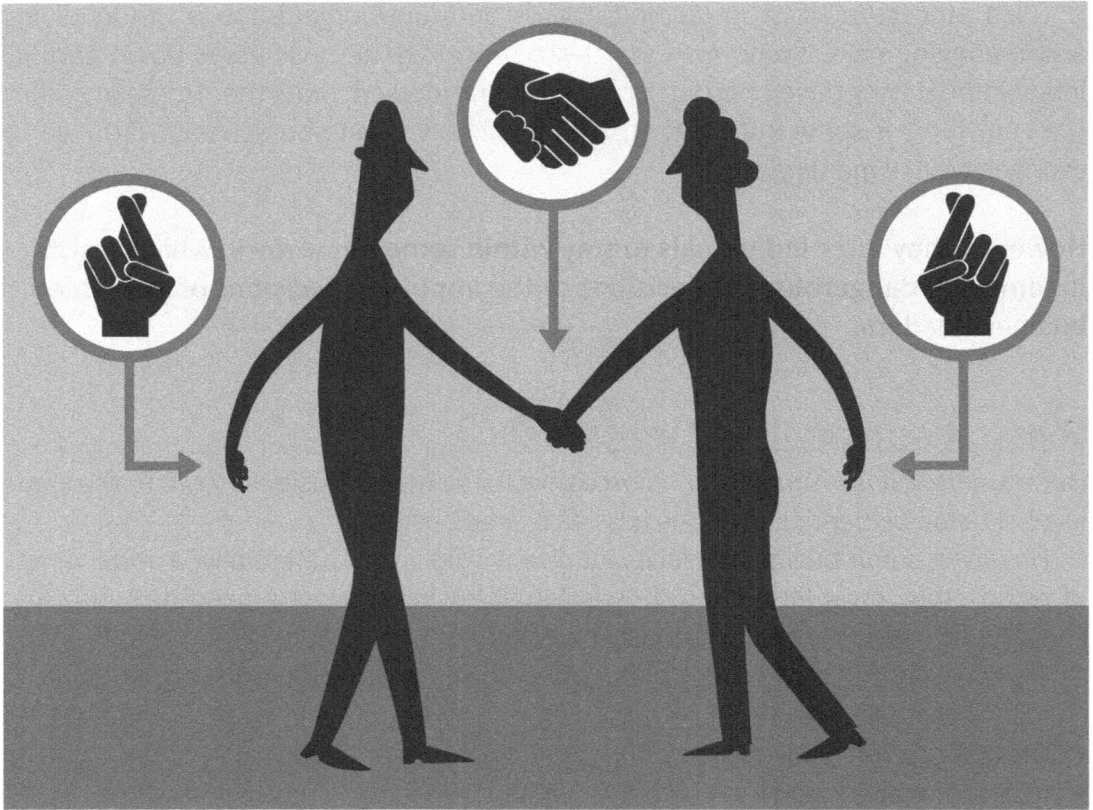

common, especially in small business.

What part does luck play in business?

What part does luck play in the success or failure of businesses?

> 66 *I'd rather have a lucky general than a smart general. They win battles.* 99
> — Dwight D. Eisenhower

> 66 *Eighty percent of success is showing up.* 99
> — Woody Allen

The *Oxford* dictionary defines "luck" as:

❝ *Success or failure apparently brought by chance rather than through one's own actions.* ❞

An even more thought-provoking definition from Michael Mauboussin's book *The Success Equation*, as it relates to business, is:

❝ *Luck is a chance occurrence that affects a person or a group (e.g. a sports team or a company). Luck can be good or bad. Furthermore, if it is reasonable to assume that another outcome was possible, then a certain amount of luck is involved. In this sense, luck is out of one's control and unpredictable. Luck is a residual: it's what is left over after you've subtracted skill from an outcome.* ❞

— Michael Mauboussin[2]

Right place, right time?

Malcolm Gladwell in his book *Outliers* challenged the rags-to-riches stories of people like Bill Gates, Steve Jobs and the oil and steel magnates like John D. Rockefeller. He argues that when they were born, the specific family circumstances they were born into and the environment they grew up in were something over which they had no control but which directly contributed to the success they became famous for.[3]

Gladwell argued that the lore of success too often dwells on an individual's personal qualities, focusing on how grit and talent paved the way to the top.

There is no question these business people grasped the opportunities they had and used their skills, passion and dedication to turn that luck into the success they sought. However, luck played a part in their success, which we need to consider.

Around half of the top 12 richest men in US history were all born within the 10-year period from 1830 to 1840. This made them well placed to be at their peak at the time the Industrial Revolution, the growth in railways and the oil boom hit the USA, after starting in the United Kingdom. Had they been born in the period that saw them peak coming into the Great Depression and World War II, perhaps we may never have heard of names like J. P. Morgan, John D. Rockefeller and Andrew Carnegie.

It's unlucky being a woman

Another lucky break for business people born in this era was that they were born male. No woman appears in the rich lists during this era. In fact, in the book *100 Richest People in World History*, only three women appear in the list — Cleopatra, Elizabeth I and Queen Elizabeth. There is likely to be a whole range of social reasons we could point to that would have prevented women achieving the same success in business as their male counterparts through history.[4]

Unfortunately, it would also seem that even in our current business world, if your goal is to reach the Forbes rich list, it's better to be born male. In the period from 2001 to 2016, only three women appeared in the Forbes top 10 rich list in any of those 17 years. These were Alice and Helen Walton from Walmart wealth and Liliane Bettencourt from the L'Oréal family.

It would be foolhardy, even insulting, to assume that only men have had the prerequisite skills, aptitude and drive to achieve success in business through history. Sadly, it would seem the business playing field has been far from equal throughout history when considering gender.

We are not always in control

Experience, skill and knowledge will always play the significant part in setting the best future path for our business. However, if past successes are assumed to be entirely of our own making, are accompanied by misguided overconfidence, or even arrogance, we could form our own **halo effect** — we could start to believe we are infallible. This may not end well the next time, if there was any element of luck in those past successes.

We often look at business people who predicted market movements or saw very risky decisions pay off and hail them as astute, insightful business people. We also usually chastise those who got it wrong. Luck is boring as the driving force in a story. We want to apportion the event to the efforts or actions of someone.

We can all be guilty of assuming we were clever when we look back on an event that went well in our business, knowing what we now know. Likewise, we often chastise ourselves for getting things so wrong, again, with the luxury of hindsight.

Many CEOs are kidding themselves

Daniel Kahneman challenges the notion that we have the level of control over our businesses that we would like to think. He believes it is an illusion that if we have understood the past, it somehow assumes we can predict and control the future. He believes these illusions are comforting but are just that — illusions.

Kahneman challenged the level of control senior executives had in the success of their business. He challenged the extent to which business leaders and their

management practices influenced the outcomes of their business. His research indicated that they certainly do, but the effects are much smaller than a reading of the business press would suggest. He found that there is only a very loose correlation between a company's success and the CEO who leads it.

As Kahneman so eloquently puts it:

> 66 *It is difficult to imagine people lining up at airport bookstores to buy a book that enthusiastically describes the practices of business leaders who, on average, do somewhat better than chance. Consumers have a hunger for a clear message about the determinants of success and failure in business, and they need stories that offer a sense of understanding, however illusory. There is a fine line between enlightened business leaders who get it right all the time and those who had an element of luck on their side.* 99[5]

Hindsight is 20/20

This is where **hindsight bias** can trap us. We can look back on past events with absolute clarity. There is no uncertainty. We can judge and question why. Hindsight is a great thing.

Hindsight is a luxury I had in writing this book. I have been able to assess the reasons for business failures with the complete clarity of hindsight. I have had to continually question myself: *"What might I have done if I were in these people's shoes when they made the decisions they did?"*

A decision or prediction looks much more obvious after it has occurred than before it happened when the outcome was a complete unknown. When things go well, we want to praise those who delivered this, and when things go wrong, find someone to blame. We do this with the benefit of hindsight. A healthy dose of luck, good or bad, could have been involved.

We want to feel like we are in control of our destinies. We admire those who have succeeded.

However, there were many business owners just as smart, with just as good an idea, who worked just as hard, and followed all the same principles, yet did not share in the same success.

One can't ignore that luck may have played a part — being in the right place, at the right time.

Luck does run out — skill does not

It is also an insult to look at a business that has exceeded all expectations and simply say *"They were lucky"*.

In examining a business's success, we need to focus on the things that they could truly control that we can replicate and be realistic about the aspects that may have been luck or out of their control.

We can never replace skill, experience, hard work and good decisions. Just be careful not to apportion all our successes solely to our skill or our failures to a lack of skill. Keep some perspective. We should stop and ask, *"Hey, was there an element of luck in that?"* If the answer is *"Yes"*, ask what happens if the luck runs out next time around.

> **❝** *To be successful, you have to be out there; you have to hit the ground running. And if you have a good team around you — and more than a fair share of luck — you might make something happen.* **❞**
>
> — Sir Richard Branson, in his autobiography, *Losing My Virginity*[6]

Regression to the mean

Daniel Kahneman, from his time assisting the Israeli Air Force, debated with the commander about his practice of chastising the cadet pilots when they performed badly. He also questioned why the commander never acknowledged them when they performed exceptionally well. The basis for the commander's view was that when he praised the pilots for exceptional performance, they would typically follow up with a lesser effort, yet when he berated them, their next effort was much better.

Kahneman argued that the reason for this was simply the pilot's performance returning closer to their normal levels of performance — when they had a really bad day, chances were this would not continue for long before they returned to their average performance. When they had an exceptional day, chances are it wouldn't last, and they would fall back to a more normal level of performance.

This normal level of performance is the *"mean"* or average level of performance and we will typically operate either side of the mean, regressing back to that mean over time. If we continue to practise, build our skills and experience, this *"mean"* will slowly lift over time, but from day to day we are likely to oscillate

around the mean.

The shifts away from our mean are likely to have elements of luck — good or bad.

A professional golfer has those days where every ball drops and the next day nothing goes well. The skill of the golfer should keep them near their handicap, but some days, good or bad luck will push that player away from this. A significant focus on practice and increased skill and fitness will see the handicap improve but this takes time, as the body and brain must adapt over time. Other examples of this are the **"Sports Illustrated *Cover Jinx*"** and the **"Hot Hand Fallacy"**.

Sports people who found their way onto the cover of *Sports Illustrated* following a standout year often followed up with a much worse year — one should not blame *Sports Illustrated* for this but the regression to the mean — the year they made the cover was exceptional and unlikely to be sustainable.

Many basketball announcers, seeing a player sink a string of three-pointers, say the player is on a *"Hot Hand"* and can't miss. Research into this by Amos Tversky and Thomas Gilovich found that each new event had very little relationship with the previous successes. While there is clearly a better chance of sinking the ball if we are an elite basketballer than the randomness of a coin toss, one should be cautious about predicting success based on recent baskets.

Scenario planning — a technique to contemplate the future

In 1967, Ted Newland and Jimmy Davidson were asked by their employer, Shell, to start what was later called the "futures" operation or the "Year 2000" study. This was the birth of scenario planning. Shell has continued to use the process for half a century and it assisted in developing a scenario that played out, for example, in the 1970s oil crisis.

Rather than predicting a single future, scenario planning assumes that all predictions of the future are, to some extent, wrong. Instead of one view of the future, it considers several credible future scenarios. This will typically include a best and worst case, and the most likely scenario based on what is known now.

The best- and worst-case scenarios are where business owners need to force themselves to go and to consider, no matter how unappealing. That is, what external scenarios both very good and extremely bad could feasibly occur, and what might happen to this business if they eventuated?

Control the controllable . . .
and ask, *"What if?"*

> ❝ *God grant me the serenity*
> *To accept the things, I cannot change;*
> *Courage to change the things I can;*
> *And wisdom to know the difference.* ❞
>
> — Serenity Prayer, Alcoholics Anonymous

We can make the mistake when things aren't going as we would like of apportioning blame elsewhere (see our previous discussion on attribution error) or worse still, directing blame, even self-loathing, on ourselves, when we should be looking to others to also be held accountable.

We can also be guilty of getting frustrated by the decisions of others, events, or activities that are external to our business and may (or may not) be affecting us. These may be the activities of competitors, the decisions of politicians or councils, world prices, inflation, employment or other economic measures.

If the issues are critical enough to warrant our time influencing them, then we should do what we can to sway things more our way through submissions, lobbying, or discussions with our business association, local councillor or member of Parliament.

However, in most cases, businesses, especially small businesses, will not have the time or resources to do anything more than accept these external issues and get on with running their business. Basically, we must look at controlling what we can control.

This is often called our **locus of control**. This is the degree to which people believe they have control over the outcome of events in their lives, as opposed to external forces that are beyond their control.

Some of us have a strong sense of our locus of control, looking to act on what we can control and accepting accountability for what we can do. Others are inclined to take on some level of a victim mentality, apportioning issues impacting them on the actions of others. The former people have a strong **internal locus of control**. The latter have a stronger **external locus of control**.

This is a part of knowing ourselves.

If we have a very strong internal locus of control, we will take responsibility

for our actions, apportion our successes to our own efforts, and avoid blaming others or external events. The caution here is that some of these events may be someone else's fault, not ours, and we can take on the responsibility that rests with others. It is a fine balance at times.

If we have a stronger external locus of control, we will find it tougher to take accountability for things that we could control and may lose opportunities while apportioning blame elsewhere.

There is no clearer example of where attribution error and an external locus of control is borne out than in the explanation of failures of business. As you will have picked up throughout our discussions, if a business fails, we should look to the owners and decisions makers.

Very few of the thousand liquidations I reviewed saw the owner stand up and say *"Yes, I got it wrong."* They may well acknowledge it privately, and it is very likely they are hurting very deeply from what they did or didn't do, but rarely do they publicly attribute the business failures to themselves.

If you were lucky, enjoy it — don't rely on it

When we assess past business events, or ponder future options, we should assess the risk, control what we can control, but acknowledge that what transpires may not always be due to our insight, hard work or experience.

There may have been an element of luck in a past event or luck could impact future events. That doesn't mean we don't continue to work hard and work smart. It just means accepting that both the good and bad outcomes may not have even been influenced by anything we did.

Next time, the circumstances may be different. You may not be so lucky (or unlucky).

As this chapter has discussed, the business world involves uncertainty. We will face risks and there will be times when things go well or go poorly that could be due to nothing other than luck (good or bad).

If we become paralysed with fear from uncertainty, then we are very unlikely to achieve the success we seek from our businesses.

There are a few key considerations when dealing with high levels of uncertainty that are also accompanied by significant consequences to the business. When embarking on a risky path that we feel is essential to the success of our business, we need to ask ourselves the following questions:

- What scenarios could eventuate that could see this path going very well or very badly?
- What are the consequences to me, my family and my business if this goes badly?
- What can I control and what is out of my control?
- Of those things I can control, what will I do to increase the chances of success?
- If a worst-case scenario occurs, what warning signs will I see so I might take early action?
- If a worst-case scenario does eventuate, can I survive it?

When you come out the other side of such events and they turned out exceptionally well, or poorly, be objective enough to accept what part luck played in the outcome, either good or bad.

Remember, if the outcome was due to things you had no control or influence on, be careful relying on them the next time around — you may just have got lucky this time and luck does run out.

CASH AND THE MOUSE THAT SANK THE BOAT

The wisdom of a child's book

I spent many enjoyable hours reading children's books to my two kids to get them to sleep when they were young. Even though they have now left home and are making a life for themselves, I fondly remember many of these stories. Some have stayed with me all these years later. My favourite is still *Who Sank the Boat?* by Pamela Allen.[1] While the illustrations are what made the book a favourite for my kids, the simple story has a few very telling messages, if one assumes the business is the sinking boat.

The basis of the story goes something like this:

A cow, a donkey, a sheep, a pig and a tiny little mouse lived on a farm and decided to walk to the bay.

The cow gets in the boat at the wharf first. All was well.

The donkey jumps in the boat and settles in the bow of the boat. Still all is well

Then came the pig and then the sheep

Then the little mouse jumps in and sadly the boat sinks.

Throughout the author asks "Who sank the boat?

She concludes the story by making the statement to her young readers that

"You DO know who sank the boat"

The debate would then ensue with my kids on who it was. Was it the cow, the donkey, the pig, the sheep or the mouse?

After all my discussions and research, the question always arises: *"What sank the business?"* Unfortunately, far too often the running out of cash and not being able to pay taxes is the (not so tiny) mouse that finally tips the business over, sinking it forever.

However, invariably there was a (metaphorical) cow, donkey, pig or sheep that was burdening the business well before the cash finally ran out, and then someone, most often the IRD, came knocking.

Who do we pay first — and last?

As with all failures, there is usually a range of factors that cascade — with the ultimate consequence being no cash to pay the bills. Small businesses that run out of cash look at ways of dealing with it — and most small businesses face this issue at some stage in their business's life. They try to prioritise who does and doesn't get the little cash they can find. Typically, the staff are paid, the bank is paid, creditors are paid, maybe the owners are paid and, lastly, the IRD is paid.

Businesses start delaying paying creditors, especially those who are less likely to pursue them. Owners may reduce or delay payments to themselves, but they can't do this for long.

The IRD is often the last on the list to be paid. This is because tax can usually be delayed, as it comes later in the form of GST, provisional or terminal tax. It also tends to be the silent cash that is accumulating in the background as, unlike creditors or staff, the IRD are unlikely to contact you if you miss a payment — at least not straight away.

To the business owners who are not watching it, tax can slowly build up to quite significant sums and become large enough to *"sink the boat"*.

Running low on cash is not something that happens overnight. There will be many warning signs. The best and first place to look when cash is tight is within the business rather than seeking external sources of cash.

Profit and cash — you need both

The basic financial formula

So, let's look at the basics of what every business needs to be looking at to be profitable (even if the profit is for social or charitable purposes).

SALES
COST of SALES
GROSS PROFIT
EXPENSES
OPERATING PROFIT (or EBITDA)

This basic profit and loss statement applies to every business, and details the most important items at the disposal of the business owner to improve profitability.

The business needs to increase sales and reduce its cost of producing those sales (variable costs) to deliver a healthy gross profit. It also needs to reduce expenses (fixed costs — often called overheads).

If only it were that simple, but unfortunately it is.

Many small business owners have limited scope to reduce expenses, as they are typically already small. This may not be the case of the big businesses (like Solid Energy, Pumpkin Patch or SCF), which can accumulate significant overheads.

The golden ratio

For any business, increasing profitability is achieved by increasing sales without a disproportionate increase in the cost of producing those sales. Therein lies one of the most critical financial key performance indicators (KPIs) in most businesses, especially small businesses — % gross profit. This is calculated as:

$$\frac{\text{SALES} - \text{COST of SALES} \times 100}{\text{SALES}} = \frac{\text{GROSS PROFIT} \times 100}{\text{SALES}}$$

Keeping this margin as large as possible is critical to a business's profitability. Too often businesses grow their sales but their cost of sales increase too much, so they make little extra money. This occurs as retailers offer bigger discounts to increase sales, construction companies reduce margins in bidding for jobs to keep their crews working, and so on.

The % gross profit will vary from industry to industry. For example, builders struggle to get much more than 15% margin on a house, electricians about 25% on a job, machinery and vehicle sales may achieve less than 10%.

Businesses that take their eye off this, especially if their overheads are also creeping up, can find themselves in serious trouble without fully understanding why.

So, if this is profitability, what is cash?

The main difference between profit and cash is timing. With cash, all that matters is when the money enters the bank account or leaves the bank account.

Profit and loss reports are usually detailed based on when you generate an invoice or receive a supplier's invoice, *not* when you get paid or pay the supplier. Most of these invoices will have credit provided. That is, we don't have to pay or we don't seek payment for several days.

We may also have people who are very bad payers, or don't pay at all.

The profit and loss statement will include the interest on loans but excludes any principal payments on those loans. If the business is carrying lots of debt, it will have to be paid out of the profits. So, the business may appear quite profitable but have none of that profit left after paying all its debts.

If the owner wants to buy plant and equipment that is of greater value than $500, they are considered assets and do not appear in the profit and loss statement. So again, these must be funded out of profits or by borrowing money.

Businesses will also take money out of the business for the shareholders in the form of drawings throughout the year or dividends.

So, from month to month, what is invoiced may look very different from the actual cash coming in and going out from the business's bank account.

While this discussion centres around small business, the principles for big business are the same — there may simply be many more zeros in the numbers.

When the cash dries up, the business dies

Whether we are running a business aiming to generate a profit or it is a not-for-profit or charitable enterprise, if the dollars aren't managed, the business won't be around for long. It doesn't matter how big or small the business is — when the cash dries up, the business will die.

Being under-capitalised

The other issue, particularly for small businesses in New Zealand, is a lack of working capital. This is, effectively, having insufficient cash in the bank from month to month to pay the bills without turning to other external sources of money.

PROFIT AND LOSS

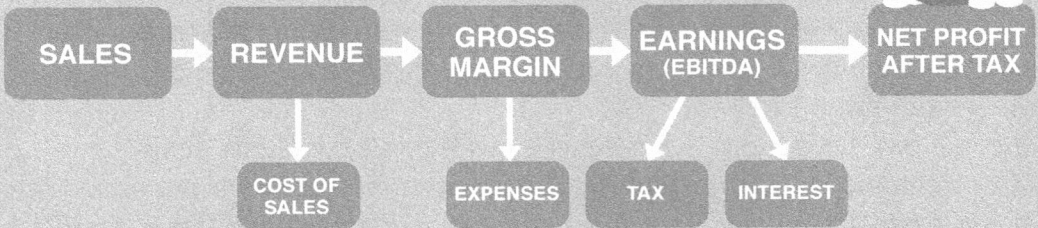

SALES → REVENUE → GROSS MARGIN → EARNINGS (EBITDA) → NET PROFIT AFTER TAX

REVENUE → COST OF SALES

GROSS MARGIN → EXPENSES

EARNINGS (EBITDA) → TAX

EARNINGS (EBITDA) → INTEREST

BALANCE SHEET

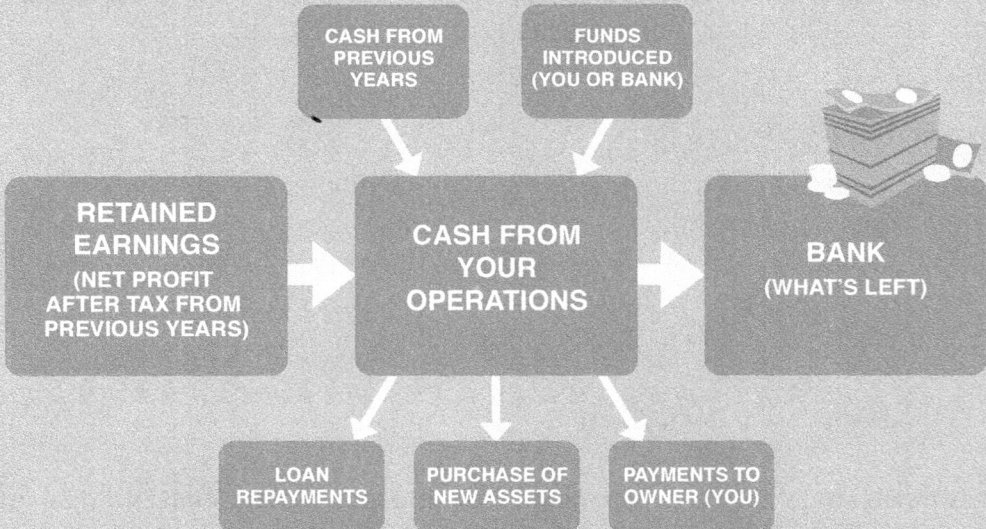

CASH FROM PREVIOUS YEARS

FUNDS INTRODUCED (YOU OR BANK)

RETAINED EARNINGS (NET PROFIT AFTER TAX FROM PREVIOUS YEARS) → CASH FROM YOUR OPERATIONS → BANK (WHAT'S LEFT)

CASH FROM YOUR OPERATIONS → LOAN REPAYMENTS

CASH FROM YOUR OPERATIONS → PURCHASE OF NEW ASSETS

CASH FROM YOUR OPERATIONS → PAYMENTS TO OWNER (YOU)

It is very common for small businesses to start a business under-capitalised. That is, they start with almost no money behind them. As I've already mentioned, New Zealand is the easiest place on earth to start a company and many businesses start with almost no money.

There are very few places in New Zealand for a small business to go to raise money to start their business. It really falls to their own personal sources of money or the bank. The bank will usually only lend to a small business if they can access equity in the small businesses owner's home, or, as a minimum, offer a small overdraft facility on their bank account.

So, the small business starts, the costs start creeping up, sales don't meet the expectations the owner had hoped for, then throw in some loan repayments and the pressures on cash, and on the owner, grow.

Things may be different for larger companies. There are likely to be other sources for raising capital to run the business. However, ultimately the principles are the same. The monthly bills are bigger, the amount of cash needed to pay them is bigger and, if the business fails to manage all this the consequences are also much bigger.

Taking too much money out of the business

An all-too-common issue in small businesses that can get them into serious trouble is the practice of taking too much cash out of the business for personal use. In the case of bigger businesses there are also numerous examples where payments, in the form of dividends to shareholders, were high, putting great pressure on the business. This was the case with Solid Energy paying the government and Pumpkin Patch paying its shareholders.

Pumpkin Patch paid its shareholders over $88 million in the seven years between 2005 and 2011, compared with reported profits of just over $90 million (i.e. 98%), adding greater pressure to borrow more money to support its growth plans rather than using internally generated cash.

Often people new to business look upon the venture as a **cash cow**. The term cash cow was first used by the Boston Consulting Group to help large corporations define the parts of their empires that were chugging along, delivering steady cash without a lot of effort, nor with a lot of excitement.

The analogy with a "cow" was from a belief that the owner of cows could produce milk readily and with little effort or maintenance. As a long-term resident of the dairy-rich Waikato region of New Zealand, I know many dairy farmers who would struggle to accept that managing herds of dairy cows was low maintenance nor an easy way to make cash. Dairy farming is very hard work.

While perhaps a poor analogy, too many people look upon a business as a ready source of cash that it may not actually have. Business owners sometimes fail to separate themselves from their business and see the business's money as their money. They freely draw money out of the business for personal use and, over time, lose track of this cash.

A sad example when too much was taken out

Here is a very real and a very sad example of what can happen if a small business takes too much money out of the business for the benefit of the business's owners.

An Auckland-based business called the High-End Pool Company Ltd (it was a pool company but under another name) was started in 2004 by husband and wife Alan and Mary Smith (also not their real names).

They were both directors and 50% shareholders. High-End Pool Company provided high-quality, award-winning pools to wealthy customers in Auckland. It was a very profitable and, by most standards, successful business. Alan did most of the design and installation work.

With the growth of the business, Alan spent all his time on the job with his small crew. Mary handled the accounts and did the administration. Alan was happy to entrust his wife with all this, as it was not his strength and he simply did not have the time. Besides, she was good at it and he trusted her completely.

Unfortunately, Mary did expect the business to provide her with a reasonably lavish lifestyle. She was also developing an unhealthy gambling habit. In the later stages of the business's life, she was taking over $4000 out each month in drawings, beyond Alan and her own wages, to support this habit. She did not tell Alan.

Alan was unaware of this until creditors contacted him about not being paid. He also soon realised, via his accountant, that the business had built up a growing IRD debt. His wife's worsening gambling habit, and the resultant impact from the lack of cash available to the business, caused significant stress for Alan, both personally and for the future of the business. It was especially disheartening when the business was growing, was very profitable, receiving awards, and had strong customer testimonials.

Unfortunately, creditors put increasing pressure on the business, forcing it into liquidation in 2017. Eventually, Alan's health failed as he experienced a severe stress-related breakdown.

In Alan and Mary's case, the drawings were substantial and supporting an unsustainable lifestyle. The occurrence of owners taking too much from their business is an all-too-common one. The impact of extracting too much money from a business and living beyond one's means can cause significant issues.

You could lose everything

Even worse is if a business goes into liquidation and the shareholders have taken more money out of the business than they put into it. In this case, the liquidator can pursue the shareholders to recover that money for the creditors. If the owners no longer have the cash, the liquidators could bankrupt the owners and dispose of their personal assets to repay the liquidated company, who in turn can then pay the creditors.

Managing the money you owe, and money owed to you

Unfortunately, many businesses get into trouble and struggle to meet their own cash requirements because other businesses aren't paying their bills.

When a business goes into liquidation, rarely is it able to pay everyone it owes. The order of priority for payments in a liquidation is firstly secured creditors — those who have security over assets. Second are preferred creditors such as employees and the IRD. Lastly are the many other businesses that are owed money but have no security or priority — called unsecured creditors.

Whether the reason a business is not being paid is the tardiness of the business that owes the money or its liquidation, unpaid bills can be hugely damaging to a business's cash situation.

A few examples

- **Oakridge Masonry Ltd** was a stone masonry business operating in Tauranga. It was owned by a husband and wife team. In November 2014, the IRD filed for its liquidation as it was unable to pay its taxes. The owners indicated they were unable to pay taxes because it was unable to get debtors to settle their accounts with the company. It in turn owed five other businesses money it could not pay.

- **A-Grade Construction Ltd** was a building and construction business based in Auckland. It was put into liquidation by its shareholders in October 2014. It indicated it was struggling but the main reason it was forced to go into liquidation was because many large debtors were not paying. When liquidated, A-Grade Construction owed over $180,000 to 30 other suppliers and businesses.

Unfortunately, there are many examples where these is a cascading impact on businesses from other businesses failing to pay their bills.

Debt collection is painful — but necessary

Even more common are businesses that stay afloat but must battle every month chasing money owed to them. This is one of the least appealing jobs a business faces and many avoid it, often with serious implications.

In addition, some larger organisations impose lengthy credit periods on its suppliers, who may have no negotiating power.

Every business, no matter its size, needs to have disciplines in place to ensure it is paid on time, every time.

This could involve being paid in cash at the point of sale (POS), getting security over assets while awaiting payment, checking the creditworthiness of clients, getting payments in advance, implementing detailed terms of trade, debt collection processes, and more.

This is critical for a business of any size.

In the end, business is tough enough without being owed money that is rightly the business's.

And when you can't pay the bills

Just as we all wish to be paid, so too should we pay those we owe. Getting a reputation as a bad payer may have long-term implications. If the business gets into a tight cash situation, suppliers who have been paid well over long periods of time are more likely to allow the struggling business some slack.

There are many examples where creditors worked with a struggling business to help it survive when they could have seen it liquidated.

If a business is not a good payer, it may find its details listed on credit registers and lenders may be disinclined to lend it money.

If a business is struggling to meet its debts with lenders or the IRD, it is unwise to hope it goes away. Both the banks and the IRD are prepared to help if a business speaks to them early.

If a business gets into more serious trouble and a creditor decides to act to recover its money, it can do this via the courts, using a statutory demand.

After a statutory demand is issued, the business it has been issued to has 10 working days to dispute the debt or 15 working days to pay the debt. If it does nothing, liquidation of the company by the court may follow.

A statutory demand can be used as a means for a creditor to get their money, as well as being a precursor to triggering a business's liquidation. If a business is owed money that is not in dispute, and it has exhausted other debt collection options, this is an option it could take. It can be expensive, as it needs to be done by people expert in the process (typically lawyers) and if liquidation is triggered and the business is an unsecured creditor it may not get anything anyway.

The IRD has the resources and the skills to instigate statutory demands on businesses that aren't paying their tax. It also ranks higher than unsecured creditors. Therefore, the IRD triggers more statutory demands than anyone else.

Businesses need to talk to the people they owe money — whether it's the bank, IRD or suppliers. Some business people who have outstanding money owing are ashamed to admit they are struggling, but staying silent in this situation is very unwise. If the business raises its hand early enough, others may be able to help.

Sticking our heads in the sand will achieve no good outcome.

16 PAYING TAXES — THE CASH OF LAST RESORT

If we discuss the liquidation of businesses in New Zealand, we must discuss the role of taxation. More small businesses face liquidation because of unpaid taxes than any other reason.

> 66 *Taxes are the price we pay for a civilised society.* 99
> — Supreme Court Justice Oliver Wendell Holmes Jr

We talked about cash sinking the business in previous chapters. If we had to establish who the failed business is most likely to owe that cash to that ultimately sinks the business, then it would be the IRD.

This is less so for large company failures like Solid Energy. Most large businesses appear to manage outstanding taxes. In the case of the majority of small to medium business failures, it is the IRD that remains unpaid.

In turn, it is the IRD that instigates the liquidation of more businesses in New Zealand than anyone else. If the shareholders trigger a voluntary liquidation, it is often to avoid the IRD doing it instead.

Therefore, we cannot discuss the failure of businesses within New Zealand without discussing taxation and the IRD. In turn, to avoid failures, all businesses must consider how they manage their taxation.

We may not like them, but we need them

The IRD is often held in very low regard by most business owners and, in fact, most tax payers. Taxation can be complicated and the IRD may not be that easy to deal with. No one enjoys seeing large chunks of their earnings disappearing into government hands. Most of us dread going through our annual tax return and kindly leave it to our accountant.

Whether we like it or not, as it is so often said (first by Benjamin Franklin), there is nothing more certain than death and taxes.

The country's ability to function relies on the efficient collection of taxation. So, whether we like them or not, we need an effective IRD.

What is the IRD all about?

Of the total annual revenue of approximately $100 billion raised by the New Zealand government (in 2016), over 70% comes from taxation. Most of the remaining 30% revenue comes from state-owned enterprises, like Solid Energy — before it failed.[1]

So, it goes without saying that the country would cease to function without an effective tax department to collect taxation.

The Tax Administration Act of 1994 describes the role of the IRD to be to:

“ *use their best endeavours to protect the integrity of the tax system.*

. . . the integrity of the tax system includes —

(a) taxpayer perceptions of that integrity; and
(b) the rights of taxpayers to have their liability determined fairly, impartially, and according to law; and
(c) the rights of taxpayers to have their individual affairs kept confidential and treated with no greater or lesser favour than the tax affairs of other taxpayers; and
(d) the responsibilities of taxpayers to comply with the law; and
(e) the responsibilities of those administering the law to maintain the confidentiality of the affairs of taxpayers; and
(f) the responsibilities of those administering the law to do so fairly, impartially, and according to law. **”**

They are expected to chase every cent

An important point we should not forget about the IRD's statutory responsibility is that it is required to collect as much tax revenue as it legally can, as described in the same legislation:

> 66 It is the duty of the Commissioner to collect over time the highest net revenue that is practicable within the law. 99

Therefore, we should not be surprised when the IRD chases every cent it can from those who should be paying their taxes.

Greece — when taxes aren't paid

The financial crises that Greece faced in the years after the GFC were given wide international coverage. There are many reasons why Greece's economy was on the brink of collapse. However, one factor that contributed to Greece's demise was the lack of tax that was paid.Greek officials described tax evasion in that country as *"a national sport"*. The worst offenders in Greece were small businesses and the self-employed.[2]

Unfortunately, that is valid throughout the world. The self-employed and small businesses are the most likely to avoid paying their taxes. It's just there appeared to be more of it going on in Greece.[3]

So, unless we want to face the crises confronting countries like Greece, we should accept paying taxation is good for all of us.

Paying taxes means we're making money

Strangely, some businesses don't like paying tax and, in a perverse way, feel satisfied they didn't have to pay tax at year's end.

The reality is if we are paying lots of tax, then the business is making lots of money. Therefore, our goal should be to pay as much tax as we can. This, of course, is noting that a good accountant should do all they can to ensure we only pay the tax we legally must, and not one cent more.

And it's not our money anyway

Whether we like it or not, as business people we are the short-term custodians of the IRD's money.

When we pay our staff, we must take the PAYE from their wages and pass it on to the IRD. That money is not the business's, even though many businesses use it for other things. When we sell our products or services, 15% of that money, the GST, is the IRD's. We expect that tax to be offset by the 15% GST on the goods and services we must buy to run our businesses. The difference is simply the money we hang on to for a short period before handing it over to its rightful owner — the IRD.

So, we need to keep the GST we owe aside and not use it for other things.

If the IRD is paying the business back GST on a regular basis, which does happen in the early stages of a business's life, it's pretty obvious that it's a situation that can't last, as the business is spending more than it is making.

Hopefully after all this, and with some expert advice from our accountant or tax advisor, we make a profit. Sadly, if we are a profit-making business, 28% of that is not ours either and, at some point, the IRD will be after it in the form of provisional tax. So, that also needs to be set aside.

The IRD lose far too much money

The IRD faces significant losses in its tax revenue when businesses fail.

Of the liquidations I reviewed, the clear majority owed tax that was never going to be paid.

For the years 2013, 2014, 2015 and 2016, the IRD lost, in unpaid taxes because of liquidations, $333 million, $220 million, $167 million and $221 million, respectively. That is, in these four years, the IRD (and all taxpayers) lost about $940 million from liquidations — money it will never see again.

The average loss for each failed business over these four years was $130,000. Remember that the clear majority of businesses that fail in New Zealand are small businesses usually with a single director. Very often when big businesses fail, their taxes are sorted. Therefore, these losses suffered by the IRD are usually due to failures of small to medium businesses.

In addition to losses due to liquidations, over the same four years the IRD gave businesses that were struggling to pay their taxes some relief to help them survive. This relief totalled almost $445 million. Most of these businesses kept operating after relief was offered. Again, this is money the IRD will never see.[4]

Every day the IRD is having to chase businesses that are behind on their taxes. Many of these businesses have some repayment plan in place because they got behind on their taxes. In addition to this, the IRD is likely to be charging these businesses interest and penalties on top of what they owe.

In June 2016, the total overdue tax debt (personal and business) was $5,755 million, which was owed by 339,000 entities (businesses and individuals).[5]

The IRD has done a lot in recent years to improve these processes, and with the advent of the cloud-based, electronic, interconnected world, it has more tools at its disposal to pursue unpaid taxes.

Even with the improvements by the IRD to collect money, small businesses in New Zealand are still not very good at managing and paying their taxes. Businesses get into trouble because they fail to understand what they owe, when they must pay it, and ensuring it is paid.

It's simple — really

It would seem immensely obvious and an extremely simple concept to grasp — we must pay tax, so we should make sure it happens.

I can't deny, the tax system is complex and not easy to grasp, and the IRD are not always the most pleasant bunch to deal with. However, there are many people who spend their careers helping people get it right — most often accountants — so there is little sympathy out there for those of us who get it wrong.

Why, then, is failing to pay taxes so common?

Is it laziness, disorganisation, denial or simply that it's another demonstration of our imperfection as humans, and that we make mistakes? We know we must do it. We know what happens if we don't, but too many of us don't do it.

So, in summary . . .

Find out what tax must be paid.
Find out when it must be paid.
Keep the money needed to be paid to one side.
Put processes in place to make sure it is paid.
And if help is needed — ASK.

17 DEBT AND HOW TO KILL A 1400-YEAR-OLD BUSINESS

The once great temple builder — Kongo Gumi

Kongo Gumi Co Ltd was the oldest company in known history. It started in AD 578 when Shigemitsu Kongo, a Korean migrant, came to Japan to build temples at the invitation of the royal family. These temples were to meet the rise of Buddhism in Japan.

The first temple was the Shitennō-ji Temple in Osaka, which still stands. This project gave birth to the construction company Kongo Gumi Co Ltd. Shigemitsu Kongo and his ancestors operated this family business continually for over 1400 years. The firm was a symbol of Japan's "*shinise*", or family-run business culture.

The company was headquartered in Osaka. Even as late as 2004, temple building accounted for more than 80% of the company's revenue, which exceeded $60 million.

During the 1980s, property prices in Tokyo were growing dramatically driven by a range of favourable economic factors, including low interest rates. In 1991, prices had risen over 300% from 1985.

Kongo Gumi, which for over 1400 years had held true to its core values and operated in the business market it knew, could not resist the temptation of this booming property market and borrowed heavily to invest.

The government and Bank of Japan stepped in with a range of initiatives to slow the market, including forcing up interest rates. This ultimately resulted in the collapse of the property market.

When the market collapsed, Kongo Gumi was burdened with huge debts (ballooning to $343 million).

It struggled on for almost two decades, but it eventually had to liquidate in 2006 under the burden of this debt. It was absorbed into its parent company and ceased to exist. So, a business that survived over 1400 years of social change, attacks on Buddhism (during the 19th-century Meiji Restoration), two world wars, and more, could not survive poor property decisions and the associated debt that it brought — very sad!

The debt burden

Rarely can a business grow or even survive without the use of someone else's money.

It is rare that larger businesses would operate without some debt. In many cases, large businesses that have a large equity in the business and little debt are frowned upon — they are failing to use that equity to access other money, namely debt, to grow the business.

It might be much tougher for a small business to attract money from external sources. They are far less attractive to lenders.

Friends, family or fools

Finding people to lend to a small business is not easy. When a small business starts, there are a limited number of options to fund the business. Typically, the first point of call is the owner's savings. Even if the owner had access to large amounts of personal wealth (which very few do), they will need to call on money from others.

Many whimsically describe the next source of funds as ***friends, family or fools***, with family members being a very common option. Very often the money is offered based on a handshake and trust. It's often a loved one who provides the money, even if the investment is a poor one.

We watch popular television shows like *Dragons' Den* where a new business owner fronts a group of wealthy individuals who quickly form a passion for the business, equal to that of the person presenting the ideas — they then hand over a large sum of money. Or they just berate the poor person and destroy their passion — great reality television.

Alas, these sources of money are rare and most of the businesses that start each year in New Zealand will never see such money.

And then there are the banks — and the "non-banks"

There are many stories of businesses that started with nothing, used some personal savings and grew on the back of money they produced solely from the activities of the business. It's great if a business can achieve growth this way.

Unfortunately, self-funded growth is not easy to achieve and more often as a business grows it will need to access money from other sources. Businesses may also need external funds purely to stay alive.

After we've exhausted our own savings, the next most common source of money is the bank.

Many people are, justifiably, nervous about borrowing from the bank.

All banks want to lend people money — that is why they exist. However, they also need to be confident they will get that money back. Business owners may be passionate about the business or the idea, but that may not translate into enthusiasm from a lender such as a bank.

The number of non-bank finance companies, like South Canterbury Finance, that a business could go to for funds are far fewer now than prior to the GFC. These finance companies were far more comfortable to lend to riskier ventures than the banks were — which came at a significant price.

While the GFC saw the end of many of these finance companies, it is very likely, with time, non-bank lenders will reappear. While I'd like to hope businesses will show more caution in how much they borrow, and the finance companies will follow better lending practices than those prior to the GFC, I fear we have short memories.

Sadly, I fear we will return to the days where money was easier to access than it has been post the GFC. Alas, as I have highlighted throughout this book, we are human, irrational, and I have little doubt we will repeat past mistakes. If business owners can more easily attract funds, they will likely take the path of least resistance and take such funds — forgetting the price paid in the past from such decisions.

Big companies have more options

Larger companies usually have more options to raise funds. If they are listed on a stock exchange they may ask shareholders for more money. Larger businesses often pose less risk to lenders, who are more comfortable to hand over their money. Unfortunately, when bigger businesses fail, the debt they owe tends to be substantial.

We have already discussed several failures where the business built up and then were unable to manage debt. Solid Energy had never borrowed money to run its business until the final years before its demise. When the cash started drying up with a fall in its revenues, it was unable to service the debt.

Sadly, lenders were far too eager to lend Solid Energy money believing their shareholders, the government, would pay them back no matter what happened — sadly they did not.

Likewise, Pumpkin Patch's move into the UK and USA was off the back of money it borrowed. The debt only became an issue when the sales they predicted, and were reliant on, did not eventuate.

Too often businesses borrow money but do not factor in options to service that debt when negative events occur. In Solid Energy's case, a fall in coal prices was not an unrealistic scenario, nor was a lower level of sales in new markets for Pumpkin Patch.

Sometimes the issue is not borrowing money but understanding what the money is for, ensuring it is borrowed for the right reasons, and considering the consequences if things don't go to plan.

A common source of funding for a small business — the family home

As already mentioned, the only realistic place a smaller business owner can go to access additional money is the bank. Unlike larger organisations, which have more assets and are more attractive to a bank, small businesses are more likely to fail, have tighter cash flows to service the debts, and limited assets within the business.

Therefore, for the banks to lend money, they will want to secure it against some decent-sized assets. In the case of most Kiwis, this will be the family home.

The Reserve Bank of New Zealand indicates that over 56% of all the lending banks do is for housing, with only 25% for business.

Statistics New Zealand highlights that around 87% of the debt Kiwis carry is on real estate.[1]

This is held by people in the middle-age bracket of 35–54 years old. Unfortunately, there are one in ten Kiwis reaching retirement still carrying debt on their homes. We would all like to reach retirement free of debt, but this is not the case for many Kiwis.[2]

Considering the number of small businesses in New Zealand, most are owned by individuals already carrying debt on their home. To get money from the bank for the business they usually must secure the loan by using equity that is remaining in that home. They may also have to increase the amount of debt on the house for use by the business.

Therefore, small business owners' personal and business lending most often centre around the family home and can keep small business owners in debt well into their later working years.

What you must pledge to secure debt

When a lender, like a bank, lends money to someone, and wants to secure that money against an asset, like a family home, they are doing this to ensure they can go somewhere to get their money back. In the case of a business failure, they want to rank highest in the priority list of who gets the money first.

Other people may also want to get security over money or assets that a business has borrowed from them. For example, a business may buy a motor vehicle on finance from the car dealer. That car dealer will ask for security over the vehicle and have first priority to retrieve the vehicle if the business can't pay.

Those who have securities over a business or specific assets within that business will be listed on the **Personal Property Securities Register (PPSR)**. (These are detailed for companies on the Companies Office website.)

General Security Agreement and receivers

It is common for major lenders, especially banks, to ask a business borrowing the money to sign a *General Security Agreement (GSA)* when they lend the money. This gives the lender security over all the assets of the business. As it gives security over everything, it is a very powerful tool the bank can use if the business gets into trouble and can't meet the obligations of the loan.

If the bank feels the business could default on the loan, it can appoint a receiver to come in and take over the business. The receiver's powers are considerable. Their goal won't be to do what's in the best interest of the business or the owner of the business. It is to act in the interest of the lender. This was the case in the Salthouse Marine failure.

The receiver can seize and also sell any or all the business's assets in an attempt to get the lender's money back. The receiver can also keep the business running if that is in the best interests of the lender. For example, if the business is midway through a building project, the receiver may ensure the project is completed to attract the best sale price rather than selling a partly completed building.

While it can happen, it is not that common that the bank will step in and sell the house from under a small business owner if they default on their business loans. Receiverships are less common when small businesses get into trouble. Receivers are usually expensive and the lender needs to have confidence the amount owed has a high chance of being recovered and the amount is worth their while.

Banks are more likely to help

In the case of small businesses getting into trouble, the bank is more likely to work with the owners to get them back on track, assuming it's not too late when the bank finds out.

To get a small business back on track, the owner may be forced to take additional equity out of their home to help the business survive. So, to the outside world the business lives on, the bank is happy (or happier), but the owner has given up a large chunk of equity in the home that they may have spent decades paying off.

When the debt starts mounting

It is likely that large organisations carrying significant amounts of debt will be operating under specific rules of the bank. It is unlikely personal guarantees will exist or security over personal assets. The bank will be backing the performance of the large business or project. It is likely to have individuals within the bank keeping a closer eye on the project and requesting details about compliance with the rules under which the money was lent.

In the case of small businesses, a bank manager may have dozens (even hundreds) of businesses it is tracking. If a small business owner starts struggling to meet their commitments to the bank, even if it is a short-term issue, they need to talk to the bank.

It is in both the owner's and the bank's best interest to find solutions. If a small business is struggling and says nothing, it will make it more difficult to deal with, especially if the issues go on for an extended period.

The bank won't have visibility of the other debts a small business might be battling with. Customers who aren't paying the business (debtors) or IRD debt that is accumulating will go unseen by the bank. If these are becoming a serious issue, it is worth talking to the bank early rather than waiting until things reach crisis point.

A bank will track a small business owner's behaviour. The first sign that you may have a problem is if your overdraft is at or exceeding its limits.

If a small business can't meet its obligations to the bank, it's very unlikely the first step will be for the bank to send in a receiver under the security provisions and take control of the business — unless of course the business owes them serious amounts of money that makes this step worth their while.

It is more likely the bank will want to discuss how to help the small business owner turn this around. They may ask for an independent opinion on the state of the business. They will want to see a plan to get the business out of the hole. They may look at changing the financing arrangements.

If the issue is serious enough, it's likely the bank will delegate the matter to someone other than the manager the business is used to dealing with. Instead, it is likely to be handed to bank employees specialising in businesses that default — and they are not usually as empathetic to a business as the small business's bank manager.

While the bank is unlikely to shut a small business down and take the owner's house, they have the right to do so and would not have had the owners sign a security agreement it they were not prepared to act on it.

Whatever the bank does, it is unlikely to act immediately and unilaterally and without the business owner's input — and usually such issues do not happen overnight.

18 DOING THE LITTLE THINGS REALLY WELL

To this point, our discussions have centred on the big issues facing small and large businesses that led to their failure. To close out the discussion on how to reduce the likelihood of business failures, let's discuss the little things that can make a big difference, especially to smaller businesses.

In a small company the shareholder (the owner), the director and the person running the business are usually the same person. This is by far the most common scenario in New Zealand, especially when 97% of businesses have fewer than 20 staff.[1]

The link between the day-to-day activities of these small businesses and success is more pronounced than in a big business. When the little things are done poorly, the impacts are more immediate and more telling. In the big businesses, such inefficiency can go on for some time before it has serious implications.

The day-to-day activities is where business owners, leaders and employees spend the clear majority of their time. They require hundreds of small, regular decisions, none of which is likely to impact the business's survival but collectively can have a big impact. We don't, nor should we, consciously stop and ponder these to any excess. The businesses would grind to a halt and nothing would happen as we scrutinise the minutiae.

This is where the procedures, policies, processes, systems and rules can bring repeatability into a business and provide consistency between the different people in a business. If it is done in excess, these processes become painful bureaucracy. If refined, they can be immensely helpful.

In South Canterbury Finance, Allan Hubbard was not a believer in systems and processes. This created many issues as transactions were not checked and things were done inconsistently.

So, it is unlikely the ultimate failure of a business will be linked to the daily activities in a business. However, getting all those little things right will ultimately deliver the big things.

Time — it is everything

When I spoke to the receiver of the Salthouse Marine case, he attributed the failure to the day-to-day management of the boat-builds — underquoting and too much time spent building the boats and failing to track and allocate time. Julie Salthouse dismissed this as a material contributor to the failure. Whether it did or didn't play a part in the Salthouse Marine failure, it is a useful reminder that wasting time in a business, especially a small business, can have serious implications.

Whether a manufacturer, tradesman, consultancy business, whether producing a product or providing any number of services, time is a critical resource too often mismanaged.

Our time is the greatest gift we can give. We have an infinite number of things we could do with our time and once given, we can never get it back.

Yet this most precious of resources is something we too often waste, especially in the day-to-day running of businesses. Time is also an expensive resource. In New Zealand, for a business of any size it is common that the single highest cost is the staff. If we and our people waste time, it is very expensive.

As owners, we waste time. We are all given the same hours in a day and the choice to use that time as we see fit. Unfortunately, once used, time can never be reused again. Let's firstly look at a few things we can do to manage our time before implementing practices in the business.

Procrastination — eat the big frog first

One major time waster is procrastination.

A great book to assist in understanding and then managing our procrastination is Brian Tracy's *Eat that Frog!* The title stems from a Mark Twain quote:

> **❝** *Eat a live frog first thing in the morning and nothing worse will happen to you the rest of the day.* **❞**
> — Mark Twain

Brian Tracy uses this concept to describe our tendency to procrastinate over that unpleasant task — the biggest frog. Taking the quote further, if you must eat frogs, eat the biggest one first. If you leave it and just stare at it, it won't go away and it won't get any smaller. It will simply look more unpleasant over time. The longer these unpleasant tasks get left undone, the worse the challenge is. We need to take more immediate action and just start eating.[2]

The aim is to understand our most important tasks and to concentrate single-mindedly on completing them — even if that task is not that pleasant.

Being action oriented will make a big difference to the business. Brian Tracey says that successful, effective people are those who launch directly into their major tasks and then discipline themselves to work steadily and single-mindedly until those tasks are complete.

The habit of setting priorities, overcoming procrastination, and getting on with the most important task is a mental and physical skill.

Procrastinators should not despair. Overcoming this bad habit is learnable through practice and repetition. As with any difficult task, it will take us, and our lazy brains, time to learn. Once it becomes a habit, it becomes both automatic and easier to do.

Multitasking — doing a lot of things badly

When our minds switch between different tasks, it takes time to become focused enough to tune out from one task before taking on the next. This is especially the case if we are switching between tasks that we find easy and enjoyable and tasks we don't but still have to complete.

This is why multitasking is so inefficient.

When we multitask, we are not doing two or more things at the same time. We are swapping between two or more things. The more we succumb to the growing temptation to multitask, the more likely we're going to see adverse effects on our ability to focus on any task, especially challenging tasks.

When we multitask, our brains don't know which task is the important one. Our brains are lazy and will gravitate toward the easy task that takes least mental energy. So, if

we are doing two or more tasks, one of which is more ingrained, we'll find our minds drifting back to that one rather than paving a new neutron path to complete the new, tougher task.

Every time we switch our attention from one task to another, we pay a price. Sometimes the price is small and we can corral our attention back easily.

But sometimes the cost is bigger than we think: instead of a switch cost, we pay a price for mixing the two tasks. The cost of mixing tasks is the extent to which the previous task intrudes into the current one.

Our failure to register an unexpected event when engaged in a fairly trivial task is called ***inattentional blindness***. We are blind to things that we're not paying attention to, even when they are directly in front of us. Daniel Simons and Christopher Chabris' gorilla experiment is the perfect way to explain inattentional blindness. It explains why we lose our wallets or keys in plain sight. And it's also exploited by magicians.

So, in short, avoid multitasking when a task we are doing is difficult, new or important. Find the environment to focus on it and do it properly.[3]

Prioritise

After you have read the preceding chapters, I hope it is now clear that we are not superhuman, no matter the elevated position we may hold. We can't remember everything. We can't process everything. To improve the quality of our choices, we need to simplify and reduce those choices to a manageable number.

In short, in executing our strategy and goals, we must prioritise. This includes placing some priority on ourselves, our family, friends and our wellbeing.

We need to allocate some time to set our longer-term goals, strategy and plans. We need to set aside time to understand the values we live and work by. We need to prioritise our time so we can disappear from the day-to-day grind and focus on ourselves and bigger-picture priorities.

Identifying and removing waste

No matter the size of a business, it is very likely there are things we are doing that add little value to anyone, including our business or our customers. At times, we are so busy doing things that we fail to see that the way we are going about it is wasting time, money or materials. At a small level this may be a nuisance and annoying. At a more serious level it could be really hurting the business and, when things get tight or extremely busy, this waste could have serious implications.

The removal of waste can be done simply by stepping back from the day-to-day activities, looking at how we are going about the things we do every day and challenging those things that are frustrating, time consuming or unproductive. If we can identify these, we then need to do something about it.

The concept of removing waste from manufacturing processes is not new — it goes back hundreds of years. It was used by Henry Ford. It probably has its strongest links to the quality processes and just-in-time processes the Japanese, particularly Toyota, took up in post-war Japan. They took some of their inspiration for this from the American engaged by General Douglas MacArthur to support Japan's post-war recovery, W. Edwards Deming.

These processes (often called "lean") are now applied well beyond traditional manufacturing processes. They are now used in establishing waste in a wide range of processes, including service-based businesses, customer processes, even start-ups.[4]

Habits and rules to assist in overcoming our irrationality

There are many practices that every modern business puts in place to assist in its successful operations. We have processes, policies and systems. These deliver consistency and provide guidance for all those in the business. They assist with consistency in delivery, clarifying expectations, ensuring quality, protecting us legally and much more.

We need these processes in our businesses to help overcome the limitations we have as irrational human beings.

Rules and policies set out what the business expects and removes any individual biases that each of us might have. We have interview processes to prevent unconscious biases or stereotyping resulting in our selecting or rejecting candidates for the wrong reason.

The culture of a business of any size describes all those unwritten rules that define the way "we do things around here".

Communications often break down because of different values, different personalities, and simply because each of us recalls past discussions, commitments and events differently. That is why we have agreements and contracts. Even though we might trust the person we are developing the agreement with, as time passes we simply forget and recall inaccurately or differently.

Building good habits that we repeat, increases our skills, and improves quality and repeatability because we are burning these neutron paths into our brains. Practising good habits will make them more permanent.

We use cost benefit calculations and get work checked by others not just to find mistakes in our work, but to ensure we are not impacted by heuristics like the *confirmation effect*, unseen *conflicts of interest* or *anchoring* driving us to the wrong result.

We develop negotiating boundaries and strategies and do our homework before entering an important negotiation. This helps us avoid being anchored to a deal that is no good for us. It also helps us avoid building such a strong attachment to what we are pursuing that we are impacted by the *endowment effect* — we become attached to it too early and are prepared to pay too much for it.

We have boards of directors to ensure CEOs are not continuing with projects based on *sunk cost effects* or are developing unhealthy personality traits like arrogance, unhealthy ego, or a lack of empathy.

So, when we feel it is necessary to bring a new process in to improve the business, explain the key reason and don't be afraid to remind everyone that it is being done because we are all irrational, imperfect human beings and we should not be afraid to accept that and put processes in place to overcome it.

SECTION 5:
WHAT HAVE WE LEARNED

To conclude and summarise

We have looked at the details of why some of the highest profile New Zealand businesses failed. Sadly, they are but a small sample of the thousands of businesses that fail each year in this country.

Our journey then explored why businesses fail by taking us through the mind of the business person and has detailed the limitations of that mind in running businesses.

Lastly, we looked at some common reasons, apart from our humanity, that lead to failures and how better to run the businesses we are involved in.

So, I will now recap and summarise why I believe businesses fail.

- We are human. Our brains are imperfect. We can take in only so much information. We forget much of it. What we recall may not reflect what we took in.
- We are irrational whether we like to accept it or not.
- Our brains are slow to learn. We must put great effort in to become experts.
- We take mental shortcuts to survive. This leads to biases that are very often incorrect.
- When we decide, we take the easy path — we use our intuition. This is great if we are experienced, but dangerous if we are not.
- Our emotions guide our decisions.
- We need to know when to use analysis and critical thinking and when to use our gut feelings.
- Being intelligent is helpful but we only need to be smart enough.
- We can never know enough about ourselves — all the good, the great and the not so good.
- Arrogance, stubbornness and over-confidence are dangerous attributes for a business person. Be self-confident but humble.
- Psychopathy, narcissism and Machiavellianism are too common. Those who suffer from it may not know they do. The rest of us should not tolerate it, as it hurts people and businesses.
- Good governance is fundamental in the running of a large businesses. This requires strong, courageous, ethical people following good processes.
- Know when it's time to move on. Great business leaders are often recognised for leaving before they needed to and are missed — rather than people being glad they are gone.
- Before making those big calls, ask "What if?".
- Not all decisions work out. If the "What ifs" are materialising, don't be afraid to say "We got it wrong".

- Those who lie, cheat and defraud do immeasurable harm. Not all people are honourable.
- Know why the business exists, and where it is heading. Drifting along serves no good purpose.
- We all have values we live by. They guide us. We need to understand what they are and live by them.
- Control the controllable.
- Taking risks is a part of business. Understand them, manage them, ask "What if?" but don't be paralysed by them.
- Luck is a part of business. Accept when luck served our needs and impacted the outcome — luck, whether good or bad, runs out. Hard work and skill does not.
- PAY YOUR TAXES.
- Debt, if managed well, is a great ally — if we borrow too much or manage it poorly, it will not end well.
- A lack of cash will be the mouse that sinks the business — watch out for all the other "big farm animals" that are causing the issues well before the cash becomes the problem.
- Do the little things well, value time — it's precious — and spend some time prioritising.
- We need to care for ourselves and care for those around us.

While the topic of "failure" provides macabre interest for us, real people were impacted by all these failures.

My hope is this journey has provided you with greater insight into how we each tick, why we get it wrong and how we might deal with this.

It is a journey I have thoroughly enjoyed taking and sharing.

I hope you find the success you seek from your business.

All the very best to you.

BOB WEIR

Acknowledgements

There are many people I would love to name who played a part in this. Unfortunately, I chose a topic for this book that made all those I spoke to uncomfortable and a little wary about talking. Business failures are painful. They often involve court action, the signing of confidentiality documents or are covered by client privilege.

I did speak to many in the legal profession who shared their wealth of general experience. I spoke to many people in the insolvency industry from the Waikato, Bay of Plenty, Auckland and Wellington. They too were steadfast in holding true to the confidentialities as part of their liquidation process. I thank you for your candour, insight and professionalism.

In saying that, I must thank business journalists from the *National Business Review (NBR)*, Fairfax and the New Zealand Listener, not only for your information on specific business failures but also your advice in the art of investigative writing — I now share the challenges you face getting to the truth.

I would also like to thank the Psychology department at the University of Otago and the senior students whose enthusiasm and intellect were inspiring and thought provoking. The same applies to those lecturers who share their insight into what makes us tick.

As you can see from the extensive reference list, I have used the insight from hundreds of people who have written an immense amount. Their knowledge, skill and research has made my journey an enriching experience.

All the following names are people who spent time sharing their stories or assisting as best they could with me, over a beer, coffee, in meetings, over the phone, or in emails — some once, others over many months: Kevin Gloag; Kim Thompson; David Ross; Jamin Halberstadt, Julie Salthouse; Barry Bragg; Stuart McLauchlan; Don Elder; Anthony Burg; Luke Bunt; Bruce Cotterill; Sandy Maier; David Patterson; Rebecca Mackie; Graeme McGlinn; Duncan Priest; John Price; Bruce Tichbon; Lachie McLeod, Edward Sullivan; Rachel Scott; Tony Bird; John Fisk; Armon Tamatea, Nigel Gormack; Scott Laurence; Steve Pearse; John Crawford; and many more.

To the team of people who helped me self-publish, there are many of you. Thanks to you all.

BOB WEIR

Appendix: South Canterbury Finance — structure of entities

The following diagram outlines the structure of all South Canterbury Finances entities. It was developed by the Reserve Bank of New Zealand at the time they were investigating SCF. I do not expect you to be able to read any of the details within this structure — but it gives you a sense of the shear complexity of the organisation. Remember, it was a structure predominantly overseen by one man, Allan Hubbard, who was in his 80s and used traditional paper-based methods.

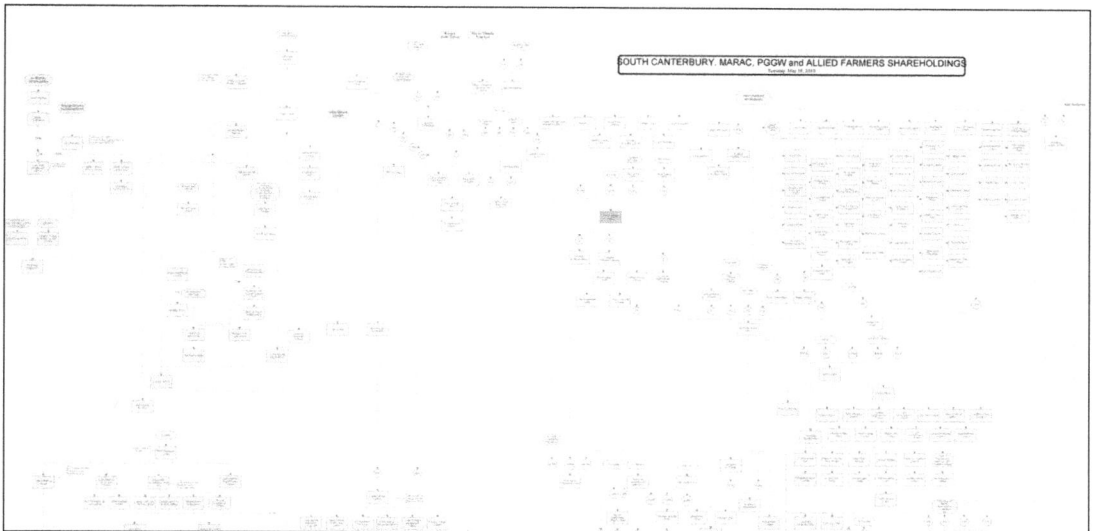

SOUTH CANTERBURY, MARAC, PGGW and ALLIED FARMERS SHAREHOLDINGS

If you want to see this in detail, you will need to go to the website, **www.whybusinessesfail.co.nz**. It is provided here not for you to analyse — the page is too small. It's to illustrate the huge complexity of Allan Hubbard and some of his associates empire.

References

Chapter 1: What is business failure — and what is success?

1. World Bank Group (2017). *Doing Business 2017: Equal Opportunity for All.* Washington DC License: Creative Commons Attribution CCBY 3.0 IGO.
2. Statistics New Zealand. *Business Demography Statistics.* Retrieved from http://www.stats.govt.nz
3. The Companies Office. *Measuring corporate health through companies that form, fail and last.* Retrieved from https://www.companiesoffice. govt.nz/insights-and-articles/measuring-corporate-health/
4. Ries, Eric (2011). *The Lean Startup — How Constant Innovation Creates Radically Successful Businesses.* Penguin Group.
5. Official information requests from the IRD on 1 July 2016 and 3 April 2017
6. Interest.oc.nz website, *Deep freeze list — Finance industry failures".* http://www.interest.co.nz/ saving/deep-freeze-list
7. Official information request from Office of Treaty Settlements in July 2017.
8. Gibbons, Ann (2017, June 7). *World's oldest Homo sapiens fossils found in Morocco.* http://www. sciencemag.org
9. Hunt, Edwin S.; Murray, James M. (1999). *A History of Business in Medieval Europe 1200–1550.* Cambridge University Press.
10. Stone, R. C. J. *Russell, Thomas*, first published in the *Dictionary of New Zealand Biography*, vol. 1, 1990. Te Ara — the Encyclopedia of New Zealand, http://www.TeAra.govt.nz/en/biographies/1r20/ russell-thomas (accessed 16 July 2017)
11. King, Michael (2003). *The Penguin History of New Zealand.* Penguin Group (NZ), pp. 225–27
12. Hunt, Carlton (1937). *The Development of the Business Corporation in England. 1800–1867.* The Academy of Political Science, pp. 463–65. http:// www.jstor.org/stable/2143404

Chapter 2: The failure of New Zealand's coal miner — Solid Energy

1. *Move to Intensive Monitoring* (June 2012). Retrieved from www.treasury.govt.nz/ publications/information-releases/solidenergy.
2. *Revised Business Plan to Minister from Palmer* (August 2012). Retrieved from www.treasury. govt.nz/publications/information-releases/ solidenergy.
3. *Update from conversation with John Palmer-Emails* (August 2012). Retrieved from www. treasury.govt.nz/publications/information-releases/solidenergy.
4. *Additional Work on Solid Energy New Zealand Limited* (February 2014). Retrieved from www. treasury.govt.nz/publications/information-releases/solidenergy.
5. Elder, Don (November 2009). *An Export-Led Economic Step Change for New Zealand.* Retrieved from www.treasury.govt.nz/publications/ information-releases/solidenergy.
6. *Further information requested on an integrated National Resources Company Questions — Letter to John Key* (June 2010). Retrieved from www. treasury.govt.nz/publications/information-releases/solidenergy.
7. CCMAU (17 August 2006). *Briefing for meeting with Chair and Chief Executive.* Retrieved from www.treasury.govt.nz/publications/information-releases/solidenergy.
8. Fulton, Tim (October 2015). *Solid Energy creditors agreement challenged by Cargill International.* Retrieved from www.stuff.co.nz.
9. CCMAU (17 August 2006). *Briefing for meeting with Chair and Chief Executive.* Retrieved from www.treasury.govt.nz/publications/information-releases/solidenergy.
10. Solid Energy Media Release (3 February 2017). *No buyer for Spring Creek mine leads to closure.* Retrieved from www.solidenergy.co.nz.
11. *Solid Energy NZ Ltd Annual Shareholder Meeting* (6 October 2009). Retrieved from www.treasury. govt.nz/publications/information-releases/ solidenergy.
12. Solid Energy Media Release (9 May 2007). *Solid Energy Enters Biodiesel Market.* Retrieved from http://www.coalnz.com/about/media-releases/2007.
13. Solid Energy Media Release (9 May 2007). *Solid Energy Enters Biodiesel Market.* Retrieved from http://www.coalnz.com/about/media-releases/2007.
14. Solid Energy New Zealand Ltd. 2010 Annual Report. Retrieved through an Official Information Request to Solid Energy.
15. NBR Business Desk (February 2013) *Solid Energy's lignite coal plans dead, all related assets for sale.* Retrieved from http://www.nbr.co.nz.

16. Solid Energy Press Release (24 September 2009). *Solid Energy and Ravensdown investigate lignite.* Retrieved from www.scoop.co.nz

17. Office of the Auditor-General (2014). *Additional Work on Solid Energy New Zealand Limited.* Retrieved from https://www.oag.govt.nz/2014/solid-energy.

18. Media Release (May 2007). *Solid Energy enters biodiesel market.* Retrieved from http://www.coalnz.com.

19. Annual Reports 2009, 2010, 2011 and 2012. Retrieved through an Official Information Request to Solid Energy.

20. Bradley, Grant (May 2012). *Solid Energy Finds Mini Maui. Business Herald.*

21. Collins, Jim and Porras, Jerry (1994). *Built to Last: Successful Habits of Visionary Companies.* Harper Business.

22. Elder, Don (November 2009). *An Export-Led Economic Step Change for New Zealand.* Retrieved from www.treasury.govt.nz/publications/information-releases/solidenergy.

23. *Proposal for an integrated national Natural Resources Company — Letter to the PM* (May 2010). Retrieved from www.treasury.govt.nz/publications/information-releases/solidenergy.

24. *Solid Energy's Proposal for Natural Resources Ltd* (May 2010). Retrieved from www.treasury.govt.nz/publications/information-releases/solidenergy.

25. *Solid Energy National Resource Company — Response* (August 2010). Retrieved from www.treasury.govt.nz/publications/information-releases/solidenergy.

26. *Solid Energy's Natural Resources Company Response* (August 2010). Retrieved from www.treasury.govt.nz/publications/information-releases/solidenergy.

27. *Business Planning for SOEs Response to draft SCIs* (May 2009). Retrieved from www.treasury.govt.nz/publications/information-releases/solidenergy.

28. *Solid Energy's response to COMU's new monitoring approach — Letter to John Palmer* (March 2011). Retrieved from www.treasury.govt.nz/publications/information-releases/solidenergy.

29. *Solid Energy's response to COMU's new monitoring approach — Letter to John Palmer* (March 2011). Retrieved from www.treasury.govt.nz/publications/information-releases/solidenergy.

30. Annual Reports 2009, 2010, 2011 and 2012. Retrieved through an Official Information Request to Solid Energy.

31. The High Court of New Zealand. *The Bank of Tokyo-Mitsubishi UFJ Ltd and Solid Energy NZ Ltd.* Judgement of Winkelmann J.

32. Rutherford, Hamish (March 2015). *Solid Energy lenders could see more losses.* Retrieved from www.stuff.co.nz.

33. *Solid Energy New Zealand — Scoping Study Report* (November 2011). Retrieved from www.treasury.govt.nz/publications/information-releases/solidenergy.

34. *Solid Energy NZ Ltd Annual Shareholder Meeting* (October 2009). Retrieved from www.treasury.govt.nz/publications/information-releases/solidenergy.

35. Elder, Don (November 2009). *An Export-Led Economic Step Change for New Zealand.* Retrieved from www.treasury.govt.nz/publications/information-releases/solidenergy.

36. *Solid Energy NZ Ltd Annual Shareholder Meeting* (October 2009). Retrieved from www.treasury.govt.nz/publications/information-releases/solidenergy.

37. *Briefing for meeting with Chair and CEO on 11 May 2010* (March 2010). Retrieved from www.treasury.govt.nz/publications/information-releases/solidenergy.

38. *Solid Energy — Draft Statement of Corporate Intent — October 11.* Retrieved from www.treasury.govt.nz/publications/information-releases/solidenergy.

39. *Business Planning for SOEs Response to draft SCIs* (May 2009). Retrieved from www.treasury.govt.nz/publications/information-releases/solidenergy.

40. *Scope for Meeting with Solid Energy — Emails John Crawford and Don Elder* (April 2011). Retrieved from www.treasury.govt.nz/publications/information-releases/solidenergy.

41. *Solid Energy Business Plan Update; the Response to the UBS Scoping Study* (February 2012). Retrieved from www.treasury.govt.nz/publications/information-releases/solidenergy.

42. Mooney, Chris; Mufson, Steven (April 2013). *How coal titan Peabody, the world's largest, fell into bankruptcy.* Retrieved from www.washingtonpost.com.

43. Vardi, Nathan (August 2015). *U.S. Coal Company Alpha Natural Resources Files for Bankruptcy.* Retrieved from www.forbes.com.

44. Smellie, Pattrick (2013, March 14). *"Miner's debt expansion all its own work, say former leaders".* *National Business Review.*

Chapter 3: Death of a Kiwi icon — Pumpkin Patch and the risk of growing

1. McGrathNicol (24 February 2017). *Pumpkin Patch Group — Voluntary Administrators' report pursuant to section 239AU of the Companies Act 1993.*
2. McGrathNicol (24 February 2017). *Pumpkin Patch Group — Voluntary Administrators' report pursuant to section 239AU of the Companies Act 1993.*
3. Katz, Bella (8 April 2014). *Time for Change at Pumpkin Patch.* http://www.stuff.co.nz
4. *New Zealand Herald* (31 August 2017). *Pumpkin Patch teases online relaunch in New Zealand, Australia.* http://www.nzherald.co.nz.

Chapter 4: When businesses fail, who decides the truth? — Salthouse Marine

1. HPL Partners. *Salthouse Marine Limited (In Receivership) Receiver's First Report on the State of Affairs.* Retrieved from the Companies Office.
2. *New Zealand Herald* (12 February 2001). *Talking Heads: Interview with Julie Salthouse — by Daniel Riordan.*
3. Fisher, Greg (2011). *When the going gets tough….* Retrieved from www.clubmarine.co.nz, Volume 26. Issue 3.
4. High Court of New Zealand. Judgement of Woolford J. December 2012. Jim Delegat vs Chris Norman, Boat 93, and Julie Salthouse.
5. Meadows, Richard (August 2012). *Rich-lister fights million-dollar yacht deal.* Fairfax Media
6. High Court of New Zealand. Judgement of Woolford J. December 2012. Jim Delegat vs Chris Norman, Boat 93, and Julie Salthouse.

Chapter 5: Dishonesty, fraud, and Ross Asset Management

1. Serious Fraud Office website https://www.sfo.govt.nz/our-vision.
2. *Serious Fraud Office/Financial Markets Authority vs David Robert Gilmour Ross — Notes of Judge D R W Barry on Sentencing* (15 November 2013). In the District Court of Wellington. Clause 14.
3. Gaynor, Brian 2017 *"Ponzi scheme fallout still being untangled"* NZ Herald.
4. PWC. First liquidators report December 2012. Retrieved from the Companies Office website.
5. Hartley, Simon (2014 Nov. 27). *"Jail term for disgraced lawyer and "consummate thief and liar".* Retrieved from https://www.odt.co.nz.
6. Stock, Rob (2015 July) *"New Zealand's history of Ponzi schemers"* Retrieved from www.stuff.co.nz
7. Laing, D; Gullery, L (2012 Aug 29). *"Notorious Hawkes Bay fraudster freed".* Retrieved from www.nzherald.co.nz/hawkes-bay-today.
8. *David Robert Gilmour Ross vs The Queen Judgement of the Court* (11 June 2014). In the Court of Appeal of New Zealand.
9. Association of Certified Fraud Examiners (ACFE) (2016). *"Report to the nations on occupational fraud and abuse"* 2016 Global Fraud Study.
10. Ramamoorti, Sridhar; Morrison, David E.; Koletar, Joseph W.; Pope, Kelly R. (2013). *A.B.C.'s of Behavioral Forensics: Applying Psychology to Financial Fraud Prevention and Detection.* Wiley. Kindle Edition.
11. Biegelman, Martin T. *"Faces of Fraud – Cases and Lessons from a Life Fighting Fraudsters"* Audio Book. From www.audible.com.
12. Ramamoorti, Sridhar; Morrison, David E.; Koletar, Joseph W.; Pope, Kelly R. (2013). *A.B.C.'s of Behavioral Forensics: Applying Psychology to Financial Fraud Prevention and Detection.* Wiley. Kindle Edition.
13. Biegelman, Martin T. *"Faces of Fraud – Cases and Lessons from a Life Fighting Fraudsters"* Audio Book. From www.audible.com.
14. McNicol, Hamish and Burgess, Dave (18 April 2014). *Wife gets $900k from mansion sale. Dominion Post.* Retrieved from www.stuff.com.
15. The World Bank (19 October 2016). *World Governance Indicators.* Spreadsheet Downloads retrieved from http://data.worldbank.org/data-catalog/worldwide-governance-indicators.
16. Transparency International (25 January 2017). *Corruption Perceptions Index 2016.* Retrieved from www.transparency.org/cpi2016.
17. Fisman, Raymond and Miguel, Edward (2007). *Corruption, Norms, and Legal Enforcement: Evidence from Diplomatic Parking Tickets. Journal of Political Economy,* vol. 115. No 6. The University of Chicago.
18. Fisman, Raymond and Miguel, Edward (2007). *Corruption, Norms, and Legal Enforcement: Evidence from Diplomatic Parking Tickets. Journal of Political Economy,* vol. 115. No 6. The University of Chicago.
19. Mead, Nicole L.; Baumeister, Roy F.; Gino, Francesca; Schweitzer, Maurice E.; Ariely, Dan (February 2009). *Too tired to tell the truth: Self-control resource depletion and dishonesty. Journal of Experimental Social Psychology* 45 (2009): 594–97.
20. Ariely, Dan (2012). *The (Honest) Truth about Dishonesty: How we lie to everyone — especially ourselves.* Harper Collins, London.

Chapter 6: Allan Hubbard and the failure of South Canterbury Finance

1. Green, Virginia (2010). *"Allan Hubbard – A Man Out of Time"* Random House, Auckland New Zealand.
2. The Timaru Herald , (2009, 30 July) *"Hundreds drawn to Knighthood campaign"*. Retrieved from www.stuff.com.
3. Korda Mentha. (2009 Aug). *"Preliminary Overview of Findings"*. Retrieved from www.treasury.govt.nz.
4. Green, Virginia (2010). *"Allan Hubbard – A Man Out of Time"* Random House, Auckland New Zealand.
5. Heather, Ben (2011, 10 Oct). *"Allan Hubbard mourned as hero"*. The Press. Retrieved from www.stuff.com.
6. McFie, Rebecca. (2010, 23 Oct) *"The Hubbard Enigma"*. The Listener. Retrieved from www.noted.co.nz.
7. Hickey, Bernard (2008 June). *"The 5 Survivability Factors for finance companies"* Retrieved from Interst.co.nz.
8. Green, Virginia (2010). *"Allan Hubbard – A Man Out of Time"* Random House, Auckland New Zealand.
9. South Canterbury Finance (2008, 19 May). *Investment Statement and Prospectus. SCF0164 Share Issue Cover.indd.*
10. Hickey, Bernard (2008 June). *"The 5 Survivability Factors for finance companies"* Retrieved from Interst.co.nz.
11. Office of the Auditor-General. (2011 Sept). *"The Treasury: Implementing and managing the Crown Retail Deposit Guarantee Scheme"* Retrieved from www.oag.govt.nz.
12. Office of the Auditor-General. (2011 Sept). *"The Treasury: Implementing and managing the Crown Retail Deposit Guarantee Scheme"* Retrieved from www.oag.govt.nz.
13. Office of the Auditor-General. (2011 Sept). *"The Treasury: Implementing and managing the Crown Retail Deposit Guarantee Scheme"* Retrieved from www.oag.govt.nz.
14. Korda Mentha. (2009 Aug). *"Preliminary Overview of Findings"*. Retrieved from www.treasury.govt.nz.
15. Radio New Zealand (2014, 1 July). *"SCF executive quit over "risky" lending"*. Retrieved from www.radionz.co.nz.
16. Gibson, Anne (2010, 2 Sept).*"Big-city nightlife helped to sink finance company"* NZ Herald. Retrieved from www.nzherald.co.nz.
17. *"Aorangi Securities Limited ("ASL")* – Offer of Securities" Letter from Securities Commission to Allan and Margaret Jane Hubbard and subsequent correspondence. Megan Blenkame and Lane Neave Lawyers.
18. Ministry of Economic Development (2010 June 18). *"Report from the Registrar of Companies to the Securities Commission – Aorangi Securities Limited, Forresters Nominee Company Limited and Associated Persons."*
19. Minutes of Meeting of the Securities Commission Board held at 4pm on Friday 18 June 2010.
20. Heather, Ben (2010, July 08). *"Bankrupt Botherway resigns"* Retrieved from *www.stuff.com*.
21. Grass, Kerry (2011, Aug). Memorandum to The Hubbard Support Group. *"Statutory Management."*
22. The High Court of New Zealand Timaru Registry (2014 Oct). *The Queen vs Edward Oral Sullivan, Robert Alexander White and Lachie John McLeod. Reasons for Verdicts of Heath J.*
23. The High Court of New Zealand Timaru Registry (2014 Oct). *The Queen vs Edward Oral Sullivan, Robert Alexander White and Lachie John McLeod. Reasons for Verdicts of Heath J.*
24. The High Court of New Zealand Timaru Registry (2014 Oct). *The Queen vs Edward Oral Sullivan, Robert Alexander White and Lachie John McLeod. Reasons for Verdicts of Heath J.*
25. Green, Virginia (2010). *"Allan Hubbard – A Man Out of Time"* Random House, Auckland New Zealand.
26. Regulatory Review – A. Hubbard (2011 June). *Press Release from the Hubbard Support Team.* Retrieved from www.scoop.co.nz.

Chapter 7: The brain of the business owner

1. Galloway, Shawn M. (Jan 2011): *"Why We Fail to See Risk (Reticular Activating System)"* EHS Today, New York.
2. Sprenger, Marilee (2010). *"The Leadership Brain for Dummies"* Indiana. Wiley Publishing, Inc.
3. Sprenger, Marilee (2010). *"The Leadership Brain for Dummies"* Indiana. Wiley Publishing, Inc.
4. Gilbert, Daniel. (2004). *"The surprising science of happiness"* TED Talk.
5. Ariely, Dan (2012), *"The (Honest) Truth about Dishonesty: How we lie to everyone – especially ourselves"* Harper Collins, London.
6. Eagleman, David (2015). *"The Brain: The Story of You"*. Edinburgh Canongate Books Ltd.
7. Viskontas, Dr Indre (2017). *"Brain Myths Exploded – Lessons from Neuroscience"*. The Great Courses. Audiobook. Virginia.
8. Bruer, John T. (1999). *"Neural Connections – Some you use some you lose"*. The Phi Delta Kappa International pp264-277.
9. Harari, Yuval Noah (2011). *"Sapiens - A Brief History of Humankind"*. Penguin Random House.
10. Boyd, Dr Lara (2015). *"After watching this, your*

brain will not be the same". TEDx Vancouver

11. Eagleman, David (2015). *"The Brain: The Story of You"*. Edinburgh Canongate Books Ltd.

12. Viskontas, Dr Indre (2017). *"Brain Myths Exploded – Lessons from Neuroscience"*. The Great Courses. Audiobook. Virginia.

13. Eagleman, David (2015). *"The Brain: The Story of You"*. Edinburgh Canongate Books Ltd.

14. Viskontas, Dr Indre (2017). *"Brain Myths Exploded – Lessons from Neuroscience"*. The Great Courses. Audiobook. Virginia.

15. Harari, Yuval Noah (2011). *"Sapiens - A Brief History of Humankind"*. Penguin Random House.

16. Harari, Yuval Noah (2011). *"Sapiens - A Brief History of Humankind"*. Penguin Random House.

17. Medina, Professor John J. (2014). *"Your Best Brain"* The Great Courses. Virginia USA.

18. Jang, Kerry L. and Livesley, W. John; Vernon, Philip (1996*). "Heritability of the Big Five Personality Dimensions and Their Facets: A Twin Study"* Journal of Personality. Duke University Press.

19. Eagleman, David (2015). *"The Brain: The Story of You"*. Edinburgh Canongate Books Ltd.

20. Kahneman, Daniel (2011) *"Thinking, Fast and Slow"* Penguin Books.

21. Kahneman, Daniel (2011) *"Thinking, Fast and Slow"* Penguin Books.

22. Thaler, Richard H. and Sunstein Cass R, (2008) *"Nudge – Improving decisions about health, wealth and happiness"*. Penguin Group London.

23. Schacter, Daniel L. (2001). *"How the Mind Forgets and Remembers - The Seven Sins of Memory"*. Souvenir Press, London.

24. Viskontas, Dr Indre (2017). *"Brain Myths Exploded – Lessons from Neuroscience"*. The Great Courses. Audiobook. Virginia.

25. Harris, Russ. (2007). *"The Happiness Trap - Based on ACT: A revolutionary mindfulness-based programme for overcoming stress, anxiety and depression"* Exisle Publishing Limited, Australia.

Chapter 8: The simple mental shortcuts we use to survive each day

1. Tversky, A. and Kahneman, D. (1982) *"Judgements of and by representativeness"*. Cambridge, UK: Cambridge University Press.

2. Linstron, Martin (2008). *"Buyology: How everything we believe about why we buy is wrong"* Random House.

3. McRaney, David (2011). *"You are not so smart"* Oneworld Publications. Great Britain.

4. Kahneman, Daniel (2011) *"Thinking, Fast and

Slow" Penguin Books.

5. Kahneman, Daniel (2011) *"Thinking, Fast and Slow"* Penguin Books.

6. Ariely, Dan (2008). *"Predictably Irrational – The Hidden Forces that Shape Our Decisions"* Harper Collins. New York.

7. Carroll, Patrick; Grace, Jodi; Terry, Meredith; Sheppard, James A. (2002). *"Exploring the Causes of Comparative Optimism"* Psychologica, 42. Pp65-98. University of Florida.

8. Statistics New Zealand. *"Marriages, Civil Unions, and Divorces: Year ended December 2016"* Retrieved from http://www.stats.govt.nz.

9. Kahneman, Daniel (2011) *"Thinking, Fast and Slow"* Penguin Books.

10. Kahneman, Daniel; Tversky, Amos; (1973). *"Availability: A heuristic for judging frequency and probability"*. Cognitive Psychology. Volume 5 Issue 2. pp207-232.

11. Kahneman, Daniel; Tversky, Amos; (1973). *"Availability: A heuristic for judging frequency and probability"*. Cognitive Psychology. Volume 5 Issue 2. pp207-232.

12. Reinhart, Carmen M. and Rogoff, Kenneth S. (2009) *"This Time is Different – Eight Centuries of Financial Folly"* Princeton University Press. New Jersey.

13. McRaney, David (2011). *"You are not so smart"* Oneworld Publications. Great Britain.

14. Kreb, Valdris*, "New Political Patterns" Retrieved from* http://www.orgnet.com/divided.html.

15. Zajonc, R. B. (1980). *"Feeling and thinking: Preferences need no inferences"*. American Psychologist, 35, pp151-175

Chapter 9: How we decide

1. Eagleman, David (2015). *"The Brain: The Story of You"*. Edinburgh Canongate Books Ltd

2. Nee, Victor; Snijders, Tom; Wittek, Rafael. (2014). *"The Handbook of Rational Choice Social Research"* Stanford University Press pp 33 to72.

3. Marshall, Gordon; Scott, John (2009) *"A Dictionary of Sociology"* Oxford University Press

4. Ariely, Dan (2008). *"Predictably Irrational – The Hidden Forces that Shape Our Decisions"* Harper Collins. New York.

5. Ariely, Dan (2008). *"Predictably Irrational – The Hidden Forces that Shape Our Decisions"* Harper Collins. New York

6. Viskontas, Dr Indre (2017). *"Brain Myths Exploded – Lessons from Neuroscience"*. The Great Courses. Audiobook. Virginia

7. Lamia, Mary C. (2010, Dec). *"Like it Or Not,

Emotions Will Drive the Decisions You Make Today". Psychology Today Retrieved from www. psychologytoday.com

8. Lerner, Jennifer S.; Li, Ye; Valdesolo, Piercarlo; Kassam, Karim; (June 2014).*"Emotion and Decision Making"* Annual Review of Psychology.

9. Finucane, Melissa L.; MacGregor, Donald G.; Slovic, Paul. (2006, Oct) *"The Affect Heuristic".* European Journal of Operational Research pp1333 to 1352.

10. Damasio, Antonio (2006) *"Descartes' Error"* Vintage Books. London.

11. Glacwell, Malcolm. (2005) *"Blink –The Power of Thinking without Thinking"* Black Bay Books

12. LeGault, Michael (2006). *"Think – Why Crucial Decisions Can't Be Made in the Blink of an Eye".* Threshold Editions. New York.

13. Graham, John R.; Harvey, Campbell R.; Puri, Manju (2015). *"Capital allocation and delegation of decision-making authority within firms".* Journal of Financial Economics 115. pp449 to 470.

14. Klein, Gary (1998). *"Sources of Power – How People Make Decisions".* The MIT Press. Cambridge Massachusetts.

15. Tierney, John (2011 Aug 17). *"Do You Suffer from Decision Fatigue?"* New York Times Magazine. Retrieved from http://www.nytimes.com

Chapter 10: Employees — they are irrational people too

1. Nevid J (2013). *"Psychology: Concepts and Applications".* Wadsworth, Cengage Learning, Belmont CA p288.

2. Mackay, Hugh (2010). *"What Makes Us Tick – The ten desires that drive us". Hachette Australia.*

3. Maslow, A. H. (1943). "A *theory of human motivation".* Psychological Review, 50(4), 370-396.

Chapter 11: Self-awareness, personality, and what we stand for

1. Ramamoorti, Sridhar; Morrison, David E.; Koletar, Joseph W.; Pope, Kelly R. (2013) *"A.B.C.'s of Behavioral Forensics: Applying Psychology to Financial Fraud Prevention and Detection".* Wiley. Kindle Edition.

2. Medina, John, J. (2014). *"Your Best Brain – Course Guidebook"* The Great Courses.

3. Watson John; 1930 *"Behaviourism"* (Revised Edition) University of Chicago Press. Extracted from Wikipedia

4. Gladwell, Malcolm (2008). *"Outliers – The Story of Success"* Little Brown and Company

5. Gleitman, Henry; Gross, James.; Reisberg, Daniel.

(2011). *"Psychology".* WW Norton & Company Inc. New York.

6. Medina, John, J. (2014). *"Your Best Brain – Course Guidebook"* The Great Courses.

7. *Lowenstein, Roger* (2001). *"When Genius Failed – The rise and fall of Long Term Capital Management".* Fourth Estate. London.

8. Richards, Steven; Paulhus, Delroy; Furnham, Adrian (2013). *The Dark Triad of Personality: A 10 Year Review. Social and Personality Psychology Compass* 7/3, pp. 199–216.

9. The Herald on Sunday *(2015 Dec 20)* "The Everyday Psychopath". Retrieved from www. nzherald.co.nz.

10. Pittinsky, Todd L; Rosenthal, Seth A.; (2006). *"Narcissistic Leadership".* The Leadership Quarterly 17 pp 617 to 633.

11. National Institute of Mental Health. "*Borderline Personality Disorders".* Retrieved from website. https://www.nimh.nih.gov/health/statistics/ prevalence/borderline-personality-disorder. shtml.

12. Vaknin, Sam (2015). *"Malignant Self Love".* Narcissus Publications.

13. Vaknin, Sam (2015). *"Malignant Self Love".* Narcissus Publications.

Chapter 12: Know why the business exists, where it is heading — its strategy

1. Iyenger, Sheena (2010). *The Art of Choosing.* Twelve New York.

2. De Geus, Arie (1997). *The Living Company.* Harvard Business School Press.

Chapter 13: Health, wellbeing, and their impact on business

1. Official Information request of ACC.

2. Website: World Health Organization: *Stress at the Workplace. http://www.who.int/ occupational_ health/topics/stressatwp/en/.*

3. Sapolsky, Robert (1994). *Why Zebras Don't Get Ulcers.* Henry Hold and Co., New York.

4. Harris, Russ (2007). *The Happiness Trap.* Robinson, London.

5. Lyubomirsky Sonja (2007). *The How of Happiness — A new approach to getting the life you want.* Penguin Press.

6. Diener, Ed; Biswas-Diener, Robert (2008). *Happiness — Unlocking the mysteries of psychological wealth.* Blackwell Publishing.

7. Weir, Bob (2017). *Success Made Small — A step by step guide to business success.* Under 5 Small Business Ltd.

8. University of Exeter (September 2013). *Go on, volunteer — it could be good for you! Mental Health Weekly Digest*, p. 31.
9. Dunn, Elizabeth; Norton, Michael (2013). *Happy Money: The New Science of Smarter Spending.* Oneworld Publications.
10. Frankl, Victor E. (2004). *Man's Search for Meaning.* Audible.com.

Chapter 14: Controlling the controllable, risk, uncertainty and luck
1. Deloitte (2014). *Risk Intelligent Governance Lessons from state-of-the-art board practices.* Retrieved from https://www2.deloitte.com.
2. Mauboussin, Michael J. (2012). *The Success Equation — Untangling Skill and Luck in Business, Sports, and Investing.* Harvard Business Review Press, Boston.
3. Gladwell, Malcolm (2008). *Outliers — The Story of Success.* Little Brown and Company.
4. Rodenberg, Jarno (2016). *100 Richest People in World History — How Wealth is Created and Preserved.*
5. Kahneman, Daniel (2011). *"Thinking, Fast and Slow.* Penguin Books.
6. Branson, Richard (2011). *"Losing My Virginity: How I survived, had fun, and made a fortune doing business my way".* Random House USA Inc. New York, United States.

Chapter 15: Cash and the mouse that sank the boat
1. Allen, Pamela (2007). *Who sank the boat?* Puffin Books, Penguin Group (Australia).

Chapter 16: Paying taxes — the cash of last resort
1. *Financial Statements of the Government of New Zealand — for the year ended 30 June 2016.* Retrieved from www.treasury.co.nz.
2. *The Economist* (November 2012). *A national sport no more — Greek tax dodgers are being outed.* Retrieved from www.economist.com.
3. Georgakopoulos, Thodoris (June 2016). *2016-06 Tax Evasion in Greece — A Study.* Retrieved from https://www.dianeosis.org.
4. Official information requests from the IRD on 1 July 2016 and 3 April 2017.
5. IRD website — http://www.ird.govt.nz/aboutir/external-stats/debt/total-overdue-debt/total-overdue-debt.html.

Chapter 17: Debt and how to kill a 1400-year-old business
1. Reserve Bank of New Zealand. Retrieved from https://www.rbnz.govt.nz/statistics/c5
2. Statistics New Zealand. Retrieved from http://m.stats.govt.nz/browse_for_stats/people_and_communities/Net worth/nz-debt.aspx.

Chapter 18: Doing the little things really well
1. Ministry of Business Innovation and Employment (MBIE) (June 2017). *Small Businesses in New Zealand — How do they compare with larger firms?* Retrieved from http://www.mbie.govt.nz
2. Tracy, Brian (2007). *Eat that Frog! 21 Great Ways to Stop Procrastinating and Get More Done in Less Time.* Berrett-Koehler Publishers, Inc.
3. Viskontas, Dr Indre (2017). *Brain Myths Exploded -— Lessons from Neuroscience.* The Great Courses. Audiobook. Virginia.
4. Ries, Eric (2011). *The Lean Startup — How Constant Innovation Creates Radically Successful Businesses.* Penguin Group.

www.ingramcontent.com/pod-product-compliance
Lightning Source LLC
Chambersburg PA
CBHW061345210326
41598CB00035B/5886